# GLOBAL
# SOUTH
# ASIA

Padma Kaimal
K. Sivaramakrishnan
Anand A. Yang
SERIES EDITORS

# THE ENDS
# OF KINSHIP

*Connecting Himalayan Lives*
*between Nepal and New York*

SIENNA R. CRAIG

UNIVERSITY OF WASHINGTON PRESS

*Seattle*

*The Ends of Kinship* was made possible in part by the Naomi B. Pascal Editor's Endowment, supported through the generosity of Nancy Alvord, Dorothy and David Anthony, Janet and John Creighton, Patti Knowles, Katherine and Douglass Raff, Mary McLellan Williams, and other donors.

Additional support was provided by the Department of Anthropology's Claire Garber Goodman Fund at Dartmouth College.

Design by Katrina Noble
Composed in Minion Pro, typeface designed by Robert Slimbach

24  23  22  21  20      5  4  3  2  1

Printed and bound in the United States of America

UNIVERSITY OF WASHINGTON PRESS
uwapress.uw.edu

LIBRARY OF CONGRESS CATALOGING-IN-PUBLICATION DATA
LC record available at https://lccn.loc.gov/2020006815
LC ebook record available at https://lccn.loc.gov/2020006816

978-0-295-74768-2 (hardcover), 978-0-295-74769-9 (paperback), 978-0-295-74770-5 (ebook)

Cover design: Camille Vance
Cover illustration: *Mustang to Manhattan*, copyright © 2019 by Tenzin Norbu
Part illustrations courtesy of Tenzin Norbu
Permission credits to reprint from various works are provided at the end of the book.

The paper used in this publication is acid free and meets the minimum requirements of American National Standard for Information Sciences—Permanence of Paper for Printed Library Materials, ANSI Z39.48–1984.∞

In memory of Jigme Dorje Palbar Bista, 25th King of Mustang

From a distance, topography is intent
as in, *Where I am from is no more.*
Blood is not a natural conclusion
to kinship despite theories and experiments
where red prefaces emotion

—TSERING WANGMO DHOMPA, "EXILE"


To create one's world . . . takes courage.

—GEORGIA O'KEEFFE

# CONTENTS

# RECOGNITION AND GRATITUDE

. . . it makes the pieces one by one in the dark
there is always enough dark . . .
one with the uneven current of breathing
with the silence untouched by the rush of noise

—W. S. MERWIN, "THE ARTISAN WORLD"

Anthropologists often speak of "key informants." I find this framework lim-
iting. Even when used respectfully, it connotes a transaction rather than an
ethics of care, let alone the co-creation of knowledge. I prefer "core relationships" to describe the people without whom this book would not exist.

Nawang Tsering Gurung and I first met each other on the playground of
a Kathmandu boarding school, when he was nine and I was twenty-two, in
1996. Born in upper Mustang, educated in Kathmandu and the U.S., and
now a U.S. citizen, Nawang is a consummate culture broker. He has been
mentored by prominent scholars, has a vast social network, and has worked
on many research projects, including ones with me. He has spearheaded cultural education efforts for younger Himalayan New Yorkers; advocated for
community rights; engaged in projects that support Himalayan and Tibetan
languages; and participated in local education, conservation, and development efforts back in Mustang. Based in New York, he continues to nurture
connections with Nepal. This is perhaps most poignantly revealed in the
ways that he's lived up to his late father's lineage, his mother's expectations,
and his three younger siblings' needs. He is engaged to a young woman from
upper Mustang. They live in Queens and, by the time this book is printed,
they will be parents.

I met Karma Choden Gurung and Yangjin Bista in 2012. We grew close
quickly. I was introduced to each of these young women through Nawang.

Now in their early thirties, for women of their generation, they are highly educated. Karma Choden (or "KC" for short) has a bachelor's degree in biology, and Yangjin has a master's degree in anthropology/sociology, both from Kathmandu-based institutions. KC's family has limited resources and social status; Yangjin was born into a branch of Mustang nobility. Whereas Yangjin and her family identify strongly with Buddhism, KC has embraced Christianity as her guiding faith. Both young women are meticulous researchers with deep knowledge of Mustang's social landscapes. After our collaborations began in 2012, they went on to work with other foreign scholars, development workers, and educational institutions. In the years since we have known one another, Yangjin and then KC have been elected to political posts in Mustang and taken on other leadership positions in their communities. I've also witnessed both of these women become wives and mothers in recent years.

Born in the Muktinath Valley and educated in a boarding school in the Himalayan foothills of West Bengal, India, Kunzom Thakuri is one of the bravest people I know. We met in 1995. I had just arrived in Mustang as a Fulbright Fellow, on the heels of graduating from college. Kunzom had returned to Nepal after completing her secondary education and had taken a job with the Annapurna Conservation Area Project (ACAP). At the time, ACAP, under the direction of the then–King Mahendra Trust for Nature Conservation (KMTNC), was charged with managing tourism in upper Mustang as well as spearheading conservation-development initiatives after the region was opened to foreigners in 1992. While this model of community-led conservation and tourism management was revolutionary, both globally and in Nepal, it was not an easy sell in Mustang.

During those early days of our friendship, Kunzom and I spent many hours talking about the intricacies of life, culture, land, and politics in Mustang. I admired how she navigated social difference. Kunzom made the transition to the U.S. in the late 1990s and, for a time, we both lived in the San Francisco Bay Area. We kept in touch as she and I spent time in America, Europe, and Nepal over the next decade. She returned to Nepal more permanently around 2011 to begin a massive undertaking: helping to envision, build, staff, and manage a new primary school in an upper Mustang village. Through this effort, she is striving to implement an innovative model of elementary education in Mustang at a time when, as this book explores, the driving cultural norm is that receiving a high-quality education requires *leaving* home. We have spent time together in research capacities in 2012, 2014, 2016, 2018, and 2019. She is a teacher, a confidant, and an inspiration.

As for me, born in California and educated in New England, I first traveled to Nepal as a nineteen-year-old undergraduate student of religion and anthropology. I lived in Nepal from 1995 to 1998 and have continued to spend time in the country each year since then. What began as a youthful connection to people and place has been sustained through my own marriage and motherhood, into middle age and through the process of becoming a scholar-teacher.

My personal, academic, and creative paths have shifted over the years. My desire to reckon the worlds in which I was raised and into which I have been welcomed as an anthropologist remains constant. I take responsibility for this book's errors—of omission, of misunderstanding, of ignorance. Although this work is centered on one relatively small community, I hope it will encourage cross-cultural thinking and invite reflection on what we share as human beings. I hope that people from Mustang will find this book meaningful—particularly younger generations who are working so hard to retain cultural footholds and to chart their own course. This has remained my guiding intention.

Aside from these four core relationships and public figures, all other names in this book are pseudonyms. Still, there are so many individuals and institutions to whom I am grateful. I name those I can below.

In and beyond Mustang: Angya, Palsang, Tsering, Dolma, Lhachi, Lumo, Karma Sherab, and *ibi* Sonam; Tshampa Ngawang, Karma, Zompa, Tsewang Gyurme, and Jamyang (Jimmy); *rokmo* Dawa, Kunga (Mahendra), Sonam Chöten, and Tenki as well as Nhunzin, Jigmi, Jigme Wangmo, and Tseyang; Jigme Singe Palbar Bista and Doyang; Tsewang and Maya *didi*; Raju and Tharik; Surendra, Karsang, Karchung, and Tsewang Jigme; Chimi Dolkar, Tshampa Angyal, Sangye Pao, and Tenkyi (Apple); Amchi Gyatso, Amchi Tenjing, Lhundup Gyatso, Tsewang Rinzin, Chimi, Rinzin Angmo, Rapsang, and Tashi Yangchen; Palsang, Tsewang Tenzin, Chimi Dolkar, Kemi, and Suresh; Amchi Nyima, Nyima Bhuti, Kunga, Yungdung, and Pasang; Nyima Drandul; Nirmal and Laxmi Wangdi; Lama Tashi, *meme* Tshultrim, and the Namgyal and Kag *khenpo*; Pema Dolkar (junior and senior), Tenzin Sherab, and Yuden; Norbu Gyaltsen, Laxmi, and Tsering; Amchi Tenjing Dharkye; Yangchen, Lhakpa, and Tashi; Chemi.

Dartmouth compatriots in and throughout the writing process: Ann Armbrecht, Dwai Banerjee, Sabrina Billings, Elizabeth Carpenter-Song,

Maron Greenleaf, Grant Gutierrez, Tracey Heatherington, Chelsey Kivland, Abby Neely, Bernie Perley, Yana Stainova, Jesse Weaver-Shipley. And a special debt of gratitude to Laura Ogden, who has taught me so much about loss and wonder.

Exemplars: Vincanne Adams, Charlotte Bacon, Keith Basso, Ruth Behar, João Biehl, Kevin Bubriski, Andrea Clearfield, Teju Cole, Robert Desjarlais, Tsering Wangmo Dhompa, Davydd Greenwood, Pico Iyer, Marianne Lien, Christine Montross, Kirin Narayan, Stacy Pigg, Harold Roth, Volker Scheid, Kathleen Stewart, Paul Stoller, Manjushree Thapa, Kesang Tseten, Mark Unno.

Mentors: Edmund Morris (1940–2019) and Sylvia Jukes Morris (1935–2020). Edmund taught me about play of form. He demanded authenticity, instilled in me a love of writing by hand, and embodied cadence and humor—in writing and in life. Sylvia was as graceful as she was meticulous. She inspired me to be ever curious about the textures of people's lives, to resist the obvious. Their love for each other—through marriage and as writers—was unparalleled, miraculous, and beautiful to behold.

Scholars and friends who have shaped my thinking: Mark Aldenderfer, Cynthia Beall, Calum Blaikie, Geoff Childs, David Citrin, Gen. Sir Sam Cowan, Fidel Devkota, Ramesh Dhungel, Carroll Dunham, Andrew Fischer, James Fisher, William Fisher, Heidi Fjeld, David Gellner, Barbara Gerke, Melvyn Goldstein, Arjun Guneratne, John Harrison, Sondra Hausner, Kabir Mansingh Heimsath, Kristine Hildebrandt, Resi Hofer, David Holmberg, Jim Igoe, Daniel Kaufman, Thomas Kelly, Stephan Kloos, Tim Lahey, Austin Lord, Christian Luczanits, Kathryn March, Carole McGranahan, Manish Mishra, Galen Murton, Ross Perlin, Anne Rademacher, Charles Ramble, Geoffrey Samuel, Martin Saxer, Tsering Shakya, Fr. Greg Sharkey, Pasang Sherpa, Sara Shneiderman, Nicolas Sihlé, Bandita Sijapati, Deepak Thapa, Tawni Tidwell, Mark Turin, Emily Yeh.

Artists: Tenzin Norbu and Bidhata KC.

Students: Hannah (McGehee) Anderson, Liana Chase, Pawan Dhakal, Phurwa Dhondrup, Kripa Dongol, Michael Everett, Katie Gougelet, Singer Horsecapture, Rebekah Scott, Edom Wessenleyeh.

For supporting the work: the John Simon Guggenheim Foundation and the National Science Foundation. At Dartmouth College, the Dean of the Faculty, the Office of the Provost, the Department of Anthropology's Claire Garber Goodman Fund, the Dickey Center for International Understanding, and the Leslie Center for the Humanities.

At University of Washington Press: executive editor Lorri Hagman, Global South Asia series editor Kalyanakrishnan Sivaramakrishnan, and two anonymous reviewers.

Family, born into and chosen: Steve Craig, Mary Heebner, Charles Rowley, Macduff Everton, Robert Everton, Regina and Brian Mair, Larry and Sylvie Bauer, Lesa Heebner, Don Davis, Lise Apatoff, Daniella Mayer, Kiki Thorpe, Lucy Raimes, Pia Baker.

Ken and Aida: my kin, my heart.

Mustang, Nepal. Map created by M. Roy Cartography, based on a hand-drawn map by John Harrison and used with permission of both.

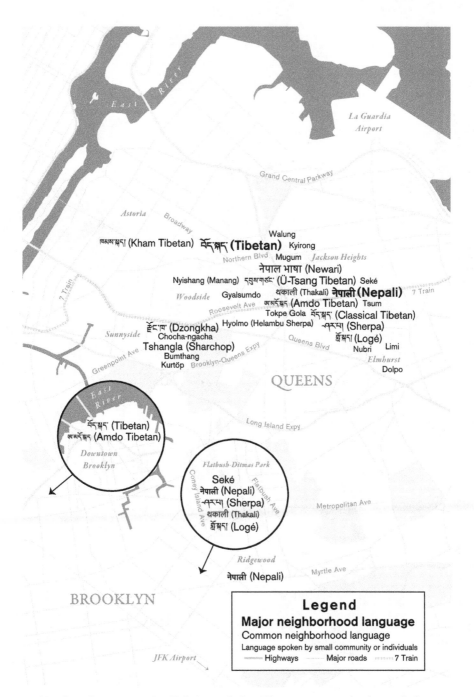

Himalayan languages in New York City, including Tibetan variants spoken by people from Mustang, Nepal. Map created by M. Roy Cartography, based on a map of the languages of New York created in collaboration with the Endangered Language Alliance.

# THE ENDS OF KINSHIP

# INTRODUCTION

> People choose, he said, people choose, and they choose on behalf
> of others.
>
> —TEJU COLE, *OPEN CITY*

ON DECEMBER 16, 2016, JUST BEFORE NOON, I WAS WALKING
through a forest steeped in snow in rural Vermont. Sun came and went
between clouds. It was quiet, spare. Crystalline light reflected off the frozen
surface of a nearby pond. The world felt peaceful, filled with grace and
presence, even as it was marked by absence: bare birch trees, pale winter
light.

I did not know it at the time, but as I was walking, Jigme Dorje Palbar
Bista, the twenty-fifth King of Lo, was leaving the shell of his body, his consciousness released. He was eighty-six years old. Although he died in Kathmandu, Bista ruled his cultural and political domain in the northern reaches
of Mustang District, Nepal, for more than half a century. I had the good
fortune to have known him, in some small way, for twenty years. We shared
an affinity for horses and a love of the place he called home.

Mustang's northern border abuts the Tibetan Plateau. Much of the district lies in the rain shadow of Dhaulagiri, the seventh highest mountain in
the world, and the Annapurna massif. This geological effect burnishes Mustang's landscape ochre, with pockets of verdant irrigated fields under a
cerulean sky. Village homes of rammed earth and mud brick, stone and tim-
ber, are whitewashed and striped with pigments that invoke protector deities who guard this land. Sand-colored ruins of castles, cairns, and fortresses
dot the landscape. These architectural palimpsests recall this area's place in
the history of western Tibetan dynasties. The kingdom of Lo itself dates to
the fourteenth century. Mustang's caves, in turn, hold much earlier histories of high-altitude human settlement, indigenous religion, and early traces
of Buddhism. The Kali Gandaki river runs like a spine through this land,
the gorge it creates a centuries-old conduit for trade between high Asia and
the Gangetic plains to the south. Until the Chinese annexation of Tibet in

3

1959, and the closing of the Nepal-China border soon thereafter, the kingdom of Lo and its leaders retained close ties with neighboring Tibetan communities, even with Lhasa, Tibet's capital.

Jigme Dorje Palbar Bista was known by many names. As a way of signaling his status, he was granted the high caste Hindu surname Bista by the royal family of Nepal, themselves descendants of Prithvi Narayan Shah, the figure whose armies "unified" the country through military and cultural conquests during the eighteenth century. Nepal's unification included strategies of alliance, including incorporation of the territory that would come to be known as Mustang. In this and other senses, the people of Mustang are, and are not, Tibetans. Like most of us, they hold multiple identities—ways of knowing themselves and being known by the world that can render the specifics of belonging transparent and opaque, by turns.

In Nepali, people referred to Bista as the Mustang Raja. He was one of four "petty kings"—including local rulers in the districts of Bajhang, Salyan, and Jajarkot—who retained regional power even as their territories were merged into a national political geography. These "raja" figures were recognized by Nepali law from 1961 until 2008, when Nepal transitioned from a Hindu monarchy and parliamentary democracy to a secular federalist republic.

In Logé, the local variant of Tibetan language, Bista was called Lo Gyalpo, wherein *gyalpo* means "king." This title evokes respect and deference akin to that given the king of neighboring Bhutan as well as royalty from the erstwhile Himalayan kingdoms of Ladakh and Sikkim in India. The fact that this nobleman was stripped of his "raja" title in 2008 by the new Nepali state did little to affect his importance in the lives of Loba, the people of Lo. To them, he was far from "petty" in his influence. Many Loba referred to this man as Kundun, which means "presence." It is the same term of address used by Tibetans to speak of His Holiness the Dalai Lama. This shows just how important he was locally. The Lo Gyalpo helped to define and defend a people, a place, a way of life, and a sense of rootedness in the high pastures and valleys, the canyons and plains, the monasteries and villages of this Himalayan enclave.

Bista's lineage dates to the founding of Lo in 1380 by Amepal, a noble from the western Tibetan kingdom of Gungthang. Amepal's son and heir, Angun Zangpo, established the city of Lo Monthang, a place named for the "plain of aspiration" on which this settlement was built and where Bista was born. In 1964, when Bista was in his mid-thirties, he assumed his title after the death of his father. He was his father's youngest son. Bista married Sidol

Palwar, a refined, elegant woman who traveled from Shigatse, Tibet, to Lo as a bride in 1950. They had no surviving biological children, so the couple adopted their nephew as son and heir. Over the past half-century, Bista ushered his community through massive political-economic and sociocultural transitions, which it is the work of this book to describe.

When I picture the king, I see his stately dignity. Framed by a broad face, his expressive lips formed words of advice or considered action for his people and, especially in his last years, shaped the syllables of Buddhist prayer with humility and devotion. He was a beautiful, intense presence. During our meetings, be they formal audiences at Khar, the palace in Monthang, or over quiet cups of tea with his family in Kathmandu, I remained in awe of him. He could be serious, even stern, but then his regal countenance would melt into a smile, his gold-plated tooth and turquoise earring glinting brightly.

One of my most cherished memories of the king is from 1997, when I traveled with him and his entourage to his summer pastures for days of sheep shearing, yak wrangling, picnicking, and ritually bathing his horses. It was here that I saw the king as a man at work, filled with purpose. I will hold on to that memory, as I do the ones of him and his male companions each morning circumambulating the wall that borders Monthang. There was a sense of routine in these movements but also dedication and communion, kinship and connection to place.

The king's heir, along with others who belong to his generation of Mustang nobility, are invested in the future of Mustang. The family remains central to many aspects of local life—cultural, political, economic—even without continued recognition of this kingdom *as a kingdom* by the Nepali state. And yet the death of Jigme Dorje Palbar Bista marked the end of an era. A Nepali media report in *República*, which came out in the wake of his death, said that his last words to his family were, "Never migrate from the village and the district."

I cannot confirm the veracity of this statement, but I believe in its essence. The late king loved his home fiercely, with his whole being. Even so, this dying wish is a promise that is impossible to keep.

◆ ◆ ◆

When I traveled with the Lo Gyalpo to his summer pastures, momentous changes were beginning to occur in and through Mustang. People were leaving their villages for the village of New York. Like so many migrants the world over, they were departing in search of economic opportunity, life experience, and the chance to offer their children a different future. As is the case for the millions of humans on the move across our Earth today, for those from Mustang, it is not easy to parse the pull of socioeconomic advancement and the rite of passage of youthful migrations from the push of political oppression and environmental change. By the late-1990s, a civil war that would last a decade had crippled many sectors of Nepal's economy. Although wage labor abroad and a deep reliance on remittances at home had yet to become the national norm, seeing migration as a pathway to economic and social well-being had taken root as an ideal.

This is not to say that people from Mustang were new to movement. Subsistence in the high Himalaya, where growing seasons are limited and weather can be fierce, demands creative strategies. For centuries, people from Mustang have combined agriculture, pastoralism, and trade to lowland Nepal and northern India as a way of life. Beginning in the 1980s, locals, mostly men, began traveling as contract laborers to Korea and Japan. Like their neighbors from Manang District, some did business in Asian centers of wealth: Hong Kong, Bangkok, Singapore. However, these moves were not viewed as permanent. Rather, they were annual or life-stage tactics for generating cash for school fees, medical expenses, acts of religious sponsorship, or investments in land or business opportunities back in Nepal. But the movements between Nepal and New York have been different. They have become more permanent, even as they are allowing for further cycles of mobility and opportunities for finding home in more than one location. This change has happened rapidly—within about two decades and one generation.

Now, as lives are forged between Nepal and New York, survival no longer depends solely on agriculture, animal husbandry, and regional trade but also on service-sector employment (running tourist lodges in Mustang, painting nails in Manhattan) and the potent entanglements of remittances. Based on demographic trends in Nepal's 2000 and 2010 censuses, Mustang District has experienced one of the highest rates of depopulation in the country. Numbers vary, but from records kept by villages and rural municipalities in Mustang as well as by diasporic social service organizations in New York, it is estimated that about a quarter of the nine to ten thousand culturally Tibetan people from Mustang District live in New York. In most cases, this number does not include Mustang-American children born in the United States. Nor does it account for those from Mustang who are living permanently in urban Nepal. The demographic transition grows ever starker when examining age cohorts of educated and able-bodied people, now gone from the mountains. Yet these numbers are nearly imperceptible when considering the immigrant populations in places like Jackson Heights, Queens. I am left contemplating the interplay between the profoundly *visible* depopulation of Nepal's Himalayan highlands and the relative *invisibility* of Himalayan migrants in New York.

New York is not the only destination for people from Mustang. In addition to those who have established residence in India, and monastic and lay youth who are educated there, others have migrated to cities in Europe and Asia. They have worked on U.S. military bases in Iraq and Afghanistan; some now serve in the U.S. military. Others work as contract laborers in Japan or Korea, as their uncles and fathers might have done before them. Many of Mustang's senior monastics take regular *dharma* tours across cosmopolitan East Asia, North America, and Europe.

At a broader level, migration and remittance defines contemporary Nepal. Since 2000, there has been a tenfold increase of Nepalis laboring abroad. Of Nepal's approximately thirty million people, about four million have migrated for work, or about 15 percent of the population. As documented by the work of Nepal's Centre for the Study of Labor and Mobility (CESLAM) and by other scholars, approximately 1,500 people leave Nepal each day, and remittances account for a third of the country's GDP. I have met Nepalis—including people from Mustang—at train stations in Lisbon, on public buses in Auckland, in Parisian cafés, and many places in between. As Nadeem Aslam describes in his novel *The Wasted Vigil*, "Pull a thread here and you'll find it's attached to the rest of the world."

◆  ◆  ◆

The embodied act of walking clockwise around a sacred space—which the Lo Gyalpo would do at dawn around Monthang and which many Himalayan people do each morning and evening around the Boudha and Swayambhu *stupa* in Kathmandu—is known as *kora*: སྐོར་བ་.

This term is linked closely with another word, *khorwa* (འཁོར་བ་), a Buddhist principle that defines the nature of desire, interdependence, and cyclic existence—what in Sanskrit and in popular culture is called *samsara*.

People walk *kora*, but this act exists, as language and as lived experience, under the larger umbrella of *khorwa*, the cycle of birth, aging, sickness, death, and rebirth through which sentient beings travel. In Tibetan Buddhism, such reckoning is often symbolized by a wheel—of life, of time, and of the Buddha's teachings. These two interlocking concepts have been crucial to my thinking about migration and social change. Throughout this book, I have chosen to use the term *khora* as a way of representing, imperfectly in an English language text, these two interwoven concepts.

At its root, "diaspora" means dispersal. It is a casting out and across, a transformation of ways of life, a re-imagining of belonging. But experiences of dispersal are not uniform. They do not run in straight lines. Instead, they figure in circles, in cycles. I have come to understand migration and attendant markers of diaspora as *khora*. Broadly, *khora* is a way of being in and moving through the world. This concept illustrates patterns of mobility, processes of world-making, and the dialectical relationship between loss and wonder around which diasporic experiences turn. To see such human movement as *khora* is to expand the affective register of diaspora beyond a one-way trajectory, toward what it means to be—and to belong—in and through forms of circumambulation and transmigration. Many lives can exist within one human lifetime and between one life and the next.

The extent to which one feels at home depends on where one is situated, with whom one walks *khora*, literally and figuratively. For people from Mustang, as with the seasonal shifts of grazing animals between summer and winter pastures, the transitions between farming and trading, or even taking the subway to and from work, *khora* signifies a routine, embedded in social networks, that provides solace, guidance, and support. At times, *khora* enables contemplation of impermanence in a Buddhist sense. The *khora* of migration is enfolded within the turning of the wheel of cyclic existence—with all its vicissitudes of ignorance, attachment, and aversion. Even so, practicing *khora* can have a centering effect. Through movement, we find stillness.

Anthropologist Carole McGranahan has described fieldwork as a type of *khora*. I concur. In fact, I would expand this idea to say that the practice of anthropology can also be *khora*, in that it is a literal and figurative circling around the sacred center of human connection, over time and across space. Through decentering cycles of departure and arrival, anthropologists learn to navigate uncertainty and practice compassion. This book traces such movements, at once internal and external. I also recognize that the terrain through which anthropologists and our interlocutors move can be uneven, punctuated by power and circumstance, by papers and politics.

All too often in anthropology, we assign the term "theory" to the ideas of (primarily) white, male Continental philosophers, and we discount or minimize theoretical work that gets done in other ways. Yet when stripped down, "theory" is simply the creation and use of concepts that help to explain social phenomena. *Khora* does such work. I have chosen to root this book in a framework that comes from Himalayan and Tibetan communities not only because it reflects vernacular understandings—not just because people speak about and practice *khora*—but also because it carries conceptual weight. The work of critical Indigenous scholars (I am particularly grateful to Zoe Todd and Bernard Perley) have helped me to trouble the assumption that theory must emerge from a Western intellectual pedigree in order to be recognizable, let alone capable of opening up new ways of knowing. The difficulties and benefits associated with the daily practice of *khora* in specific Himalayan contexts reflects the complexities of migration in a more catholic sense, from its legal obstacles and economic prospects to the ways it reshapes families and communities, including their connections to land and lineage, to language and culture.

As a category of experience, *khora* stands for the pathways we travel from one life or one country to the next—and back again—and how we are changed through these processes. The concept resonates with anthropological discussions of modernity and mobility: circulations of capital and labor across the globe. In this sense, *khora* connects to dynamics variously described as *globalization*, *transnationalism*, and the *worlding* of people, ideas, and things. Globalization is a gloss for the circulation of resources and neoliberal ideals, transnationalism emphasizes the dissolution of geopolitical boundaries, and worlding troubles assumptions about how or in what directions global movements occur. Onto the bones of these intellectual ideas, *khora* adds a layer of muscle memory: of cyclic movement, of ethical action, of a walking temporality that links the past and the present to possible futures.

Still, *khora* is not simply a mode of explaining something, in the ways that a term like "transnationalism" becomes a shortcut for intricate, varied experiences, nor is my use of *khora* about making a universal claim. Instead, consider *khora* a way of doing and being, a mechanism for action. *Khora* can help us to see how the circulation of people, things, and ideas is affectively and materially complicated. The *khora* of migration interweaves threads of care and belonging as lives are stitched together through time and space. In this sense, *khora* is rooted in relatedness, in kinship.

◆    ◆    ◆

Migration at once depends on and works on kinship, the genealogical bonds of descent and alliance that shape humanity. We follow the paths and the footsteps of those who have moved before us. People call upon kinship networks to facilitate the logistics of migration—visas, jobs, apartments—and to help one another through less visible but equally challenging emotional transitions. No matter where people from Mustang find themselves, the cultural obligations that anchor community mean that one's first effort in any situation is to establish—through a recitation of place-based social history and by speaking names—where and how you fit into networks of kin. In Himalayan communities as elsewhere, such webs of belonging keep people at once beholden to, and endeared to, one another. This says something about love and understanding, and about home.

*The Ends of Kinship* explores what it means for people from Mustang, including those who have migrated to New York, to care for one another, steward a homeland across time and space, remake households elsewhere, and confront distinct forms of happiness and suffering through this process. How do people honor and alter their shared responsibilities and senses of connection to one another and to a particular geography, not only in spite of but even through the turning of the wheel of migration? How do different generations abide with one another, even when language fades and people struggle to comprehend? I ask these questions across distinct social ecologies, from high mountain villages of northern Nepal to some of the most diverse urban neighborhoods on Earth, at the heart of America's immigration story.

This book's engagement with one small region of the world speaks to broader dynamics. Immigration is a lightning rod issue of our time. Whether located in New York or experienced in the places from which *new* New Yorkers hail, immigration articulates with legal rights and claims to property; the division and reunification of families; legacies of state violence, processes of settler colonialism, and dynamics of political uncertainty; and aspirations for living beyond what is captured by the terms "refugee" or "economic migrant." This is true for highly visible groups—Central American migrants, Syrian refugees—and for those, like people from Mustang, who remain nearly imperceptible within the demographics of New York and the greater United States but whose presence in America has dramatically reshaped their home communities.

What do I mean by *the ends of kinship*? At its heart, this book focuses on the fabric of duty and desire that *is* kinship, as it is experienced through the transformative process of migration. By definition, "ends" references more than one place. It bespeaks physical distance—points on a map, say—even as it signals temporal shifts, notches in a time line, moments of initiation and completion. This book is not only about people who have moved from one place to another. It is also about how people live in and through multiple places, about what it means to leave, to remain behind, and possibly to return. I am not speaking of an *end*, singular. Quite the opposite.

The relational dynamics of kinship can give meaning to people's lives in accordance with, or even in spite of, physical and political abilities to move—the warp and weft of citizenship and identity. As with rope or thread, some relationships fray through migration while others are newly knotted. The ends of kinship are ties that bind people to one another in dialogue with the emotional and structural forces that can sever or reformulate these bonds. In this sense, we are *all* living at the ends of kinship—if for different reasons. I feel the ends of kinship with my parents, even as I sense these ends within the families with whom I have lived, worked, and learned, in and through Mustang, over the past twenty-five years. One aim of this book is to highlight the lived experiences of pain and loss inherent to the ends of kinship and to illuminate the senses of possibility and hope that can occur through the *khora* of migration.

◆ ◆ ◆

True to the nature of *khora*, the book's structure follows the turning of the Wheel of Life: from pregnancy, birth, and childhood to making a living and creating families to old age, death, and forms of rebirth. The text proceeds in six parts, each of which includes a fictional short story and a chapter of narrative ethnography. A short essay and an ink line drawing by the Himalayan artist Tenzin Norbu frames each part. Taken together, image and text distill an essence rather than make a neat argument. With the exception of Jigme Dorje Palbar Bista's portrait that opens this book, I've chosen not to include photographs. In opting for likeness over literal realism, I am making both an ethical and a creative decision. Also, I have foregone conventional footnotes for an essay on methods and sources at the end of the book along with a bibliography of works that have shaped my thinking and writing. This is an aesthetic choice about how words occupy a page and a creative response to the politics of citations in academia.

Speaking of creativity, I believe it takes imagination and, sometimes, the crafting of fictional accounts to *see* social truths. As method and form, fiction reveals the strengths and limits of ethnographic knowing, specifically when it comes to fostering empathy and curiosity. Anthropology enfolds distinct human dramas within larger webs of meaning. Fiction shapes the stories held within "data" into complex sensory, affective, and dramatic experiences that speak to and beyond the generalizations of theory, the specifics of culture. Each mode illuminates the other. As Walter Benjamin insists in *The Storyteller*, the power of stories rests precisely in what is evoked rather than explained. To couple fiction with ethnography is to resist singular interpretation.

I drafted the stories first, writing from memory. The stories guided me as I reviewed more than two decades of material to craft the ethnographic chapters, which are written purposefully as fragments, without neat beginnings or endings. Like a tile mosaic or a quilt, pieces that may initially seem temporally or geographically dissonant are stitched together, revealing intricate patterns of life forged between Nepal and New York. Though narratively neater, the stories allow for a different kind of honesty. In them, I write about intimate things from multiple perspectives. To be clear, the events described in the stories are fiction, but they emerge from my years of relationship with people from Mustang. As such, these stories are real in the sense that they are credible. They have been crafted into form in a different way than field notes or interview transcripts become ethnographic text. Both processes involve distillation, culling, coding.

I am inspired by writerly anthropologists and by writers whose art reflects the thickness of life in ways that could be called ethnographic. Tacking between short stories and ethnography provides an opportunity to consider what each genre offers as well as the limits of that offering. What is seen. What is elided. One form reveals the negative space of the other. And, as my painter mother has taught me, negative space is not empty but filled with possibilities for new ways of seeing.

◆  ◆  ◆

In Tibetan, *lam* means "road" or "path," but it also signals consciousness: a way and the Way. The word indicates effort, practice, progress toward a goal. In Tibetan Buddhism, this goal is spiritual enlightenment. My path—of learning, collaborating, and writing across languages and cultures—began in Nepal a quarter-century ago. In many ways, people from Mustang are the family I've chosen, rather than the family into which I was born. Even so, I have learned so much from Mustang about what binds families together and what can wrest them apart.

Yet while I may be "big sister" to some people and "little grandma" to others, I will state the obvious: I am not from Mustang. And what I *am*—a white, educated, middle-class American woman—is reflective of a politics of difference. These optics are worth stating plainly, since anthropology has a long and checkered history of writing the words and worlds of others. Yet for all its faults and fissures—its colonial legacies and its reflective turns— anthropology remains a vital way to practice humility and to listen.

*The Ends of Kinship* is an effort to represent the lives of people about whom I care deeply. I hope to share a fraction of what I have learned from these remarkable individuals whom I respect, but in whose shoes I will never walk this *khora*. Honoring the confidences that have been entrusted to me has shaped how and what I write, where I let silence breathe. I admire the capacities of those from Mustang to maintain and transform who they are in Nepal and through diaspora—this wrenching dispersal, this liberation. Telling these stories requires shedding light not only on creative and courageous capacities but also on insecurity and conflict, disappointment and trouble, power and authority. To *not* do so—to idealize or over-expose— would not serve those about whom this book is written.

The individual and collective memories that form this book might be thought of as an archive of experience. Like any archive, it is incomplete. It amplifies certain voices over others. It has blind spots. No matter who makes the archive or who does the writing, no treasury of lives can ever be wholly representative. So much remains untranslatable, hidden. Anthropology has taught me this much.

Still, there is value in the telling.

# PART I

# ATTENDING TO BIRTH

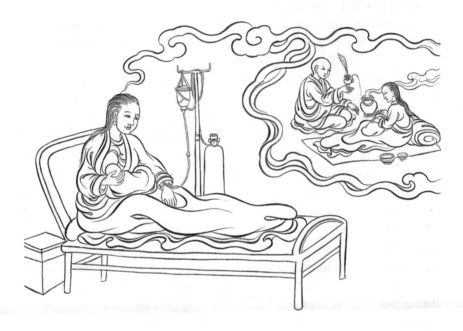

Each thing
I did, then, I did for the first
time, touched the flesh of our flesh,
brought the tiny mouth to my breast,
she drew the avalanche of milk
down off the mountain, I felt as if
I was nothing, no one, I was everything to her, I was hers.

—SHARON OLDS, "FIRST BIRTH"

PREGNANCY AND EARLY CHILDHOOD ARE FILLED WITH PRECARITY AND joy no matter where they occur. Like women across the Himalaya and Tibetan Plateau, those from Mustang have faced many challenges in bringing new life into this world. Geography can create obstacles to care. Roads can be inaccessible and unreliable, as can hospitals and health posts. To practice medicine of any sort in rural Nepal remains a challenge. To proceed with knowledge and skill, under material conditions that meet the needs of women and children during pregnancy, labor, and delivery, sometimes proves impossible. The *khora* of migration is shifting Mustang women's experiences of pregnancy and childbirth. Migrations have allowed access to city hospitals and Cesarean sections, birth certificates, and contraception. These transformations, in turn, have shifted aspects of what it means to be a woman and a mother in Mustang itself.

The short story, "Blood and Bone," introduces three generations of Mustang women: a grandmother, her daughter, and her daughter's daughter. In culturally Tibetan circles, blood, *trak*, comes from the mother, whereas the father passes on his bone, *rü*. This is a way of speaking about kinship and belonging, one's biological and cultural inheritance. This story moves across time and space—from Monthang to Kathmandu to Queens. In so doing, it explores what is remembered and forgotten, shared and silenced, of women's experiences over the last half-century.

The ethnographic chapter, "Finding the Womb Door," describes how women's reproductive histories have changed over the past few generations. Its title refers to the ways that people from Mustang speak about reincarnation and what it means to be human. In other cultural contexts, birth might be framed as the nascence of life. In Mustang, it is viewed as a circling, another form of *khora*. After death comes rebirth. After the *bardo*, the in-between realm between one life and the next, a consciousness passes through an available womb door. Then, if karmic and biological circumstances align, it rests here, forming into new life.

But this Buddhist way of knowing says little about the lived experiences of pregnancy, birth, and young childhood. To this end, the chapter also examines how forms of harm, at once spiritual and structural, can shape these processes and considers how the *khora* of migration reconfigures family relationships. Social reproduction begins with a biological imperative—a primal intimacy that shapes humanity. It matters where and how this occurs. What falls out from these couplings? How is new life caught and held?

# BLOOD AND BONE

GRANDMOTHER

Diki had carried the child for half a year before she acknowledged her pregnancy to anyone, including herself. Winter helped. People dressed in so many layers during the season that the contours of bodies—the slope of a hip, the plum fullness of breasts, the bulge of a belly—could be masked.

Snow drifted across the walled city, settling on parapets, dusting livestock, straining roof beams. Diki spent her days predictably: meting out straw and food scraps to the animals, weaving, cooking dried turnip stew, drinking tea with her neighbors, gathering dung before it hardened to ice, stoking the hearth, feeding the animals again, sleeping long nights under the watch of so many stars.

But even had it been summer, she would not have spoken about the nascence in her womb. To do so would have risked another death.

Diki's losses lived within her like stones. Perfect round handfuls of hardened grief, ten of them. She would not allow herself to feel the weight of the eleventh. If this tiny tangle of blood and bone could survive the hardened landscape of her interior, so be it. Diki ate what there was to eat, always saving the fleshier bits of meat for Dhondrup, her husband. She did the work expected of her.

Dhondrup felt the quickening after Losar. He returned from a trip to the village of Kimaling, smelling of burnt juniper, horse sweat, and new barley beer, to find Diki asleep in their nest of sheepskins and rough wool. The only other person in their house was old uncle Wangdu, a monk who could sleep through anything. Dhondrup sidled in beside his wife, wrapped his rough fingers around her abdomen. She had fallen asleep fully dressed. He untied Diki's *chuba*, loosened her petticoat. Diki stirred, but she did not fully wake. Dhondrup sighed. He had hoped for some sort of love—a physical release after the pent-up energies of ritual—but he let his exhausted wife sleep. Still, her body felt full and alive, unlike her skinny legs, her hardened expression. With his hands on her belly, Dhondrup felt the child inside flutter. Movements as delicate as moth wings. Dhondrup stiffened with surprise. He held his breath, now hoping his hands would not wake his wife.

Dhondrup's training as a *ngakpa* and an *amchi* was limited. People did not refer to him as either a tantrist or a doctor. Yet he often assisted the men who appeased the spirits, who examined pulses and gave medicines. On the night in question, the ritual had been for an old nomad woman who was down from the high pastures to live with relatives for the winter. She was suffering from *tsadrip*, a shaking that sometimes led to frozen limbs or the inability to speak and that everyone knew was the consequence of spiritual pollution.

In the winter of 1961, it felt as if defilement was everywhere. People spoke of this time as a degenerate age, marked by war and new forms of greed. Chushi Gangdruk, the Tibetan resistance soldiers, had begun to arrive in Mustang. Loba understood these soldiers' desires to challenge Chinese encroachment on Tibetan sovereignty. Still, it was difficult to quell these warriors' hunger—for firewood, food, munitions, even women—or to predict what the government in Kathmandu would do in response to their presence. It was a tempestuous time.

Dhondrup withdrew his hands from his wife's body. This did not seem like an auspicious moment for new life. Still, he prayed for the being in her belly. In the coming days, without letting Diki know, he performed rituals to remove obstacles. He requested a divination. The *lama*'s dice and rosary revealed reasons for hope.

By the time the snow began to melt, everyone could see that Diki was pregnant, but she refused to speak of her condition. As the days lengthened and her belly continued to round, other women whispered, "It looks as if she is carrying a son." This was the tenth time she had conceived, but she had no living children.

Diki's first pregnancy had come on the heels of her engagement to Dhondrup, which had been arranged by their parents. That one ended before the sickness wore off, her stomach still a plane of adolescent flatness. She was only eighteen. The second, third, and fourth pregnancies passed through her just as quickly, coming in with Losar and departing before the warm winds of spring. Some believed she worked too hard. Others gossiped that Dhondrup's male substance, his *khuwa*, was weak. "It must not mix well with her blood," they said. The fifth she counted twice, for they had been twins, delivered too early and without breath. Dhondrup was off trading.

Had it not been for old *ibi* Kunsang and the medicine the *amchi* gave her, she would have bled to death.

Before the twins, she had simply carried sadness. After them, she gave in to anger. She could not bear to look at Dhondrup, let alone lie down with him. He left her alone for a year, finding comfort in drink. Some said that so much death must have its root in spiritual misdeeds, in this or previous lives.

The seventh and eighth pregnancies were conceived in drunkenness. She willed them to leave her body.

Then came the winter of pilgrimage. Dhondrup stopped drinking. Diki reclaimed an appetite. On the lama's advice, they made the journey to Kathmandu, hoping to purify the negative *karma* that had gathered around them like storm clouds. She remembered their visit to the cave at Yangleshö, her prayers to Guru Rinpoche and Yeshi Tsogyal, this divine couple, so perfect in their union. She carried the ninth pregnancy to term, but their daughter lived for only a few days before fever took her. They buried her small body in the walls of the house, as was custom.

It is understandable, then, why Diki would not speak about the life inside her now. She was thirty, but she felt much older.

As spring ripened and the stars moved toward Saka Dawa, this most holy of lunar months, Diki could sense the basin of her pelvis, her groin, opening and closing, the ways that she and other villagers kneaded *tsampa* and tea into a hard ball of dough each morning for breakfast. At first, she thought these contractions were the onset of labor and, perhaps, the end of this life. But then they settled down into the vessel of her body.

The baby turned on the day that *namdru*, "sky boats," flew over the northern horizon. It was late spring. Dhondrup and several other men were sitting on the roof of their home, repairing bridles, weaving rope. "They must be sending arms for the soldiers," said one of the men. Diki cared little about these battles, but she did notice that the child's haunches seemed to have slid down toward her womb door, his head prone, as if he too were watching the sky.

Her waters broke during Tenpa Chirim. This ritual cycle rallied the protective deities of this land to drive out negative forces that might interfere with good harvests. Rituals such as this provided a rare moment of entertainment, a release from the demands of subsistence. Diki and other village women squatted together against the rammed earth walls of the palace, watching and listening. A massive silk brocade *thangka* fluttered from the roof of one of the tallest homes in the village. The abbot and the king's priests made offerings, recited texts, sounded trumpets, drums, cymbals. Monks transformed into wrathful *dharma* protectors, twirling across the open-air courtyard that became a ritual stage.

Diki was so absorbed in the spectacle of these dances that it took her a moment to realize that the dampness she felt between her legs was not spilled tea. It was the beginning of her labor. Fortunately, *ibi* Kunsang was not far away. This village widow was twice Diki's age. They were not from the same social rank. Kunsang was a commoner, a *phalba*, whereas Diki was a *hremo*, a noblewoman. Still, Kunsang was the person most women called when labor started.

Diki rose and Kunsang followed. Other women's crouching limbs expanded to fill the small space their bodies had occupied. Few took notice of the wetness at their feet.

"The pain has not started, but waters released," said Diki. Kunsang nodded and took Diki by the elbow. They walked steadily toward Diki's home.

Diki helped Kunsang boil water, warm oil, and prepare an area away from the hearth, with old blankets and rags. Contractions began in earnest. Diki groaned. Kunsang handled the laboring woman. "Sit. Rest your head here. Let me feel the child." The old woman's palms offered a practiced dexterity. In addition to all the other women she had attended during birth, she had been through this routine ten times herself. Although only half of those children had made it to adulthood, they had all survived their first years of life. In fact, she'd even given birth to one of her children completely on her own, in a rapeseed field at dusk.

Kunsang sculpted Diki's inner form. She did not say anything when she realized that this child's back end, rather than head, was near the pelvic floor. She had helped to turn several breech births and sensed that this child could still be moved. Kunsang began this delicate work, her hands riding the waves of each contraction.

"This feels different," Diki managed between moans.

Kunsang had few words, but she repeated them as minutes turned to hours. "Don't cry. Breathe. Child will come." She was surprised, actually, that Diki's body tempered itself. Kunsang's wrinkled fingers had not been washed, but she coated them in oil and felt for the child, coaxing the womb door to widen. She could feel a feathery softness. Hair. The old woman let out a sigh. "Push. Push when the pains come."

Diki's son came into the world alive, yes, but with the cord wrapped around his neck. Kunsang worked it like knotted yarn, then blew her own breath into the mouth of this infant, sucking and spitting away what remained of the watery world he had left behind. He cried, loud and pure, and with that Diki burst open.

"Don't cry. Hold him." Kunsang placed the newborn on Diki's chest. The placenta slipped out like a fish.

MOTHER

On the night Dolkar learned that her only daughter was pregnant, she had fallen asleep in front of the television. Routine brownouts, "load-shedding" in local parlance, meant that the Kathmandu electrical grid went dark, on schedule, across the city. The generator whirred to life, waking Dolkar. She wiped drool from her cheek and straightened the pillows at her back. Chinese actors playing Tibetan warriors and light-skinned Lhasa girls dressed as nomad princesses moved across the flatscreen. This Tibetan teledrama beamed into her Kathmandu living room from Lhasa, via satellite. Even half awake, Dolkar picked up the plotline. It reminded her of the *Ramayana* soap opera—a version of the Hindu epic that aired on Star TV last year—except for the language. She'd learned Hindi during winter trading trips to India, selling sweaters in roadside stalls back in the 1980s before she and her husband bought this plot of land and built a guest house. Now she practiced Hindi by watching Bollywood films. She could manage the Sinicized inflection of official Lhasa Tibetan, but she had no desire to learn Chinese.

The young girl who helped in the guest house kitchen had cleared the dinner dishes. Dolkar's husband had retired to their third-floor bedroom, carrying his own mother on his back up the stairs. Such was the nighttime routine. Dolkar yawned, arched her back, reached for a thermos of hot water. She'd been on her feet since five in the morning, making apple pancakes and omelets, vegetable fried rice, endless pots of hot lemon-ginger-honey for tourists. This little hotel did not have attached bathrooms, but it offered the refuge of a peaceful garden and a clean kitchen. It was rarely full, but it had never been empty since the day Dolkar opened its doors thirteen years ago.

Thirteen years. In her half-sleep, Dolkar spun numbers in her head. She could write 2013 in standard English numerals at the top of the receipts that tourists requested, but Devanagari was the only script she navigated with some degree of confidence. Dolkar was nearly fifty. She'd had one year of government schooling, hardly enough for literacy, but had secretly studied her daughter's Nepali primers during the girl's early years at Little Angels School. Once her children were older, Dolkar took to sounding out

*Kantipur* newspaper headlines after her husband had drunk his tea and set aside the morning paper.

Thirteen years. With half a century behind her, Dolkar was now thirteen years older than her mother, Diki, had been when she died, after giving birth to her younger brother, the third live birth gleaned from thirteen pregnancies. Unlike other women of Dolkar's generation who had made lives for themselves in the city but still carried nostalgia for the village, Dolkar did not miss Mustang. Even all these years later, she felt that the land itself had taken her mother. A life hard as stone and soil, a place steeped in ritual but bereft of modern health care. It had swallowed her mother whole.

People said that Dolkar shared her mother's face. She found the comparison difficult to reckon from the one photograph she had of the woman who birthed her. That, and shards of memory: hands, hair, voice. In the black-and-white portrait taken during her mother's only trip to Kathmandu, the woman did not smile. She stood, formal and erect, beside her husband, against a painted backdrop of the Himalayan range. They both looked so young.

Dolkar had come into this world as a *labruk*, a back-to-back child, just a year after her elder brother's birth in 1961. Both had good appetites and bright eyes. Everyone thought this family's bad luck was behind them, but a clutch of barren years opened up after Dolkar and her older brother were born. Dolkar's younger brother was about a month old when their mother died. Diki's milk trickled, halted. Then chills and fever came in waves. Dolkar, who was eight years old and therefore mature enough to care for baby goats and baby humans, began taking the infant to a paternal aunt who nursed the child. They consulted the *amchi*, hoping the sickness would lift. At first, it was just that Diki's postpartum stomach did not seem to deflate. Instead of breathing a sigh of relief after birth, it was as if her body was a sheepskin bellow filled with air. Pain distorted Diki's face when Dolkar or her elder brother hugged her. Then the fever spiked, as did the smell of rot emanating from that most private place. *Ibi* Kunsang came with boiled herbs and poultices, but it was too late. Dolkar held her mother's hand long after the feverish flush had drained away, replaced by an ashen stillness. Dolkar's father, Dhondrup, sat beside the hearth, a widower reduced to tears and drink. He would remain this way for years.

Dolkar's mobile buzzed. She reached into the pocket of her loose cotton pants and pulled out the smartphone that had been a gift from her son, Tsepten. That boy had a sense of drama and timing. He had been born on a bus.

He should have been a *ngakpa* like his father. Instead, Tsepten managed a Nepali restaurant in Queens.

Dolkar still thought about the moment he came into the world. Very pregnant, she had been halfway through an overnight ride from Kathmandu to Benares, India, for winter trade. Her contractions started soon after they crossed the border. For the next few hours, Dolkar held on to the seat in front of her and eventually moved into the aisle. Despite her travel companions' protestations, the driver refused to stop. The teenage ticket boy, strung out from sniffing glue, began to cry. Two chickens walked up and down the aisle, calmly pecking at spit, snot, and instant noodle crumbs. A woman from lowland Nepal, her muscled arms like mahogany, offered Dolkar sips of water and shouted, "Don't worry! The baby will come soon!" A Brahmin astrologer stayed clear of the polluting mess of birth, but he began calculating the child's chart.

The scene was so chaotic that Dolkar forgot her fear, forgot the memories of her mother's face at death, visions that she had not divulged to anyone but that haunted her. This was her second pregnancy but her first true labor. After the miscarriage, she was terrified that whatever caused her mother's misfortune had been passed on to her. But then came Tsepten. One of Dolkar's cousins caught the child, whose strong cries pierced the morning air. Dawn came swiftly, flamingo pink clouds hovering above the Ganges. Dolkar became a mother. Once the newborn had been bathed and swaddled by an Indian nurse at a government hospital, the other Mustang women with whom Dolkar had been traveling joked that Tsepten must have liked the Bollywood songs blaring from the bus speakers. "He wanted to come out and sing," they said. "He will bring joy."

That was about three decades ago. Now, Dolkar thought, Tsepten spends good money for people to carve strange pictures in ink across his arms and back, he wastes time in some place where he pays to run around in circles and lift heavy things, and he refuses to get married. Tsepten had decamped to New York after earning his School Leaving Certificate (SLC). Dolkar no longer understood her son, but she had set aside anger. Tsepten inherited his father's charisma and discipline, but his father couldn't see it. They had not spoken to each other in more than a year.

Their daughter, Tsering, was tame by comparison. She'd done well in school and hoped that, after some years as a babysitter in New York, once her papers came through, she would enroll in nursing school. Dolkar's phone vibrated again. Tsering Chori lit up the screen in crisp Helvetica.

"*Ama*, are you sleeping?"

"No, *chori*. Watching television." Although Tsering could understand Logé, she and her mother had slipped into the habit long ago of speaking to each other in Nepali. They exchanged simple words, about weather in Kathmandu and weather in New York, about tourists in the guest house and the two young American children Tsering nannied for a living, Aiden and Lucy. *A-den, Lu-chi*, as Dolkar called them. Through her daughter, Dolkar had learned about strollers and sleep training, monkey bars and peanut allergies. Tsering seemed enamored by the lists of dos and don'ts her American boss posted on the refrigerator, the well-oiled management of it all. In hearing Tsering describe these children's lives in America, Dolkar marveled at the amount of attention they received but wondered how they would learn to manage pain and disappointment when it came for them. She kept these thoughts to herself.

"*Ama*, there is something to tell you," said Tsering. Dolkar's stomach tightened. "*Ama*, my period stopped two months ago. The baby will come in summer."

Dolkar breathed out. A baby. No illness or injury. No immigration officers knocking on the door. Across the world from her own baby, she smiled. This was good news.

"Are you eating well? Do you feel sick? What did the doctor say? Do you get to see a picture? Have you told Jamyang?" Dolkar was not usually effusive, but the questions tumbled out. Tsering, whose name meant "long life," was twenty-six and engaged to her cross-cousin, Jamyang, a taxi driver who worked nights. The arrangement had been secured several years ago, but the couple had grown up together and had been friends before their families bound them to each other. Affection evolved. This child would cement their bond. As was becoming common these days in New York, Dolkar thought the couple might combine a formal marriage ceremony with the child's first birthday. Dolkar could imagine the envelopes of cash and piles of *kathag*, the buffet line and pale orange walls inside that Punjabi banquet hall near Roosevelt Island. She had never been there, but she'd seen videos.

"I want to eat everything and then nothing at all, but the doctor says the baby is healthy. She's nice. Born here in New Jersey, but her parents are from Himachal Pradesh," answered Tsering. "We speak Hindi plus English together, *mix and match*. And, yes, Jamyang knows. He is so happy. We haven't found out boy or girl, but it doesn't matter. We only want good health."

"Don't tell many people," Dolkar advised. She had not planned on saying this. "You don't want gossip to cause harm."

"*Ama*, you believe that?"

"Believe that gossip is powerful? Certainly!" Dolkar flushed. Her daughter sensed this passion through the phone.

"But how could just saying something cause problems? The doctor says it is important to take vitamins, eat well, not get too much *tension*."

"Yes. That is important. And go to the doctor for *checkup*," responded Dolkar. "But what people say matters. Just *take care yourself*." Dolkar spoke little English but she used what she knew to reach her daughter. Just as the power of people's talk was real, so was the need for *checkup*.

Tsering's next question surprised her. "*Ama*, how was it, when I was born?" Dolkar did not answer right away. "I know the story of Tsepten," Tsering continued. "Everyone knows that story! But what was it like with me?"

Dolkar took a deep breath. Tsepten's birth, so dramatic, so public, had allowed Dolkar to set aside her fear. With Tsering it was different. She had been in Mustang, no longer in her natal village but in the unfamiliar hamlet of her husband's family. She had been terrified.

"You were born at home, in the same house where your father was born," answered Dolkar.

"I know that *Ama*, but what was it like? Did you go to the doctor when you were pregnant? Did you feel sick and then hungry? Did you have strange dreams? Who helped you?" Now it was Tsering's turn for questions.

"No, no doctor. It was summer. Hot, out in the wheat field. They told me stay home, but I made snacks. Carried them to the workers. Then pains started. Aunt Karsang brought me back to the house. She took good care. Cousin Sonam too. Massaged my back. Gave dried fish from Mapham Yumtso. They say it helps to make the baby come quickly. You came quickly. You were good on the breast. Father cut your cord and put medicine butter on the roof of your mouth to make you cry well. Lama Tharchen made the *kyekar*," Dolkar said, recalling the natal horoscope that augured long life, suggesting the name Tsering. "He made incense offerings too," said Dolkar, "to purify."

Dolkar remembered the smell of juniper, the sense of accomplished exhaustion at the sight of her daughter. She remembered the taste of bone broth and of falling in and out of sleep with her newborn. Dolkar was happy when the Nepali health workers arrived with vaccinations because many children had died of fever and pox in previous years. She shared some of these memories with her daughter.

But Dolkar did not tell Tsering about the miscarriage she had about a year before Tsepten's birth. She did not tell her daughter about the blood on the walls of the district hospital where she'd gone that time, after she began to bleed, or about the cold metal cot, the clumsy doctor, the frigid speculum. She did not tell her daughter about the injections she began to receive once they moved to Kathmandu, to stop the possibility of another pregnancy. She did not tell her daughter about the arguments with Tsering's father about this decision, how he called such medicine a sin. She did not tell her daughter that she longed to be present in America when her first grandchild came into this world. Part of Dolkar wanted to share all of this with Tsering, but she felt there was too much space between them.

"Don't worry, *chori*," said Dolkar. She wrapped her free hand around her abdomen, held her phone to her ear with the other. "Everything will be fine."

DAUGHTER

"This won't hurt, but it will be cold." The ultrasound technician held a bottle of lubricant above Tsering's belly and squirted. Tsering grimaced. Jamyang stood beside her, holding her hand and staring at the monitor.

"I am going to move this around a little bit," the technician continued, working the sonogram probe. "There's the little face! Are you sure you don't want to know if you are having a little princess or a big boy? Oh, I just love this part of my job!"

The technician, who seemed younger than Tsering, looked vaguely Asian but spoke with a decidedly American accent. Her words ran together. Although Tsering had been in New York for a few years now, she struggled with the pace of American speech, the assumptions. If she ever became a nurse, she would remember to speak slowly, with clear precision.

"No, we want surprise," Jamyang answered.

Tsering was into her third trimester. She could no longer tie her shoes with ease, but her days with Aiden and Lucy passed smoothly and brought comfort. She felt, more than ever, like these American children were helping to prepare her for her own imminent motherhood. She was beyond the hormonal waves that had left her irritable, and she was so visibly pregnant that people gave up their seats for her on the subway.

Tsering was also grateful that she worked for a kind American couple. Many of her friends had not been as fortunate, sharing stories of verbal abuse, withheld pay, even outright sexual harassment as fathers cornered them in bathrooms, groped them in garages. Tsering dealt with none of this. Instead, she had a beautiful woman for a boss who ran an art gallery in Chelsea. The husband taught at Columbia. They were generous.

The family she worked for had promised a crib, baby clothes, even a party. Tsering wanted to accept these things, but she heard her mother in her head when she told her boss that, while she appreciated these gifts, could she please hold off on giving them until after the baby was born? Too much preparation, like too much talking, could bring bad luck. Before she'd told her mother about the pregnancy, Tsering had never considered this particular pattern of cause and effect, but this idea followed her like an echo.

"Is baby position good?" Tsering asked.

"Let's just take a look, shall we?" The young technician found the heartbeat, hummingbird quick and just as strong. This made Tsering relax. Her breathing slowed as she imagined her child nestled within her waters.

"Hmm." The technician paused. "Hmm." She said again. This did not inspire confidence. "Dr. Sharma will be here soon. You just hang tight there for a minute, little mama. Everything will be fine."

Tsering shot Jamyang a look. It was a look of both fear and incomprehension. His English was better, in part because he listened to harried New Yorkers from the front seat of his cab all night and into the early morning hours. His job was a television serial: fast paced, full of drama and innuendo. She practiced her English with a toddler and a preschooler.

"Is something wrong?" Jamyang asked.

"I am sure everything will be fine," the technician repeated, her tone now flat. Jamyang reached for Tsering's shoulder. The technician left. Ten interminable minutes passed before Dr. Sharma came into the room. She smiled at Tsering, her almond eyes probing, generous.

"*Namaste!* It is good to see you, Tsering. Jamyang. Now, let me take a look." Dr. Sharma turned her attention toward the ultrasound machine, running the wand over Tsering's belly, exposing her inner world. She worked for a moment in silence, breathing slowly.

"Yep," she said. Then, kindly but with a directness that unnerved Tsering, she asked, "Do you have a history of difficult pregnancies in your family? This is your first child. You're young and healthy. So, what I'm seeing is a bit unusual."

Tsering stared at her, unsure of how to respond. After a few moments, she said, "My mother had my brother and me. There was no problem from what I know." Tsering did not mention that her brother had been born on a bus, that she had come into this world on the dirt floor of a village home. "My grandmother died when my mother was young, so I don't know about her. I never met her."

"Okay," Dr. Sharma said. She could sense Tsering's fear. "Please do not worry. You and your baby are going to be fine. But you will need to take extra care, and you will probably need to have a Cesarean section—an operation to get the baby out."

Tsering sucked in her breath. Her boss had Lucy by C-section, and Lucy was gorgeous and clever. She knew other women from Mustang who had given birth this way. But she had also heard stories about doctors telling women that their hips were not wide enough to have a natural birth. She remembered her mother and other elder women criticizing those who gave birth by operation. *Could they not bear the pain? Were they not strong enough?*

"Is operation necessary? Will it make me weak? Is something wrong with my body?" Tsering welled with tears.

"Let me explain what I see." Dr. Sharma smiled again and reached for Tsering's hand. "You heard the heartbeat, right?" Jamyang and Tsering both nodded. She took up the wand, turned their attention to the monitor.

"And you see here, how the baby has settled this way, with his bottom toward your pelvis?" The couple strained to see the curve of buttocks, then nodded again.

"This is called breech position," she explained. "That means that the baby's head is up, and his bottom is down."

Tsering had gone to all of her prenatal checkups. She had taken her vitamins. She'd avoided books, but that was mostly a question of literacy, time, and the potent mix of inertia and culture. Some of her friends had also recently become mothers. Nobody had ever explained to her that this could happen, that a baby could be pointed the wrong way. She felt angry. Why was she learning all of this for the first time? Why didn't her mother, her friends who were mothers—anyone—ever talk about this? She took care of children for a living. How was it that she knew so little about how they came into this world?

"Many babies turn around in their mother's uterus," Dr. Sharma went on. The word "uterus" hung heavily in the air, at once distant and familiar to Tsering. "Sometimes they flip and face down before labor starts, all on their own. Other times we can turn the baby." Dr. Sharma was looking straight into Tsering's eyes. There was trust between them.

"But I'm also seeing that you have something called placenta previa. It is not as severe as it could be, but the placenta—the sac that helps feed and care for your baby inside your belly—the placenta is covering up your cervix. The cervix is sort of like the lock on the door that has to open in order for your baby to come out. This can be dangerous."

*If spoken words can change the course of things*, Tsering thought, *then what does naming the cause of this danger do?*

"You are at thirty-three weeks now," continued Dr. Sharma. "That means as many as seven weeks to go for a full-term baby, but your child can be born earlier and still be fine." She paused before continuing. "I am going to recommend bed rest for a month and then that we deliver the baby by C-section."

Tsering tried to imagine what "bed rest" meant. Did this mean sleeping later? Taking time to get up in the morning or going to bed early?

"Bed rest means that you need to stop working now," Dr. Sharma continued. "You need to stay lying down at home as much as possible for the next four weeks. Jamyang, you are going to have to do more things around the house. Can you do that?" The stunned young man just nodded. He would take care of her during the day. They would rest together. He would drive his taxi at night.

"But what about Aiden and Lucy?" Tsering blurted out. Dr. Sharma looked confused.

"The children Tsering babysits, for work," Jamyang explained.

"Well, I can write you a letter to their parents, so they know what is happening. They should understand."

Tsering felt panicked. Stuck. Her boss had said that she could have her job back after the baby was born. Tsering had even arranged for another Loba woman who was between jobs to take over for a few months. But this was too quick. "I can't stop work," she said.

"If you want to have a healthy baby, you need to." Dr. Sharma's tone changed. It was still caring, but she'd lowered her voice an octave. She no longer smiled. The obstetrician set down the ultrasound wand and squirted antibacterial solution on her hands. As she wrung them dry, she repeated, "You will be fine. Your baby will be fine. But you need to follow my advice. I want to see you again in a week." Dr. Sharma turned to Jamyang, her face stern but kind. "Take care of her, okay?"

"Yes, doctor."

Once outside the hospital, Tsering burst into tears. "Don't cry. Don't cry," Jamyang pleaded.

Tsering's phone buzzed. She pulled it out of her pocket. *Ama.* She could not talk with her mother now, even though she'd told her to call today, after this doctor's visit. The phone continued to pulse, then went quiet. A voice message came through a few minutes later. "*Chori*, how are you? How was *checkup*? Have you eaten?" Tsering sent a short voice message in return. "*Ama* baby is good. I am going home to rest now."

For the next month, Tsering followed Dr. Sharma's orders. She lay in bed or on the couch, watching Bollywood movies. When she grew bored with these, she turned to American medical shows: *Grey's Anatomy, ER, House, Nurse Jackie.* Anything that could tell her something more about the mysterious landscape of human accidents, illness, and frailty—and the American response to these conditions. Was she crazy to think she might one day become a nurse?

Tsering told only a few close friends and her brother, Tsepten, about her situation. Still, this made her feel vulnerable. Although her community knew how to handle death and acute sickness—showing up with food, prayers, money for funeral fees or hospital bills—they did not do as well with this sort of uncertainty. Nothing bad had happened yet.

She tried to keep her communications with Kathmandu minimal. She did not want to raise alarm. Her paternal grandmother was withering, and she knew most of the caregiving fell to her mother. It was high tourist season, too. A week after the fateful visit with Dr. Sharma, Tsering had collected herself enough to call home. She did not tell her mother that she'd been confined to bed or that she would have to have an operation, but she did say that she felt the baby would come early. In this, she was not lying.

Tsering had avoided looking up placenta previa, but one afternoon into her third week of bed rest, she Googled it. Much of what she read just reiterated Dr. Sharma's explanation and advice. But a paragraph on the World Health Organization's website scared her.

> Placenta previa is a life-threatening complication of pregnancy and an important public health problem worldwide. Its impact in under-resourced settings is much greater than its impact in developed countries. In under-resourced settings, there is often a lack of awareness of the danger signs of placenta previa, which can lead to delays in seeking medical care. In addition, poor transport facilities and the need to travel long distances to reach a health unit (which may have only limited resources to deal with the problem) increase the risk of hemorrhage, which is one of the leading causes of maternal death in Africa and Asia.

Tsering felt dizzy. She set her phone down and closed her eyes. Had her mother or grandmother been in her situation, they would have likely died. Instead, she had a kind doctor in a hospital, a birth plan. This was something beyond *karma*, wasn't it?

A week later, a nurse pushed Tsering by wheelchair into the operating room. She saw Jamyang's kind eyes above the surgical mask and Dr. Sharma, her raven-colored hair tucked back, her mouth covered, her expression alert with empathy and focus. Tsering stayed partially awake through the operation. Jamyang could not look behind the curtain covering her abdomen. He stared at Tsering's face.

Incision. Extraction. Suction. She heard the nurse say, "Apgar 9. Good!" She did not know what that meant. "Sutures," said Dr. Sharma. All this passed for Tsering in a fog. And then there was her daughter, puckered and beautiful, fists kneading the air, eyes still closed.

In the days to come, there would be hand and footprints, a birth certificate, a knitted cap in pink and white, the rawness of nipples. Tsering would tell her mother that she'd had an operation for the safety of the baby. That it was what the American doctors recommended. Her mother would understand.

As for the lost ones, these remained too, singular yet collective, like stones that line the riverbed.

# FINDING THE WOMB DOOR

Karchung stoops over her handmade distillery: stainless-steel pots glued together with mud and ash to make a double boiler, a length of hose through which naked barley is transformed into alcohol. The operation is fueled by an open fire, crackling in the shade of a poplar tree. Karchung is fifty-something. This woman from the village of Drakmar has a narrow, weather-worn face. Her midriff is wrapped in striped woolen aprons over an old *chuba*. The style in which she wears her aprons, the weighty knot of turquoise around her neck, and the conch shell bracelet on her left wrist mark her as married.

Yangjin and I watch Karchung work, waiting for a break in the rhythm of her efforts to explain that we are doing a research project with women in Lo, and we would like to ask her about her family, about her experiences with pregnancy and birth. In Logé, we talk about the special ways that people from Tibet and the Himalaya have had their bodies changed by this place, over long stretches of history. We speak of blood and bone: about how lineage passes through bodies and how, from the perspective of Western science, they call this "gene." We share that we want to learn more about the relationship between Himalayan women's bodies and the circumstances of their family life.

Squatting beside the poplar, her spine against its trunk, Karchung takes a gulp of salt butter tea. "Life here is difficult for women and children, so I will talk with you about these things."

We ask Karchung's permission to write down the names of people in her household and make a list of her pregnancies and births—including miscarriages or children who died—and to draw her kinship chart. We also ask permission to collect a sample of her saliva, to measure her pulse, to take her temperature, and to find out how much iron and oxygen is in her blood. We explain that we do not need to take her blood to do this but that a small machine, put at the tip her finger, can reveal this information. "The machine will tell us some numbers," Yangjin says. "We will write them down and tell you what they mean." Yangjin goes on to say that this research will not benefit Karchung directly but that the information we learn may be helpful for future generations.

"What will you do with the saliva?" she asks.

"We will send it to America," Yangjin answers. "There, the scientists will learn more about how Himalayan people live so well in our places. To learn what makes us different from other people who live by the ocean or down in the valleys." She pulls out a small plastic vial, into which Karchung will be asked to spit.

Karchung laughs. "My son is in America. Now my saliva will go to America too! But this old *ama* stays here, making *arak*, doing the work."

Over the next hour, we listen and take notes as Karchung shares details about her family and her household. She recounts her siblings, her husband, and his family. She recounts her eight pregnancies, including the three children who died between infancy and their toddler years. We ask her to explain what happened.

"There was a time, about ten years ago, when an old grandfather *nöpa* claimed many children. He took my two-year-old son and the child belonging to my cousin and his wife. Several others."

"When you say, 'took them,' what do you mean?" I ask. "How did it happen?"

"He drowned them in the river," Karchung continues.

"Why would he do that?"

"The grandfather *nöpa* was lonely and jealous because in [the neighboring village of] Ghiling they built a daycare center for the young children and got a beautiful Tibetan girl to take care of them while their parents worked. This grandfather *nöpa* thought he should also have children to keep him company. He took them through the element of water. We lost five or six young ones before he stopped."

"How did you get him to stop taking children?"

"We did many rituals. This appeased him." Karchung speaks with assuredness about a dynamic of causality that in other cultural contexts might be called a tragic accident: children drowning as they played unattended beside the river while their parents worked in fields. But for Karchung, the death of her child in this instance is linked to the destiny of other young children in ways that bespeak neither disease nor neglect but rather an act of ill will by an infamous being who belongs to this place.

Her story is also a claim to knowledge and what counts as an authoritative explanation for such a death. Others in the village affirm what Karchung has shared, noting that these drownings were the impetus for founding daycares throughout Lo.

Karchung explains that her second child succumbed to pox, like many others in this village in previous decades. We interpret this as measles. "In those days, we did not have vaccinations," she says. Had there been such medicine available, maybe she would have six living children now.

The third child "died after a few days." When we ask Karchung why this infant had died—not "What happened?" but "What was the reason for the death?"—she touches her brow, answering this question with a gesture. This happens countless times during that summer of 2012, as we interview more than eight hundred Mustang women about their reproductive lives. To touch the forehead is to acknowledge *karma*. Sometimes the course of a life is written here.


### THE COUNTENANCE OF HARM

In mid-July 2012, deep into data collection for this project on Tibetan adaptation to altitude and women's reproductive histories, we leave Monthang early in the morning. Today, we hoped to complete our work in Namgyal and Phuwa and then move on to Thinkar by foot. The jeep lets us out in Phuwa, just in front of the home of the village headman. We go inside to review the list of households in this hamlet and plan the day.

Usually bright, one of our local research collaborators, Yangdron, is subdued. She leans her head on KC's shoulder. "I feel aches in my chest and back," she says. "Like *electric shock* going through my body," she confides as we are served butter tea and *tsampa*. I sense her growing discomfort as we eat our breakfast. "I think it is *nöpa*," she adds.

As a verb, *nöpa* is the act of harming. It means to injure or damage, to disturb the peace, to feel ill will or to cause illness. It can also indicate a sacking: of places, of people, but also of logics. In Tibetan Buddhist debate, monks slap and stomp, crimson robes flaring like petals around the stem of thigh and knee, throwing down *nöpa* as argument, as philosophical contradiction. This form of harm is refutation, that which discredits or disproves. Here, injury is ontological impairment, by which I mean an idea impaled. The world is this way. The world is not this way. Skewered.

But *nöpa* also live as beings, manifestations like the old grandfather spirit in Drakmar who was so lonely, so neglected and disgruntled, that he drowned those many children. In another case, a *nöpa* living above the village allowed the headman's horse to be attacked by a snow leopard. The horse was maimed but not killed, as if for fun. This *nöpa* was mischievous. Here, *nöpa* can be understood as the failure to protect, the failure of protection.

By the time we leave the headman's house, Yangdron's quiet conviction about what is ailing her is known by all. The headman's wife kindles juniper fronds as incense, fumigates Yangdron with the smoke, and prepares a weak *tsampa* broth. The juniper is to appease the *nöpa*. The broth is to bring back strength.

Yangdron rests in this house while the rest of us work. Later, we all walk slowly to Thinkar. Usually strong and graceful, Yangdron moves as if through mud. She is rigid. Her eyes glaze. When we arrive in the neat home of a village widow, behind the king's summer palace, Yangdron collapses in a little heap. KC and Yangjin stretch out her long legs, stroke her head, cover her with blankets. The widow—a wise and skilled woman—keeps watch on our friend as we go about our afternoon of work.

At the end of the day, the widow reports that Yangdron felt better for some time but is now feeling worse again. Like the headman's wife, the widow bathes Yangdron twice in juniper incense and feeds her thin *tsampa* gruel. I am rubbing Yangdron's back when she rises abruptly, possessed by nausea. She makes it to the front stoop before retching. The next hour passes in trepidation. We had planned to walk back to Monthang at the end of the day—two hours against a dusk wind—but now must find transport for Yangdron. After various failed attempts to locate horses (all are out at pasture) or find a motorcycle or jeep (most are on their way to Ghami for a big soccer tournament), we begin to walk, one person taking either one of Yangdron's arms.

We make it as far as the impressive gnarl of poplar near the village center before we hear the familiar rumble of a motorcycle engine. Our one male researcher, Lhawang, all energy and gangly limbs, takes off in search of its source. We continue toward Namgyal. Lhawang returns with the borrowed motorcycle just in time, as Yangdron has again begun to grow weak and stiff, her eyes vacant. We bundle her up in our scarves, shawls, and my windbreaker. Off they go.

The rest of us walk back to Monthang. Upon arrival, Kunzom searches out the local biomedical health worker. She finds him drinking beer and playing cards in the Annapurna Conservation Area Project (ACAP) kitchen, his eyes red rimmed and foggy. Instead of asking him for help, she locates the woman who assists him and asks her to examine Yangdron.

The assistant confirms that Yangdron's illness is a mixture of *nöpa* and gastric upset. After a few brief pokes at Yangdron's belly, the woman is about to give her a range of medicines, including an IV antibiotic injection. Kunzom insists on a pregnancy test. Yangdron is newly engaged. We have all been wondering. The test is positive.

Yangdron's fiancé, a jeep driver, rushes to Monthang after hearing the news. The day before, he'd been sent all the way down to Pokhara to fetch a specific medicine for the king. He comes to Yangdron's bedside after making his delivery to Khar, the Monthang palace. Given this news, and Yangdron's state, we decide that she should go home, to her fiancé's village. The next morning, we send her off with oral rehydration solution, multivitamins, and Tibetan medicines. The previous evening, Amchi Pema confirmed a pregnancy pulse but found imbalances. She diagnosed both bile- and *nöpa*-related disorders, in addition to the pregnancy, and agreed that the women in Phuwa and Thinkar had been right to offer incense.

As we send Yangdron off, into the home of her mother-in-law, I feel protective. I wonder what sort of care she will receive. I also marvel at the ability of Tibetan medicine to recognize what biomedicine cannot see and at the divinatory capacity of peeing on a stick and being told about your future.

As this story resolves into the fact of a pregnancy, I am left thinking about a certain quiescence, between shyness and shame, that surrounds sex, reproduction, and women's bodies here. As we speak with women that summer, we learn that conception often occurs unexpectedly, invoking fear and joy.

But there is more to it than that. Embedded in Yangdron's story is a brush with danger—*nöpa*. As was the case with Karchung, many of the women with whom we speak that summer name *nöpa* as a primary cause of all sorts of trouble: miscarriages, stillbirths, infertility. However, to speak of *nöpa* does not mean *not* to speak of other causes of harm. Some women tell us that newborn deaths occur when they are made to work in the fields too long into pregnancy or work too hard. They connect intimate hardships— the diminished production of breast milk, for example—to larger structures and cycles of precarity: poor harvests, family debt, anger between husbands and wives. The ultimate cause of an untimely death may be a *nöpa* or may be written on the forehead, but this does not preclude a recognition of the material forces that shape human lives.

## AUTHORITATIVE KNOWLEDGE

In reflecting on Yangdron's story, I see Kunzom's insistence that she take a pregnancy test as care-*full* and bold. Although Kunzom is not a mother, she possesses enough of a certain kind of knowledge to assert herself for Yangdron's benefit. In some ways, Yangdron had been resigned to let the reality of her pregnancy unfold to the slower rhythm of an expanding belly and to *not* talking as a form of protection, even as she was, at the same time, learning through this research project about the difficult experiences that previous generations of Mustang's women have lived through and how those hardships are intertwined with silence.

This leads me to the relationship between silence and sharing. In Mustang, as in many other parts of the world, women's status—as reproductive beings but also as human beings—are subject to a kind of scrutiny that is rarely applied to men. In homes and villages, or in the communication pathways that link Mustang to Kathmandu to New York, privacy can be a thin curtain, pleated by gossip. Sex and sexuality are tossed tacitly back and forth in village melodies, hearthside innuendo, text messages. The question "What is happening to me?" hangs in the air.

I thought I was dying when my blood came for the first time. My mother handed me some wool and told me nothing.

My body burned when I squatted to pee in the fields. What did it mean?

Sister-in-law held me as I pushed that first baby out. She was more scared than I was.

The man's substance is sticky! After my husband finished his effort, it felt like he had glued my legs together, so nobody else could open me up.

To please a man, rock back and forth like when you thresh grain. To please a woman, let the man drink enough so he falls asleep!

If the afterbirth is slow to come, danger.

These are the voices of older Mustang women, those mostly in their sixties, seventies, eighties. But confusion, contradiction, and disjuncture between what is known and what is practiced also effect younger women:

I thought I could not get pregnant the first time I had sex. But I did.

I lost one baby when it was four months inside me. The doctor in Kathmandu said he would take care of me, but he put in something that caused me pain [an IUD]. He didn't tell me. I bled so much, I thought that I would die.

I studied global health and feminism in college, but there I was at the clinic anyway, waiting for something I never thought I'd need.

A woman in her forties was sterilized by tubal ligation. She tells me that her womb was removed but that her monthly cycles continue. A new mother wipes away her colostrum. She has been told that this yellow liquid is impure, that she should wait to feed her infant until the white milk comes, sweet and salty on the tongue.

We live the knowledge we are given.

## REPRODUCTIVE HISTORY (A *HUNDREDS* EXPERIMENT)

In the beginning, water. Remember, what are now mountains was once sea. After this, Tibetans describe a coupling of monkey and ogress. He sought crags, a place to cultivate mind. But place breeds desire. She *was* crag, rock, plain; forest, river, peak. Soon, she birthed the multiples. Later, they will say the *bodhisattva* of compassion engineered this union, that Buddhism tamed the wildness of a place once known as feminine ground. Over time, bodies made peace with the lightness of air, the thinness of atmosphere. Local biologies hold many possibilities for survival. Still, genetic forgetting happens quickly in the lowlands.

I listen to hundreds of women recount reproductive histories—songs of innocence and experience. Calculations overwhelm: thirteen pregnancies, six living children; eight pregnancies, two miscarriages, a stillbirth, four living children; more rarely, five pregnancies, five living children. A friend has five children but had nine pregnancies. The twins died. A third child succumbed after a seemingly endless labor that my friend was lucky to have survived. She bore three more pregnancies, two more children. The names of her children come to me easily. I know each of them. But, that summer, I learn the ghost numbers. It takes a different kind of asking.

After many tries, we fail to read the pulse of an ancient woman wearing Chinese Ray-Bans, as fake as she is real. Is it blood coursing through her, or memory? The grandfather she calls "husband" does not speak. He spins his upright prayer wheel, sinks into a natty carpet. Children, near a dozen born, fade into the revelation that this woman has spent nigh eight years, a century of months, three thousand days spinning the wheel of blood and bone, waiting for a blessed gasp: breath to last beyond the present; breath thick with possibility; breath seared by loss.

A night of sickness in a Lhasa bathroom. Then, the ultrasound conveyed what I could already picture: watery womb, fuzzy tangle of new life. I carry her across the wrinkle of a year. Before I leave the high country, a doctor predicts she will be "big and dumb," karmic payback for my remaining in the mountains. My body tells different stories. Still, her warning nestles in. She has mopped up so much death. My labor unfolds in a hospital on the other side of the world. Forty hours can be a lifetime. Here, forty hours might have taken my life.

### FAMILY PLANNING

The lama and I sit on a grassy knoll beside the village water tap. The cliff out of which his monastery protrudes towers over us. The monk's shaved head is covered by a rust-colored wool hat, and his robes are tea stained yet neatly folded. He is telling me about the school he runs—a hybrid institution that includes monks, nuns, and a few lay children in one of the hamlets north of Monthang. He has adopted this mode of education because, otherwise, he fears that all the young people will leave the village for boarding schools or monasteries elsewhere. He is worried, among other things, about religious lineage.

The monastery in his charge is a Kagyu institution. "But everywhere these days it is only Sakya," he says, exasperated. "The parents see that they can get their kids a free education if they send them off to one of the big monasteries in Kathmandu or India, but they don't think about our own places. They just send them down. And what do we do? We bring in kids from outside. *Import-export.* Look at Chöde in Monthang or the Tsarang *gönpa*," he says. "Do you see Loba kids there? Not many. Most are from Dolpo. They are Gurung or Tamang or the children of laborers who come up to do construction or work in fields. Mustang kids fill up Tibetan monasteries in the south, and our own *gönpa* become places for outsiders. It should not be this way!"

The lama rolls his prayer beads between his palms and blows on them out of habit, before wrapping them around his wrist. He speaks of the well-educated monks from Mustang, the ones who have gone off to Singapore, Malaysia, and Hong Kong to attend senior Tibetan Buddhist teachers or expound the *dharma* themselves. "It is good to spread the Buddha's teachings," he says, "But for every opportunity, there is an obstacle. For every act of virtue, the possibility of sin. Too often I think these people are '*om* money *padme hum*.' They lose their humility and forget the land they come from." I laugh at his pun. From *mani*, "prayers," to "money," cash.

"The other big problem is the medicine women take. You know, those injections and pills to stop babies from being made. This is sinful. Since women started this practice, we've had trouble in the monasteries."

I swallow and wonder how to respond. "What kind of trouble?" I ask.

"Families used to have five, six children. Older sons would become *ngakpa*, and middle children went to the monastery or nunnery. But now, people are only having two or three children. This is not enough!"

He tells this story of demographic decline as a morality tale. I think of other stories.

The great expanse of territory that stretches from Mustang and other Himalayan borderlands across the Tibetan Plateau was once envisioned as the supine form of a wrathful demoness. She needed to be subdued—literally staked down to Earth—for Buddhism to thrive. Mustang is marked by the demoness's dismemberment. Her entrails are reborn as a row of *mani* stones. That chalky mountainside is her liver. Her heart becomes the 108 *chöten* that radiate out from Lo Gekhar, one of Mustang's oldest monasteries, a place associated with Guru Rinpoche and the building of Tibet's first monastery, Samye.

Much can be said about this story. Buddhism emerges from these acts of gendered violence, even as it is a practice of peace, a way of supplicating and sharpening the mind. I am left considering the need to tether agentive feminine power in order that enduring structures of Tibetan and Himalayan society could be built, could flourish. This says nothing about what it feels like to be pinned to place or to be tethered to one's body and its wily capacity for making life.

"Sometimes it is difficult for women to have many babies," I say. "It can be hard on their bodies and their heart-minds." I remember stories of miscarriages and maternal deaths, secret abortions and efforts to keep contraception hidden from husbands. I think, also, about the Tibetan word for "woman," *kyemen*, and its etymological parsing: *kye* is birth and *men* indicates something that is lower, below, lesser than.

"I'm a monk!" the lama answers. "What do I know of women's bodies?"

## THE GRANDMOTHER HYPOTHESIS

In the summer of 2014, I visit Dolma in the two-bedroom walk-up in Queens, where this friend from Lo Monthang now lives. I've come to meet her first grandchild: a baby girl born five weeks prior in a New York hospital.

"Come inside," Dolma ushers me into her small living room. Nyima, her daughter, sits on the floor in front of the TV, looking tired and proud. I coo at the swaddled, sleeping child and place a *kathag* and other gifts beside this newborn. As the baby sleeps, Dolma and I sit on the couch, speaking of the pathways that have led to this new life.

Dolma was born in Tibet and came to Lo as a teenager to attend the queen. Eventually, Dolma married a local man. She gave birth to three daughters and another child who did not survive. For three of these deliveries, Dolma labored at home in Mustang. She delivered one of her daughters in a Kathmandu hospital, not because she necessarily wanted to but because the family passed that winter in Nepal's capital. After various forms of gynecological complication, Dolma had a hysterectomy in her early forties. She is not the only Mustang woman I know to have gone through this procedure at that relatively young age.

"It is easier not to bleed," she tells me. "But it feels strange to have the place where my children once grew taken out of my body. Now I just have this belly. It grows, even without a baby inside!" She pats her T-shirt, rubbing her hand across her girth. "If I were back in Mustang, I'd be doing enough work to make it go away," she muses about the weight she's gained since coming to New York. "But here, we just take little walks around the neighborhood."

"Maybe you can take walks with the new baby in the stroller," I suggest.

"Yes, we go to the park," she answers. "I know how to get there." Dolma has spoken to me in the past about the smallness of her New York world. After living apart from her husband for close to a decade—he laboring in New York restaurants, she laboring at home in Monthang—Dolma and her daughters came to the U.S. They arrived through the family reunification visa program, the same chain visa category that Melania Trump's parents received and which her husband has sought to eliminate. Although Dolma speaks four languages, none of them is English. Her urban American life is circumscribed. She spends her days in this apartment, taking care of children who belong to other Loba women. It is an informal daycare arrangement, a new type of village-based labor exchange.

"When will you go back to work?" I ask Nyima.

"I am lucky. I can take two months," she answers. "The family I had been working for is moving, but they've helped me find another family. The lady in that house also just had her first baby." This new employer, like the previous one, is a white family living on the Upper West Side of Manhattan.

"So, you will both be getting used to being mothers and working," I say. Nyima smiles, says nothing. Many women from Mustang make their living as caretakers for New York children, some as live-in nannies and others as daytime babysitters. They have entered into an enduring stream of economic and affective relations that combines the need, or desire, of many American women to rejoin the workforce after having children with the need that immigrant women have for reliable employment. The emotional labor that constitutes such work, and the negotiated intimacies that can ensue in these arrangements, can be at once rewarding and challenging.

This conversation with Dolma and Nyima attunes me to the shapeshifting nature of parenting and young childhood in response to the *khora* of migration. I think about the circumstances under which people are relying upon networks of extended kin to raise families between Nepal and New York. Grandparents as well as other elder and younger female relatives have certainly shared childcare responsibilities in the past. However, caring for other people's children as an economic strategy in New York shifts the balance of care between New York and Nepal. This is not a situation unique to Mustang, of course, but it is changing how the work of parenting gets parsed between the youngest and the oldest in Mustang society.

Dolma and Nyima are fortunate that they live in the same city. For many young couples from Mustang, having the support of elder relatives to care for their children means sending kids back to Nepal, once they are weaned, often until they are school-aged. But this added work of childcare is coupled with other forms of strain on the elderly who remain in Nepal, particularly in Mustang. There, the work—of planting and weeding and harvest, of milking and making cheese, of repairing roofs and attending to ritual practice—continues, unabated. Money might be sent back to help hire laborers for some of these tasks, but the labor of raising children is not outsourced.

"The little one will stay with her grandmother," says Dolma. "She will learn from the bigger kids. She will be so good. And when she goes to school, maybe her grandmother will also learn more than *ABC123*," she laughs. This is a different sort of grandmother hypothesis.

As I think about Dolma saying her ABCs, I consider language. This strategy of sending young children on a global *khora* during childhood is also shaping the acquisition of word and gesture. Young Mustang-Americans may begin with Logé and some Nepali. They may learn to love their mother tongue as they learn to love the elder generation. They may even acquire the rudiments of written Tibetan or Devanagari in a Mustang daycare or an urban Nepali preschool before returning to New York, where they will enter the swiftly moving current of English and ESL. On the one hand, this strategy of sending young children who are born in the U.S. (and therefore have U.S. passports and the possibility to enact this *khora* with relative ease) builds a certain firmament of belonging. On the other hand, the transitions can be jarring for everyone. As illustration of these dynamics, two moments come to mind.

The first involves a grandmother I met in 2012, on a trail outside the village of Ghami. Her slight frame, already bent by age, was weighed down by a squirming toddler strapped to her back. She walked slowly, herding her two cows toward home. The woman fingered the front flap of her *chuba*, pulling a package of biscuits from the folds of fabric covering her sagging breasts—breasts that had undoubtedly nursed many children. She reached around and gave one to the child. Her expression was dull, exhausted.

The second example involves a friend from Lo who lives in Elmhurst, Queens. He is about my age. He has lived in the U.S. for eighteen years, during which time he has not been back to Nepal. His son spent four years of early childhood between Mustang and Kathmandu. When he arrived back in the U.S., he spoke no English. Three years later, he refuses to speak anything *but* English. "Don't be hitting. Do now your school working," my friend coddles his child in precise and imperfect English. He tries to ply his rambunctious boy off the iPad. He promises candy. He pleads. The child ignores him. This father works long hours, as does his wife. While there is no shortage of love in the household, there is little energy left to build boundaries of discipline and inter-generational respect, to cultivate family connection.

Dolma has made *dal bhaat*. She serves lunch on the heavy copper plates like the ones I once ate from in Monthang. We eat quietly, as an Indian version of *American Idol* suffuses the room with Bollywood ballads. Mouths pucker with the acidic delight of pickled radish, but Nyima avoids this relish for the sake of her child. "If I eat it, the baby spits up half the milk I feed her."

Dolma and I nod, knowingly. *"Yes,"* we drawl in tandem. It has been a decade since the birth of my own daughter and almost two decades since Dolma's youngest was born, but bodily memories remain.

"How was your labor?" I ask Nyima, who has finished eating and now picks up the child to nurse.

"There was no problem," she answers. "The pains started in the afternoon, and I gave birth about twelve hours later. At first, I thought that I would want to have medicine for pain, but then I thought maybe it was not good for the baby," her voice trails off.

Dolma cuts in. "There was no medicine for the pain in Monthang. Just some village friends giving massage and smooth words to keep going."

"When the baby was close to coming out, I wanted the medicine, but the doctors said it was too late," adds Nyima. Dolma had been in the room with her daughter, along with hospital nurses and the obstetrician on call. The nurse had cut the cord, swaddled the baby.

"What happened to the placenta?" I ask.

Nyima looks at me, befuddled. "I don't know."

Dolma understands my question. "It was not like at home. No earth burial. No river. They probably just threw it away."

"Why is the placenta important?" Nyima asks.

"In the village, we say it needs to be taken care of well, so that the baby will not get sick or be attacked by *nöpa*," Dolma explains.

"Really, people believe that?" Nyima responds.

"Yes," Dolma answers. "Does it help? I am not sure. But if we *don't* do this and then there is a problem. . . . I have seen that happen."

Nyima says nothing, her eyes wide.

"Was the hospital nice?" I ask.

"It was *neat and clean*," Dolma uses one of her English phrases. "But home is more comfortable."

"I would be scared to give birth at home," admits Nyima.

"How has it been with nursing?" I ask. I have just seen Nyima feed her child, but I also notice formula under the coffee table.

"She nursed for the first month," Dolma answers for her daughter.

"But the doctors said I did not have enough milk coming," continues Nyima. "So I started feeding her *lactose* too."

"What would you have done back in Mustang if this had happened?" I ask Dolma.

"We would feed *tsampa* mixed with butter early, like this," she mimes the motion of putting a little bit of dough in her mouth and then feeding it to a baby. "We do this not only if there is not enough milk but to make babies strong. It is food from our place. But here, the doctors told us not to feed anything but breast milk or this powder for six months," says Dolma. "We are in a new place now. The wind and water are different here. The customs are different. So, we have to change what we do."

As we talk, I learn that the family performed a simple purification ritual in their apartment after the birth but that more elaborate rituals for the baby girl took place back in Nepal. She was given her name by a lama in Kathmandu. The *khora* of migration is also the circling of ceremony across place, through social networks, at a distance.

I ask Dolma if the lama made a *kyekar*, a natal horoscope, for the child. Dolma nods.

"What is a *kyekar*?" Nyima asks. The newborn has fallen asleep again, and Nyima lowers her gently into a bassinet.

"The astrology you need for your life," Dolma answers. It is, to me, a perfect translation.

"Do I have one?" daughter asks mother.

"Yes. You and your sisters all have them."

"But where is it? Do I need it?" Nyima crosses and uncrosses her thin legs, pulls her baggy sweatshirt close. She looks worried. New motherhood can be like flint, igniting a sense of the miraculous, kindling fear.

"They are all at home, in the shrine room in Monthang," Dolma answers. "I have not looked at them in many years, since you grew up. But they are important."

"Why?" Nyima asks.

"It helps to know what to do, if anything happens." Dolma pauses. I wonder what she feels in that moment, how she has reckoned her own loss, the child who died. I also wonder why, if they are so important, these documents have been left behind in Nepal. Do these recorded calculations that help to frame cause and consequence, particularly at the beginnings and ends of life, have less relevance through the long stretch of adult years?

My friend surprises me with what she says next. "It is sort of like the papers that come with a new TV. A paper to explain things." She laughs. "Not really. It doesn't *guarantee*. It is written by a lama, not a company. But we should follow the advice of what is written there. We remember these things in our minds."

I sit with this simile as I watch mother and daughter communicate across language, generation, and culture.

The baby whimpers, and in an instant, the whimpers crack into a bawl. Dolma scoops up the child from the bassinet. "Don't cry, don't cry, little one. Grandmother is here."

## HALLMARK HOLIDAYS

A Facebook notification appears on my computer screen as I sit writing in the library in early June 2018. It is Choesang's first birthday. He is Yangjin's son.

What is remarkable about this event is neither the substance of the pop-up notification nor the time-space compression that brings me heart-to-heart with his mother in Kathmandu nor is it the ability to virtually peer into a private family celebration. No. What is remarkable is the marking of the birthday itself.

Yangjin and her husband are not the only young couple from Mustang who have adopted this cultural ritual. Birthday parties have become a *thing*. From Nepal to New York, people are sending out invitations, renting halls, or reserving banquet rooms in fancy restaurants. At times, they are connecting a *first* birthday with the official consecration of a marriage. They are celebrating with sparklers, streamers, and elaborate meals. Birthday parties have become a site of conspicuous consumption and also a new form of ritualized reciprocity—a moment to give money, always an odd number for good luck, placed in an envelope marked with your name. As with weddings and funerals, people keep records of the giving.

A generation ago, a first birthday would not have been marked at all. In fact, to call attention to such a moment could have been viewed as inauspicious. It would be considered dangerous to shine a spotlight on a new human being, one who might still be vulnerable to *nöpa* and other forms of harm, who might not survive to age two or age five, let alone into adulthood.

This is to say nothing of dates and calendars. Among people in their forties or older from Mustang, knowing the precise day of your birth is unusual. In contrast, the day of the week you were born often lives as part of your name. Lhakpa, for instance, means "Wednesday." This can be useful for astrological calculations. Likewise, the time of birth, the season, the animal year in which your birth occurred, and the relationship between your birth moment and the coming of Losar, the lunar new year, are all important. But assigning a birthdate in the Gregorian or Nepali Vikram Samvat calendar systems has been, for many generations from Mustang, an *ex post facto* act. It wasn't that important.

So, too, with birth certificates. To be born at home, especially in the village, meant that you did not receive a birth certificate. This form of "making paper"—getting the government to recognize your existence in official terms—took effort and was not always successful. A turn toward clinic or hospital births has been coupled not only with the creation of a paper trail but also with a demographic transition away from larger families and a public health turn toward infant and child survival. As I stare at the Facebook pictures of birthday hats and candles, of a cake bedecked in sugar roses beside platters filled with more traditional offerings of nuts and fruits, I think about the radical nature of this cultural turn toward celebrating the very young, away from the elderly.

*Tharchang* celebrations are markers of liberation from householder responsibilities for people who have made it into their seventh decade of life. Just as first birthday parties are on the rise, *tharchang* rituals are becoming rarer in Mustang. In great part, this is because the aging generation cannot really afford to "retire." Even with remittances, there is work to be done: farms to manage, animals to husband, hotels to run, village meetings to attend, grandchildren to care for.

Although Mother's Day has not taken on the social import of birthday parties, it is a holiday moment that people from Mustang, particularly those in New York, are beginning to celebrate.

In May 2017, I attend a Mother's Day party at the Elmhurst Community Center. It is organized by several young women—themselves unmarried and not yet mothers—who have gone to college in the U.S. and whose fiery adoption of feminism, along with a sense of devotion to their community, moves me. When I arrive at the community hall, *kathag* in hand, the African American security guard at the entrance asks, "You lost?" I assure him that I am not.

Spring coats are strewn about the foyer. The hall has been decorated with banners and balloons. Long folding tables line the sides of the room. One table has been set up at the entrance. There, I buy a $15 ticket. I am told that, after recovering expenses for food, a Nepali DJ, and decorations, any remaining funds will go toward the language and culture classes held for Loba children each Sunday in the basement of an apartment building in Queens.

The room is filled with women of different ages. I recognize some only vaguely; others, I know well. I see Tenzin, the wife of an old friend. She brings me a flimsy aluminum plate piled with fried beef jerky, pounded rice, spicy chickpeas, and a donut made of rice flour. This woman's sister-in-law, whom I have not seen in many years, but with whom I had spent time long ago in

Pokhara, comes up next. She smiles, wraps her arms around me. We sit together, holding hands. Soon, there are selfies.

Some in the room wear *chuba* and woven aprons. Others sport skimpy off-the-shoulder shirts, tight pants, stilettos. All fashion sensibilities are welcome here. One of the organizers explains, "We decided to have the party on actual Mother's Day, Sunday, because we wanted it to feel special. But we knew that some people wouldn't be able to come, because they have to be back at their live-in jobs by Sunday."

I see another familiar face—a face from the past. A late-twenties nail technician and a mom of two reveals herself as the girl from Dhi who was adopted into the home of a trekking lodge owner in Jomsom. We used to make tuna sandwiches together in the German bakery on the far side of the Kali Gandaki. I remember her navy blue school uniform, her plaited hair.

We eat, talk, dance. I am asked to make a speech. "It will be good," one of the organizers says, "for them to hear you speaking Nepali and our language. It will encourage them to value their culture." I am embarrassed and nervous, but I take the microphone. I speak, mostly in Logé, telling them how happy I am to be here, how hard they all work, how difficult it is to be a mother. I say that it makes me feel old but also glad to see people whom I knew when we were younger, back in Mustang, and that I am encouraged to know they are doing well here.

Everything I say feels inadequate. When they ask me to sing, I freeze up. All I can muster is *"Happy Mother's Day to You . . ."* repeated to the tune of "Happy Birthday."

Later that evening, I recall a poem I once wrote to my mother, on the same annual occasion, when I was about seven. At that time, our small household was fracturing. Divorce was imminent. I was at once too young to understand motherhood and old enough to intuit something of what it means to be a mother. The poem went like this:

Moms. The people who hold the world together.
They take care of their joy through all sorts of weather.
They take care of the house, every last toy.
I'll learn from her as she learned from her mother.
And someday, I'll pick up a toy, and I'll know
I'm a mother that holds the world together.

# PART II

# PARENTS AND CHILDREN

Education is a social process; education is growth; education is not
preparation for life but is life itself.

—JOHN DEWEY, *EXPERIENCE AND EDUCATION*

EDUCATION-DRIVEN OUT-MIGRATION FROM NEPAL'S HIGH MOUNTAINS TO
boarding schools and monastic institutions in urban Nepal or India is not
unique to Mustang. It is a cycling out the mountains but not necessarily
a cycling back. These patterns are bound up in money, obligation, and

love—with parents and sponsors, both foreign and domestic. Likewise, the *khora* of migration exists through seasonal movement between summer schools in Mustang and winter schools in Pokhara or Kathmandu and through the slower turning of the wheel of time as children are sent away, only to return once a year, or less, to their village roots.

The relationship between parents and children is a form of *khora*: a circling of support and obligation, expectation, surprise, and care. But education portends broader social change. It demands answers to new questions: What does one need to know? What does one *want* to know? What counts as knowledge? Is education necessarily a pathway to socioeconomic advancement?

Education opens up new possibilities even as it changes the world, by changing ways of knowing the world. Sometimes children born in New York spend their early childhood with grandparents in Nepal, returning to New York when they are school-aged. Meanwhile, their mothers may be caring for American children as an economic strategy. Here, the ends of kinship include the fraying of connections between parents and children, people and place. But these ends can also be refashioned: through school "families" as well as within extended families across time and space, through the dance of language.

In the short story, "Letters for Mother," Wangmo is born into a position of low social status in Monthang. Her life is changed when a Swiss man decides to support her education in Kathmandu. What does this opportunity come to mean? How does it shape her sense of self and her place within the wider Mustang community? Where does it lead? How different is Wangmo's experience from that of her daughter who is growing up in Queens?

The ethnographic chapter, "Going for Education," begins by describing the ways in which outsiders—individuals and institutions—are implicated in education-driven out-migration. It explores the logics by which parents have made decisions about their children's futures. This includes considerations about the shortcomings of the Nepali national education system and the role of private as well as faith-based institutions in educating Mustang youth. Mustang's cultural connection to Tibet shapes educational futures as well as senses of identity. Even so, American educational ideals become assimilated into Mustang-based institutions, and efforts to retain linguistic and cultural knowledge from Nepal are being carried out in New York. Still, education, even in its most advanced forms, does and does not transform social values: the ways we see ourselves and the ways we treat one another.

# LETTERS FOR MOTHER

WANGMO SINKS INTO THE CUSHIONS OF HER SLEEPER SOFA AND contemplates the birthday card. To be more precise, she stares at the letters. They begin, as usual, to float and wobble. Wangmo squints and sucks in her breath. It makes the words sit still. This act is more instinct than thought— an old habit that she used to get through school.

Wangmo holds the note with both hands. Alone in her apartment, she reads the words aloud.

*I love you mom wangmo because you are my mom wangmo. my MOM. happy birthday.*

She exhales. Wangmo not only feels proud because her child at age seven can form these letters, clear and beautiful, but also because she knows that, if her daughter were unable to do so, some well-mannered teacher's aide would pull the girl aside. The school would offer tests. Her child would get help. The problem would be named and hopefully managed, if not cured, rather than handled with an inevitable rap across her knuckles.

The birthday note is written on lined paper. Printed blue, pink, and purple hearts run across the top of the page. Her daughter has copied these hearts, making a neat row along the bottom of her message, in lieu of a signature.

Wangmo is not convinced that today, March 30, is her actual birthday, but it became the date inscribed on her *nagarikta* identity card and, now, her green card. It would do. Her mother said she had been born in spring.

Wangmo holds this endearment from her small child. The note dissolves the residue of an argument they'd had earlier this morning about which leggings her daughter would wear to school. But the note also does something else. It brings back memories of her own boarding school days in Kathmandu. Decades compress into these minutes of quiet. Before her journey on the 7 train, before the start of a twelve-hour workday at Nu 4 U Nails, Wangmo finds herself inside a twenty-year-old memory.

◆ ◆ ◆

In the days before monsoon brought thunderstorms to settle dust and cool temperaments across the Kathmandu valley, everything felt hot, edgy. Wangmo was not alone in her discomfort as she sat in her classroom. Still, she felt the flush of embarrassment as her English teacher, a feather-thin Nepali man who rarely smiled, announced an assignment: "Write an essay about your parents and why you are grateful for them."

This assignment posed two problems for Wangmo. First, she did not really *know* her parents. She was not allowed to know her father, and although she had lived with her mother until age seven, several years had passed since they'd seen each other—a veritable lifetime for a child. The truth was, she felt more pity than love for her mother. Wangmo worried for her mother's welfare, but she did not miss her.

Second, Wangmo struggled to write in any language but especially in English. The neat line that ran atop Devanagari script seemed to keep the letters in check, tethered them to one another like a rope. They only had Tibetan class twice a week, and much of this time was spent reciting the alphabet, memorizing prayers, and singing songs. She could find reliable shapes in the graceful lines of this, her natal-yet-not-natal language, and could reproduce, fairly faithfully, these shapes when asked. But English was unhinged. Shapes turned backward and forward. She couldn't wrangle the words.

As soon as the teacher turned his back to the chalkboard, Maya poked Wangmo in the ribs. They always sat side by side, sleeves of their crimson blazers brushing up against each other, ankles entwined in a clandestine hug. This intimate act was made possible only because the classroom was that crowded. The poke meant that Maya would help Wangmo with this impossible assignment.

Maya was Wangmo's best friend. They were not from the same part of Mustang, but this didn't matter. As children, the differences in their local dialects fused quickly into a vocabulary of sisterhood, wherein mother tongues mingled with the lilt of Nepali.

Maya was only a year older than Wangmo, but she seemed much more mature—maternal even. When Wangmo had been fairly new to Buddha Heart Boarding School herself, a six-year-old boy from Tangye was deposited at the school by an uncle and enrolled in kindergarten. With no empty cot in the dormitories, nine-year-old Maya volunteered to share her bunk with this terrified creature, his ankles pockmarked by bedbug bites, his cheeks mottled by wind and sun. The boy loved her, instantly. Even after a bunk became available, the boy resisted this move, wetting his bed each evening and being scolded each morning until the housemother returned him to Maya's nocturnal care.

Maya came from an important family. Her father was a Tibetan doctor and a Buddhist priest, someone who commanded respect. Her mother was loud, big bosomed, hilarious. Both loved Maya and her siblings unconditionally and took more than the usual interest in their education. In other words, Maya had something to write about when it came to parents.

Perhaps it was because they spent so much energy in school on rote memorization, and maybe it was even a gift, but Wangmo's memory rarely failed her. She could still recall with alarming accuracy the English essay she turned in all those years ago.

> Parents is extremely essential for all human being. If they didn't give birth to us, we can't come into this life. They are like a God. Our parents give us whatever whenever we wanted. They solve our problems and help us to get success in our goal. They do hard work night and day. This is all for our future. In our life they are nearest and dearest friends. Our parents is really good and kindness for us. They always support us till our last breath. We all are so lucky we got such a parents like ours. So, we should respect and love our parents. At last, always love your parents because their face got wrinkle by giving time for us.

Wangmo really liked the line about wrinkles. She remembered gripping her pencil, following the motions of Maya's hand, one beat behind her friend. Wangmo copied each of the letters, each of the words. These two girls deposited their completed essays on the teacher's desk at the end of class, careful to let several other students turn in their assignments in between their identical compositions. When the teacher handed back the essays the following week, he said nothing of plagiarism. More concerned with form than content, he noted the improvements in Wangmo's penmanship and corrected Maya's grammatical scrambles of the verb "to be." In his mind, these were students with very different prospects. They couldn't have written the same essay.

◆  ◆  ◆

Now that Wangmo has become a parent herself, such memories carry a different weight. From the relative comfort and security of a one-bedroom walk-up in Sunnyside, she takes a sip of sweet tea and closes her eyes.

She thinks of the tiny two-room dwelling that had been her childhood home. It was a crook in the elbow of Monthang, tucked into the neighborhood known as Potaling. It had a hearth, a place for sleeping, a nook for storing grain, one small window, and a wooden ledge that served as a shrine. The interior shone a lacquered black by candlelight, painted by years of dung smoke. A poplar trunk, into which had been carved footholds to form a ladder, led to a rammed earth roof that stitched this dwelling to her neighbors' homes, a row of brambles partitioning the differences between them. In the summertime, Wangmo used to scamper across the stacked firewood divides between houses, stealing handfuls of cheese set out to dry on other people's roofs. She recalled her mother's heart-shaped face underneath a tight woolen cap, the dull black braid that hung down her back, the fraying edge of her woven apron.

Her mother said that their family had been poor, "from the beginning of the beginning." Both of her grandparents had died when her own mother was hardly a teenager, her grandfather from drink and her grandmother from work and an illness of the heart. All these years later, Wangmo still wondered what this really meant. Her mother's elder brother and only sibling had been killed in a road accident in Lucknow during a season of winter trade. This further propelled her mother into an orphaned indentured servitude. She worked for one of the noble families of Monthang, weeding fields, harvesting grain, collecting firewood and manure for fuel.

Wangmo vaguely understood that she was not allowed to know her father because he had power, because he did not claim his paternity. But she would never hear the story of her father from her mother. Instead, it took two decades and ten thousand miles before someone laid bare the circumstances of her birth.

◆ ◆ ◆

It was at a Losar party, late in the evening, during her first year in New York. She'd been in the bathroom, smoothing her *chuba* in the mirror. An older woman emerged from one of the stalls. Instead of adjusting her own outfit, fixing her hair clip, or washing her hands, she just stared at Wangmo with a look that hooked incredulity to compassion.

"Whose daughter are you?" the woman asked. Her speech was slightly slurred, as if a shot of Johnnie Walker Black Label, meant for the men, had made it into her Coke. Perhaps it was the slow medicine of drink that made the woman pause, that made her notice Wangmo in the first place.

There was no escaping kinship here. Wangmo knew that the woman expected the name of her father, but she gave a different answer. "My mother is no longer. She was from Monthang."

The woman fixed her gaze on Wangmo's features. "She was poor, from that little corner house, right? I remember her, and the family she worked for. You must be that nobleman's *nyemo*! Your eyes are just like his! How old are you? About twenty? I remember how hard she worked in their fields. *Nyingjé*, your mother died when you were young. I knew her brother—the one who was killed in India. But you found a good foreign sponsor for school in Kathmandu, right? At least you got an education."

The woman gestured to her forehead. She did not have to say anything for Wangmo to know what she meant. Karma was written here, inscribed in invisible ink on the swath of skin above the eyes. "And now, here we all are, rich and poor, yoked to the promise of money in New York."

In this place of public secrets, a woman she had never met—of whom she had no memory—had just succeeded in giving voice to so many things that Wangmo wanted not to hear, not to name, and yet ached to know. She had done so with a turn of phrase that dizzied Wangmo but that also made her strangely satisfied with the ways their language could harness truth.

Pleased with her discovery—this falling into place of another piece in the mosaic of kinship that stretched between Nepal and New York—the woman now seemed disinterested in Wangmo. She adjusted her apron and headed out the door.

Before that encounter, Wangmo had often wondered if the man this woman named was her father, but she had never received direct confirmation. The moment opened up so many emotions, from outrage to compassion. As she used to do with Maya when they had lain awake in their dormitory cots, she finds herself spinning stories about people she did not know, the people who were her parents.

◆  ◆  ◆

Wangmo imagines her mother at the end of a long day of weeding, her father coming to inspect the work. Her mother's back is soaked in sweat, her *doko* brimming with new fodder for his animals. He sees her, a young woman who works hard but is not yet weathered by sun and wind. He takes an interest. He comes to call on her in that crooked little house. Maybe there is sweet talk after he takes a swallow of the milky *chang* she has borrowed from her neighbor. It is unthinkable that she would not offer him libations. What unfolds after that remains veiled. There is nobody to see.

Maybe a singular visit plants the seed of her. Maybe the affair goes on for months. Wangmo cannot know. She wonders about rough words, tears, the violence of a slap, talk of responsibility. She wonders about tenderness. She imagines that her mother would have found herself as startled by the cessation of her monthly bleeding and the swelling of her belly as Wangmo herself had been when the blood began to flow from between her legs at fourteen.

Thankfully, Wangmo does not remember feeling shame during the years of her life that she spent in Monthang. She remembers hunger and the wisps of winter air that slid under the door and through the one small window. She remembers how her mother filled the water offering bowls each morning and lit a butter lamp each evening, never thinking about the butter she might have spared for tea. Now, Wangmo understands that this act of faith could be many things: a reclamation of dignity at the bookends of long, invisible days; an enacted sense of duty; a hope to win favor with the gods.

Wangmo also remembers joy. She and her friends used to play games: finding the nests of Himalayan snowcock and sucking out the warm, yellow life from their eggs; building towers of stone with the flattest rocks they could find; using patties of frozen cow dung to sled down snowy embankments at the edge of the village; making bouquets of wildflowers and placing them on the household shrine.

◆ ◆ ◆

Robert, the Swiss man who became Wangmo's sponsor, discovered her while she and her friends were giggling and gorging themselves on sweet peas. He had been wandering through Monthang's fields in midsummer, taking pictures. The foreigner had a strange face: a reddish beard that reminded Wangmo of the wrathful masks worn by monks during festivals but green eyes that seemed kind. In their unequally imperfect English—she with the words *one photo, chocolate, pen* and both of them with phrases like *How old are you? What is your name?*—they made some sort of connection.

Still, Wangmo registered alarm when a knock on the door revealed this foreigner again, along with a local young man who spoke some English. She realized the door to their house was small only when she watched Robert fold himself in half to walk across the threshold.

Her mother spoke no English, but the message was communicated over cups of weak butter tea. This foreigner was from a place called "Swiss" but may as well have been from another universe. He would like to send her daughter to school in Kathmandu. Wangmo's mother smiled, nodded. It was a gesture of imperfect consent. Wangmo remembers her saying, "I hope that education will give her a better life than her mother."

It only occurs to Wangmo after that chance encounter in a New York bathroom that the young intermediary who appeared at her door with Robert was the nephew of her father, that they were unacknowledged cousins.

Several days after Robert's visitation, Wangmo found herself bundled up in all the clothes she owned, with *tsampa* and dried cheese stuffed into recycled instant noodle and powdered milk bags tied with string, heading south. She had never before left the village. She could not have imagined the worlds she would see in the capital, a place many from Mustang simply called "Nepal." In retrospect, she found the trust implicit in this transaction as astounding as the release of parental responsibility. What, now, was her mother to do?

Those first few months at Buddha Heart passed slowly. Each new experience had a vividness to it: the damp cots, the delight in steamed buns and curried goat every other Friday, but also the sharp edges of loneliness. Until Maya befriended her.

When Wangmo left the village, she did not know that she would never see her mother again. Some part of her understood that the lack of contact was a function of distance, poverty, and language. Still, she felt like an orphan during holidays when family members would arrive to collect their kin. But she knew that she wasn't an orphan.

When the principal of Buddha Heart summoned her to his office on a rainy day in class three and told her that he'd had a visit from someone from Monthang who said that her mother had fallen ill and died, Wangmo herself fell into a silence inside a silence. She held her chest. It felt like the time she had fallen off a horse back in Lo. *No breath, no breath.* When she took days to recover from the fall, people had said that she must have TB, but this, too, remained mere speculation.

Over the years, Robert wrote Wangmo letters into which he would fold chocolate bars and a few francs, but these gifts came infrequently. He told her that there were mountains in Switzerland, even yak. She drew pictures of white-faced herders beside yak wool tents. She did not tell him about her mother, although she guessed that the principal may have passed on the news. Robert never mentioned it.

As the years went by, though, Wangmo began to wonder about this relationship. She heard peers talking about their sponsors, comparing the letters and gifts they received, wondering about their lives in other countries. As she grew older, Wangmo remained grateful for Robert's generosity, but she wondered how he talked about her. She was grateful for the education, but she began to imagine herself as a curiosity, a burden, a charity case. Wangmo asked Maya to help her read Robert's letters and write thank-you notes in return. Their exchanges became formulaic. Robert was someone she had never really known but who had changed her life. In this way, he was like her father.

When Robert wrote his last letter, it was to say that his wife was ill and that he needed to take care of her. This was in the middle of class nine. He told her that he was sorry but that this would be the last year he could pay her school fees. He knew she only had one more year to complete her SLC. He hoped she would forgive him. He wished her well.

It was her friend Maya, of course, who read these words aloud to Wangmo. Before this news had softened into air, Maya had already planned a response. She would ask her uncle—a wealthy trader who moved between Nepal and Hong Kong—to pay for Wangmo's last year of school. Wangmo had spent enough time with Maya and her extended family during vacations that a request of this sort did not seem unreasonable.

"My uncle will do it," Maya said when Wangmo could say nothing. "My aunt will like to brag about helping a poor student." Their friendship could tolerate honest irony. "She'll think she is earning merit."

Maya and Wangmo made it through class ten together and, each in their own way, found passage to New York. That was a decade ago.

◆   ◆   ◆

This sense of time astonishes her. Wangmo thinks about the fact that her daughter is now the same age she was when she arrived at Buddha Heart. This child over whom she frets. This sweet girl who can write birthday cards. This Mustang-American who, as a toddler, was sent off to live with her father's parents in Kathmandu for two years. This was during the most difficult phase of a new marriage, with no money to speak of and the daunting process of immigration paperwork a daily stress. Still, there is a continent of difference between her own childhood and that of her daughter. She is different than her own mother; she has always had a plan. The separation that she and her daughter endured was not permanent. And yet . . .

Wangmo's husband is a good father. He treats their daughter gently and enjoys reading bedtime stories, which he does each night after he comes home from his job at a Thai restaurant. He is not from Mustang but shares, generally speaking, Wangmo's Himalayan roots. For Wangmo, meeting him and falling in love has been a great and enduring gift. There would have been nobody to arrange a marriage for her anyway, even if she had wanted that.

Together, Wangmo and her husband are figuring out what this word "parent" means. They speak with each other about what has and hasn't changed between their childhoods and that of their daughter. Wangmo knows she can be judgmental about the ways some in her community raise their children—here in New York and back in Nepal. Still, she bristles when she hears news about Himalayan people, now transplanted to New York, being called in by Child Protective Services because one of their children reports a slap or a spank to a teacher at school. She thinks about the distances between parents and children, the ways the ends of kinship can stretch and fray, and about the different forms of love and anger and grief.

Wangmo gets up from the couch and clears the breakfast dishes. She should have left for work ten minutes ago. The train will be packed at this hour, hurtling immigrant workers into Manhattan. The birthday card sits on the coffee table. She picks it up, folds it in half, and then in half again. Wangmo keeps folding until the card becomes as small as an amulet, as small as a prayer.

# GOING FOR EDUCATION

SITUATING SCHOOL SPONSORSHIP

I had not realized how small Phurba was until I bought his school outfit from a uniform supply store off New Road in Kathmandu. The navy blue trousers stretched from the tips of my fingers to just above my elbow. To this was added a matching blue sweater, a short stack of creased white polo shirts, a white button-down shirt and a tie, lace-up leather shoes, several pairs of dress socks, sneakers, and a tiny track suit. The entire collection fit easily into my backpack. By Tibetan reckoning, Phurba was seven. This made him five or six in Gregorian terms. I was twenty-two.

Phurba is the youngest son in a family of five. His father is an *amchi*. During my early extended stays in Monthang, the *amchi* and I grew close. After some time, he approached me about sponsoring Phurba to attend boarding school in Kathmandu. I considered this request, before agreeing, but not as deeply as I should have.

This was the mid-1990s. Everyone and their brother—literally—were trying to arrange sponsorship for their children to attend boarding school, preferably outside the district. At the time, the balance still tipped toward boys, although this changed within the decade. The rationale went like this:

> Government schools provide poor education in an unfamiliar language
> that does not prepare children well for life within or outside Mustang. The
> teachers are long-nosed lowlanders who don't understand our culture,
> who think people from Mustang are backwards, and who only show up
> for a handful of months each year, when the weather is nice. And then,
> they complain about everything and don't teach well.

> The only high-quality education in Lo is through the monastic system,
> and that is only a good option for middle children or kids from poor
> families. Jomsom boarding schools are acceptable, but Thakali kids from

lower Mustang tease Loba and eventually take all the good government jobs anyway. So, if you can afford it, or if you get a sponsor for your child, send them to a boarding school in Pokhara, Kathmandu, or India. They might feel shy. You will miss them. But it is better than keeping them home for education.

In the city, some schools teach Tibetan along with the Nepali national curriculum and English, and this is good for cultural preservation. Our people should know Tibetan language. Beyond culture, if your children go out for education, they will have better chances in life. They will *jagir khane*—eat a salary, plow with a pen—instead of becoming farmers and herders for a living, like their parents. They might also get a good enough job so that you won't have to worry about money in your old age. If we educate our children well, then they will manage better in the world. They will have what it takes to develop Mustang to its full potential, and they will come back to do this work.

The logic of such narratives was, at one level, undisputable. Yet these stories were neither complete nor without their half-truths and complications. For one thing, this logic did not account for the extent to which foreign or monastic sponsorships began to circulate as forms of social capital among parents, even as the ability to pay for a child's education oneself could be viewed as a sign of social prestige. It did not account for the possibility that education would transform young people, leading at least some of them farther away from Mustang, not back home, and away from cultural norms and parental expectations. Nor did it address the enduring emotional impacts of boarding school life and the dynamics of sponsorship on many other aspects of the young self.

In addition, like most stories, this narrative supports many possible endings. It could lead to a more "developed" and self-reliant Mustang. It could lead to brain-drain as well as losses of language and attendant forms of cultural trauma. It could foster parental pride in children's educational accomplishments and produce a small but growing number of highly educated global Mustang intellectuals. It could foster the fragmentation of family ties and a sense of abandonment across the generations. It could support gender equality and new possibilities for young women. It could support an already pervasive notion that a girl who had too much education would not make a desirable wife. These narratives might also spark a reaction against sending kids out of Mustang for school and foster the formation of higher quality private and community schools in Mustang itself. It could facilitate the influx of children from other parts of Nepal to fill these new Mustang-based institutions, particularly once the *khora* of migration between Nepal and New York is in full swing.

Each of these possible endings has borne out over the past two decades, and the story is still being told.

As I consider these realities, I hear the voices of Mustang educators. "To depend on *jindak*, sponsors, to educate our children is a shame," said the monk-principal of a private lay school in 2014. "There are more than thirty schools in Mustang, including government schools, monasteries, private boarding schools, but there is no *future* school—no long-term vision," said another educator from Lo that same year. "The concept of sending kids to school is in the mind of the parents," noted a young Loba who was in charge of the Upper Mustang Hostel in Jomsom, "but what 'education' means is not." In field notes from 2016, I record a telling calculus: *At the Tsarang government school, number of teachers = 5; number of local students = 0.*

At the same time, older Mustang friends—including parents of children who have left home for education and those whose children were educated in the district—remain divided on the tricky question of what schooling is "good for." Some bemoan the lack of vocational training:

> We want to build our own tourism industry, but we have to bring up cooks and carpenters from the lowlands.

> It is easy to say that people with more education should replace others with less, but I could be a microbiologist, and I still might not know how to plant a field!

Others insist on the superiority of education elsewhere yet consider the loss of vision and work ethic among Mustang youth:

> You can't even learn to write your name properly in a local school. The private schools in Mustang don't give good education. They are just about making money.

> Education is good, but if the end result is our children just say that they don't want to do any real work, they just want to sit in a chair and play on a computer, then what good is that? If they don't have ideas, capacity, and motivation but they have a +2, BA, Master, then this means nothing.

I have been struck by two particular refrains, two sides of the proverbial coin:

In our day, we learned everything we needed from a class five government education. Class five back then was like class ten today.

What children used to learn in class five, they learn in the daycares today.

These divergent visions reflect deeper questions about what education is and what it is for. The elder generation, mostly men, did master much of what they needed in terms of formal, standardized education by class five. They were reasonably literate in the national language. They learned to assimilate and navigate and negotiate, to be successful on the state's terms and simultaneously retain their cultural moorings. And yet, what one needs to know now—of the self, of Nepal, of the world—has continued to change. Dual truths are nestled in these competing visions.

When I was in my early twenties and still fairly new to Nepal, these questions about the scope and purpose of education remained nascent. They were difficult for me to see. It also is worth noting my personal blind spot: I had, after all, left home for college at seventeen without any thought that I would return, post-graduation, to the place I was raised. I also embraced the liberal arts ideal, a valuable if romantic notion of intellectual exploration for exploration's sake, without recourse to vocation. Just as education is changing the trajectories of my contemporaries in Mustang as well as their children, so, too, did it change me.

The dynamic of "going for education" in Mustang also has been shaped by several high-profile cases of sponsorship, connected to the Tibetan Government in Exile and the late twentieth-century groundswell of global Tibetan Buddhism. In the early 1990s, just as upper Mustang was opened to foreign travelers, a delegation from Dharamsala, led by a renowned Tibetan *rinpoche*, visited Monthang. This pilgrimage, captured in a documentary film called *Mustang: Journey of Transformation*, included the *rinpoche* selecting two Loba children to be enrolled at the Tibetan Children's Village (TCV), an institution founded by His Holiness the Fourteenth Dalai Lama's sister, Jetsun Pema.

The film follows these two boys out of Mustang, toward what is portrayed as a precious gem of an opportunity: to be educated in a Tibetan cultural milieu, with the blessings and support of His Holiness. Never mind that such overt linking of Mustang and the Tibetan diaspora could generate mistrust and political uneasiness within the Nepali state—particularly as Nepal has continued to edge, in geopolitical terms, toward China. Never mind that Dharamsala might feel alien or alienating to children from northern Nepal. Never mind that these children are not, and yet sort of are, Tibetan. One of these boys is Phurba's cousin. Now, both of the young men in the film live in New York.

When Phurba's father asked me to help educate his son, I entered into a bond of cultural and economic relationship, a form of reciprocity that felt at once good and bewildering. It has taken me, and Phurba for that matter, years to unravel the consequences of this action.

### VISITING DAYS

The road up to Mt. Kailash Boarding School in Kopan wound along the backside of the Boudha *stupa*, through Mahankal, and then edged left before the *pipal* tree that marked Tinchuli Chowk. Sometimes I would bicycle up. Other times I would walk from Boudha. Every time I made my way to Mt. Kailash, I felt as if I could make a wrong turn at any moment. More than once, I did. One time, I found my way to the school by scrambling up the incline on the backside of the dusty soccer grounds, following the sounds of children playing. I still recall the look of bewilderment on the kids' faces when I hitched myself up over the edge of the field, sweating in my cotton *kurta*. Sometimes I'd catch a ride on the back of a motorcycle that belonged to one of the older expatriate sponsors of high-mountain children at Mt. Kailash. Regardless of the method of approach, I always entered this institution feeling embarrassed and shy.

On visiting days, I would arrive laden with awkward offerings of sweets and colored pencils for Phurba. He would be called out to greet me. In those first years, he seemed so vulnerable that I often regretted this decision. He would cast down his eyes, his hands reaching for the treats I'd brought. Phurba's round face recalled that of his uncle. His lips crested and fell when he spoke in ways that reminded me of his grandfather.

Although I was not yet a mother, I realized when confronted with Phurba's youthful dislocation that I had not considered what his mother might have felt about having one of her children taken away from her and sent to the capital—a place she ventured rarely. Facing a schoolyard filled with mountain children, I felt responsible for Phurba's timidity and the distinct possibility that he was homesick. I shared my feelings of discomfort with his father; he sloughed them off. "Phurba is little now. He may cry sometimes, but he'll be fine. And he is not the only child from Mustang in the school." This was true. Over the years, dozens of children from Mustang have received a Mt. Kailash education. But still.

The school principal always met me with kindness and tolerance. It was in conversations with this older Tibetan refugee, at once erudite and grounded, that I first began to comprehend the magnitude of my decision to sponsor Phurba's education. The principal's whole world revolved around managing the importation of mountain children to the capital city as well as managing relationships with sponsors and parents. In those early years, he assessed Phurba's sense of displacement without hyperbole and with compassion, even as he recounted the ways that he was growing, the young person he was becoming.

During the years when I lived full-time in Nepal, after Phurba had been taken to Kathmandu, I felt awkward confiding to anyone that I was his sponsor. Part of this reflected the politics of patronage in Mustang— *jindak* could evoke jealousy. However, more than that, I didn't feel like I should be *anyone's* sponsor. In my early twenties, I was happy to be in Nepal but not ready to be responsible for anyone other than myself. At that time, I was living on $500 per month—about what Phurba's tuition cost for a year—and I had to ask my parents for help with the first few years of this commitment.

This sponsor relationship would last for fourteen years, through Phurba's completion of his School Leaving Certificate and two years of +2 "college." As school fees got more expensive, and as Phurba's family became more established in the cash economy, this arrangement would become a joint venture between his father and me. It would last until my own child was a toddler and, ironically, until I had a permanent job. In the early years of this arrangement, I recall being acutely aware of my privilege—the fact that a modest financial contribution by U.S. standards could provide a good quality education to a young Nepali—and confounded by the emotional mechanics of this transaction.

Despite the constancy with which I paid his school fees, I don't believe that I ever did enough for Phurba. I deepened my relationship with his father and uncle. I knew other members of his family well. But I was never in a position to bring Phurba home with me during school holidays, like some expatriate sponsors (themselves aid workers and artists, entrepreneurs and academics) did for their charges, and I knew that his parents could not manage to bring him to Monthang each year. I worried that he felt forgotten as he was shuttled around, in the care of other relatives.

After I returned to the U.S. to begin graduate school and married life, Phurba and I did not deepen our relationship. He would send me sweet, if generic, dear sponsor letters. I would review his report cards and send him equally saccharine responses. Perhaps we both failed to break through, but I recognize the steep unevenness of this affective terrain. It took the better part of two decades before we offered each other something genuine, spoken from the heart.

## RECKONINGS

In the autumn of 2016, Phurba and I find ourselves standing together, shrouded in the soft rain of late monsoon, on the roof of a private boarding school in Pokhara. His father and uncle built this school, with donor support from Europe and North America. This institution is an extension of a school they opened in 2000, in Monthang, that now educates more than fifty students. It is a project envisioned by Phurba's grandfather, an *amchi* of renown, and that was realized, in part, to honor his memory and the family's lineage. Phurba's elder brother is the principal. Like their cousin, he was educated in Dharamsala.

Consonant with the creation of several other private boarding schools in Mustang, this institution developed a dual mission: it offered poor and younger children a culturally resonant and government accredited primary education; for the older students, it brokered new methods of institution-based Tibetan medical training with an opportunity to earn an SLC. Initially envisioned as a way to keep more children in Mustang through childhood, while also providing them with a better education than the government school, and continuing to teach Tibetan medicine *in situ*, this vision has shifted over time.

Phurba is still young, but he is a grown man. He carries the round face of his uncle, but he sports a moustache. He is still shy, but something of that early embarrassment has been sloughed away. For several years, we have been communicating regularly, in part because Phurba serves as the school's secretary. He accompanies and assists his uncle in his role as a global practitioner of Tibetan medicine. I have come to know a small bit of Phurba's ambition, a sliver of his sense of humor.

"How has it been since the earthquakes?" I ask. We are more than a year and a half out from the devastating spring of 2015. Pokhara did not experience as much destruction as other places, but the school sustained some structural damage.

"We had to repair parts of the dining hall. There are some other problems, but we are almost ready for when the younger students come for the winter," he answers.

"How do the young ones manage?" I ask. Phurba and I are standing beside the water cistern and the row of solar panels on the roof. Verdant hills stretch out beyond the school. If I close my eyes and listen, I can hear waters of the Seti Gandaki and the incessant *ping ping ping* of low-caste women cracking boulders into stone, stone into gravel by the riverside.

"Most students like Pokhara," Phurba answers. "It is good to be studying *only*, especially for the ones who live in Monthang." At home in Mustang, their learning is often challenged by the exigencies of village life: collecting firewood, caring for younger siblings.

At this school, like several other private institutions in Mustang, children now spend the winter in more temperate climes. This idea of a mobile school—an educational model that is its own form of *khora*—was conceived as a way to keep kids learning without seasonal disruptions to curriculum that would inevitably come when non-local teachers decamped for the lowlands once Mustang grew cold. Now, winter schools in Pokhara or Kathmandu have become an expectation. They provide different educational opportunities and exposure to the world outside of Mustang and can make teachers, both locals and lowlanders, more likely to continue in their posts and can afford them additional teacher training. Winter schools allow parents to see their children but not be directly responsible for them as they move south for seasonal petty trade. Majority opinion definitely favors these winter schools. However, this innovation is contributing to the idea—disproved elsewhere in the Himalaya—that the only way to receive strong primary schooling is to leave the mountains. It can also add to the cost of education. This, in turn, may manifest as another area of financial stress for parents or increase a sense of competition between schools: Who has the more generous *jindak* when it comes to winter accommodations and activities?

"Now that we have our own building," Phurba continues, "it feels more like coming home." For the first five years of this school's seasonal migration, they rented a house on the outskirts of Pokhara, from which they ran the winter program. The roof leaked in places. The water supply was unreliable. There were challenges with the landlord. After concerted fundraising and planning, the family was able to buy land and build this permanent structure near the Tibetan refugee settlement of Pasang Ling and not far from Pema Tsal Monastery, a place where many young monastics from

Mustang study. The senior students now live in Pokhara year-round, whereas the younger classes join them from October to March.

"When the little ones come, the older students *take care* nicely. Like *family*," continues Phurba.

From my visits to this school, in its various locations over the years, I know this to be true. Even so, I know other truths: that the school struggles to retain talented teachers and manage donor-driven budgets, given the demands of inflation, corruption, and the disaster of everyday life that can unfold in Nepal; that children who fail government exams can be called out as dim-witted or lacking motivation; that the founding *amchi* find it challenging to balance the demands of running a school with other community responsibilities. Nor is this family immune to, or innocent in, the weaponized deployment of gossip—kept in a quiver, released like poisoned arrows—that criticizes the work of others and blames their own shortcomings on systems beyond their control.

Phurba leads me from the roof down through the girls' and boys' dormitories with their hunter green mattresses and the acrid tinge of monsoon mold, through the library with its pale-yellow walls and hand-me-down computers, into the classrooms for the younger children, painted with alphabets and animals. The institution has a clear sense of purpose. Yet as I contemplate where education has, and has not, gotten Phurba, I feel like I'm back at Mt. Kailash.

"Phurba," I say, "sometimes I think about how small you were when we took you to school in Kathmandu. It must have been difficult. The decision is in the past, but sometimes I wonder if I did the right thing. You were so young."

"It was hard," he answers. "I cried a lot. Sometimes the teachers scared me."

"Did you ever get hit?"

"Only twice." This honest answer stings.

"Mt. Kailash was a good place," Phurba continues. "We had many Loba there. It was like whole villages in our schoolhouses."

I flash on a memory of Mt. Kailash's metal gate. I recall meeting the children of others I knew from Mustang, including Nawang Tsering, during visiting days. He was as gregarious then as he remains now. I remember seeing the eldest daughter of another Mustang *amchi*, who possessed in her early teens a sense of maternal devotion for the younger kids and an incisive intellect, both qualities that seemed to be being nurtured.

"You were always so shy when I came to visit."

"I was! I didn't realize that *you* were my sponsor until I was in class three or four. I just thought you came because you knew my father and some of the other children. Then the principal explained."

"Really?"

"Really." We speak to each other in a mixture of standard Tibetan, Nepali, and English, itself indicative of the sociolinguistic mix that emerges through boarding school life.

"I am sorry to have caused you suffering when you were a child," I say.

Phurba flushes. "It was a good education."

Even though this may be true, the benefits of schooling have not necessarily led to secure employment or the fulfillment of his higher education goals. Phurba toyed with the idea of studying Chinese medicine, but the costs and the language demands were prohibitive. Instead, he has made a place for himself within the family business of education and clinical Tibetan medicine. I am left, all these years later, holding the contradictions of pedagogy's promises, considering the entanglements of kinship, real and imagined, that facilitating his education has produced.

"Now that I am a mother," I offer, "I think about the heart-mind of your mother, at that time when you were small."

"I missed her," he answers. "We did not see each other for some years."

"Do you think she was glad you were going to school in Kathmandu?"

"She was happy for that. She never had education. I don't know if she could think much about the difference between the government school and going to Mt. Kailash, except that one was near her and one was far away. Sending me to Kathmandu was my father's decision. He was not the only one who thought this was the right thing to do."

"But now they have a school themselves. Where they give education in Monthang," I respond. We are standing in the courtyard. Behind Phurba, affixed to the second-story balcony, is a neatly painted sign with the school's name and founding date, 2000.

"I know," Phurba says. "But people with money and power still send their kids away. We take care of the ones with less. So, it is *same same, different different.*"

## DAYCARE

Dolma leads my daughter, Aida, by the hand. She is just shy of four. Her head levels with Dolma's knees. They walk down the narrow steps of Dolma's home in Monthang. Dolma ducks under the lintel. Aida jumps over the threshold. They continue past a row of prayer wheels and through the arched gateway of this walled city. They pass another row of prayer wheels, skirt the few storefronts that have, by this time in 2008, been built outside the town's ramparts. I walk behind them, close enough to listen to Aida chatter, in English, about flowers and horses and cows and to hear Dolma, in Logé, comment on the weather, the weeding she must do in her sweet pea fields, what she will cook for lunch. Each seems to sing their words. They speak to, and past, each other.

As we round the southern corner of the town, Dolma leads us toward a little structure tucked behind a mud brick wall near the ACAP greenhouse. A sign—yellow block letters on a tar-colored background—lets those who read English know that this is the local daycare. Dolma just knows the place. She needs no sign to tell her.

Established in the early years of the new millennium, with support from an American foundation and a local community-based organization overseen by Lo nobility, these daycares began in response to a moment of crisis: the drowning deaths of several children while their parents were occupied with agricultural work, as described in Part I. Fourteen daycares now exist in the district. They have become durable institutions—places to learn languages through song and dance, take naps, eat snacks, and be inculcated into other "techniques of the body" and "technologies of the self," as social theorists Marcel Mauss and Michel Foucault describe, respectively. Children learn to wash hands, brush teeth, recite ABC and *ka kha ga*, and play with blocks and puzzles.

These institutions have taken the place of less structured if differently immersive models of youth, in which younger siblings are cared for by elder siblings or cousins, in which unsupervised play materializes from found objects and, significantly, in which doing household chores is a norm from a very young age. In other words, these institutions have laid the foundation for a shift in the focus of early childhood learning out of the home, away from extended family, and into more professionalized spaces. These shifts cannot be decoupled from education-driven migration and demographic change. In most villages, older children and teenagers have become something of an endangered species.

The foreign foundation has funded Tibetan language teachers for the daycares, as they have in other Mustang schools. The daycares are also providing employment for educated local and exile Tibetan women. Children learn to recite the Tibetan and English alphabets, although they sing local songs. They are taught the basics of Buddhist moral education. These daycares encourage expressions of individuality through art, socialize kids to share, and impart public health messages. They have created the conditions for a different sort of childhood in Mustang—one based on Tibetan ideals and on models imported from Europe and North America.

The messaging and skills learned at the Mustang daycares filter down to adults. In some instances, they have inspired or encouraged mothers' group literacy classes, even as they highlight the social divides between the lives of older women and the girls coming of age today.

> I am as stupid as a cow. I can't even sign my name. But now even little
> children know so much!

I've heard variations on this refrain many times, from mothers and grandmothers. Despite this recognition of the unevenness of formal education across female generations, these daycares are appreciated by adults and kids alike. For those grandparents taking care of young children whose parents labor abroad, the care provided by these centers—approximately six hours per day, five days a week—is a lifesaver. And for Mustang-American kids or local children who may well find themselves in New York later in childhood, they provide a form of cultural preparation for that move, even as they are decidedly local places.

On this day in 2008, Dolma ushers Aida into the group of twenty children, ages three to six. "Go, sit," she says, with her few words of English. Aida finds a place beside two boys her age, on a wooden bench made for tiny bodies. Although she doesn't know the language, she knows exactly what to do. In the shade of poplar trees, she begins clapping, stomping, and counting with her Mustang peers.

Many of the things Aida has experienced on this trip to Mustang are disorienting, if fun. I have carried her over mountain passes and have ridden horses with her on my back, this Vermont girl delighting, demanding, "Mama, go bumpity bump. More horsey." She has been coddled by a Hindu *sadhu* on his way to the holy lake of Damodar Kund. She has made bouquets of cosmos and offered them to household shrines. She has squatted in fields and forced herself to poop into little holes that lead down into the dark abyss of dry toilets, their smell masked by rarefied mountain air and ash. But the daycare is familiar territory.

The Monthang daycare teacher asks if Aida would like to sing an American song. We decide on "Itsy Bitsy Spider." My brave little girl and I get up in front of the children and begin. To Aida's surprise, many of the kids know the melody and hand gestures, if not all of the words. When we finish, I hear one of the older kids, a girl, sitting on a bench toward the back. "That is not an American song. That is our song!"

## POSTER CHILDREN

She is a mother of five, although only three of her children lived to be school-aged. One "had no breath," as she explained. Another drowned. The girl had been three, curious. "That was before we started the daycares," says this woman in her fifties. Her eyes are dark and moist with memory.

"Where are the other three, *didi*?" asks KC. It is the summer of 2012, and we are deep into our reproductive history research.

"All in India," she answers. "All monks." The woman gestures toward a poster tacked to the mud wall of her home in Drakmar. The laminated image bursts with the color red, as if hundreds of young monks clustered together for this portrait were a bouquet of roses, gathered around a central figure, His Holiness Sakya Gomang Rinpoche, blooming and regal in crimson and saffron. This mother rises from where she is sitting on a low wooden stool near the hearth. She points out her children in the picture. "There is the oldest one. That is the youngest. Two went to *Der-dun*. The middle is in *Mun-ghot*," she says, speaking of monasteries in the Himalayan foothills of Dehradun and the South Indian town of Mundgod.

I note that while two sons are in Sakya institutions, the third has been ordained in the Gelug tradition, even though there is no Gelug lineage in Mustang. We learn that her sons range in age from eleven to twenty-one and that none has returned to Mustang since leaving the village. Sometimes she meets her children in the winter, when she and her partner, the father of her two youngest children, head south for trade. She explains that it is difficult to talk with them because they no longer speak Logé. "They grew out of our language like an old pair of shoes."

KC pauses, then asks, "Why did you send them all to be monks?"

The mother shrugs and casts her eyes toward the floor. "I sent the older one as an act of faith, for the two who died. The middle and the younger, I didn't think, I just sent them. I'm poor. It is a free education. The monastery will teach them virtue."

"Yes, but who will care for you when you are old? What about this house?" KC says. The questions are as piercing as the answer.

"I don't know," says the woman. Her hands knot in her lap. Her eyes fix on the door. "I hope they will remember their mother."

SUNDAY SCHOOL

On an early August morning in 2013, before their Mustang language and culture class in New York, Nawang and one of his co-instructors, an artist originally from the Muktinath Valley, meet me at a coffee shop on Cortelyou Road. The Brooklyn streets are quiet, but they have already begun to heat up. As I listen to Nawang and his co-instructor make plans for the morning's session with anywhere between ten and twenty-five Mustang-American kids, aged six through thirteen, I realize just how overwhelmed Nawang is by having taken on this responsibility.

"I've rented this yoga studio for a few months, but it is difficult with their schedule," he explains. He sips a mug of French roast and looks tired. He'd been at his restaurant job until one in the morning. It is now just after seven. "The parents want the classes to be longer, a few hours, to make it worth their time. But then they give me looks when I tell them we need to charge $40 a month per child. They think I am making money!" he says, exasperated. "But it is hard to find a space for that long on the weekend."

Nawang is not the only person who has helped to run language and culture classes for Loba and other Himalayan youth in New York, but he has been a pioneer in these efforts. His impetus for such work has come from observing how younger Mustang-Americans become disconnected from their parents and their cultural roots as they struggle to integrate into New York life and as their parents work long hours and remain preoccupied with other aspects of the *khora* of migration. These "Sunday School" classes sometimes happen on Saturdays, but they are meant to serve a similar purpose to the cultural education that occurs in church basements, synagogues, and other faith-based community centers around the U.S. They at once distill "culture" into particular forms of performance—the ability to sing a harvest song from Lo, to offer long life prayers for the Dalai Lama, to introduce yourself in Tibetan—and provide opportunities to celebrate aspects of where you or your parents come from as well as to grasp, perhaps a bit more fully, who you are.

Nawang arrived in the U.S. as a young adult and is well networked in the exile Tibetan community in New York. He can slip into a generic sense of Tibetanness, as if putting on the uniform he wore for years at a Tibetan high school in Kathmandu. Yet he also knows the names of his household deity and village protector. He knows Mustang's wind and water, having spent his early years herding sheep and goats above the hamlet in which he was born before being enrolled in a Kathmandu boarding school.

He narrates the challenges of what he calls his "social service works." "Sometimes I have to bribe my friends to volunteer," Nawang confides. "They don't want to give up free time. We need teacher training. Otherwise, people just teach the way they were taught, with only memorization. But this is boring for these kids who are going to school in a different system.

"And even though I'm doing this for the good of community, there is still politics. How much to talk about Buddhism? Do we teach Tibetan or Nepali? Right now, we are doing *ka kha ga* and some prayers to Guru Rinpoche and His Holiness. We build from there. Some parents like that their kids are learning Tibetan, but other parents say, 'We are actually from Nepal, so the kids should be learning Nepali!' It is difficult. When people say things like that, I like it because I can reply to that question. I can tell about our true Mustang heritage."

"Do you ever talk about Bön?" I ask, knowing that Nawang is from a family lineage associated with these pre-Buddhist currents of Tibetan religion.

Nawang chuckles. "No way! These kids hardly know the difference of Sakya, Nyingma, or what sect the Dalai Lama is. Besides, if I talked about Bön, then the parents would say I am doing these works for some sort of personal benefit."

"Do you think the parents appreciate what you are doing?" I ask.

"Many do, but some . . . I don't know. It is like I remember when I was little, when I would return to the village. Parents would ask kids, 'What did you learn? Did they treat you well? Did they steal money? Did they teach you anything useful?' The same thing happens here!" he laughs. "They want their kids to know language and culture, but they don't want to pay for it, and they are not sure what is the use, except to dance at Losar parties. We are trying to convince the parents of what culture education is for."

Later that morning, I watch Nawang and his artist friend work the room of rambunctious youth. A giant Sanskrit *Om* may be painted on the wall, but this scene is far from serene. After prayer recitations and several Tibetan songs, Nawang moves the kids into a circle. He walks around them, asking them to say their name, their parents' names, their ages, and what grade they are in—all in standard Tibetan. Some of these young people really struggle. Nawang moves on to naming parts of the body, having them mimic him, correcting pronunciation. Next, small groups of children are tasked with reading a short parable in Tibetan. Most strain over simple sentences. After this exercise comes art. Everyone seems to breathe a sigh of relief.

Nawang's friend takes over, handing out colored pens and photocopied sheets of Tibetan auspicious symbols, which the kids are encouraged to copy.

I meet Pema. She is nearly fourteen and will be an eighth grader at JHS 62 in Brooklyn. She likes math. The first school she went to was a one-room government schoolhouse in her village east of Monthang. She was fortunate to go to school. Her elder sister and brother herd the family's sheep and goats. At nine, she was sent to a boarding school in Pokhara, her family having secured a foreign sponsor. Eventually, she made it to New York. Now, she sits cross-legged on the wood floor of the yoga studio beside other children, most of them half her age.

Pema is shyly pubescent in her Britney Spears T-shirt. She shows me a collage she has made. It is an image of the Buddha. She has traced the outlines from a stencil and pieced Sakyamuni's body together from a New York City subway map. This is Pema's rendition of work by contemporary Tibetan artists, people like Tenzing Rigdol and Gonkar Gyatso, who make Buddhas out of cut-up scriptures, dollar bills, Pokémon stickers.

"The Buddha is like the culture we protect," Pema says, in English. "He is like our soul. But inside, we live New York." I imagine the A-C-E line as veins running blue; the 1-2-3 trains red as arteries; the purple, yellow, and orange lines that stretch across Brooklyn and Queens—the 7 train, N-R-Q, and B-D-F—as *sogtsa*, lifelines. I wonder what Pema would make of a map of Mustang, how she might orient herself to its topography.

Toward the end of the class, I speak with the mothers who have gathered outside to collect their children. One is from Dhi. She is a distant relative of Nawang. She has an eight-year-old girl and a ten-year-old boy. Through our conversation, I learn that the girl was born here and has only known school in America. The son was also born here, but he was sent to TCV in Dharamsala a few years ago, and he is now back in the New York public school system. I sit with the dizzying nature of this educational *khora*. Another young mother collects her six-year-old, who speaks beautiful Logé and is comfortable in English. "We only speak Mustang language at home," she explains, in Nepali, when I comment on his fluency. "Everywhere else, it will be English," she says, "but without our language, what do we have?"

## THE VILLAGE AS FOREIGN TERRITORY

The girl sitting across from me in Nawang's family home in Ghiling looks like she is about to cry. On this cool summer evening in 2012, she fingers a mobile phone listlessly, staring down at the floor. A mug of butter tea is placed in front of each of us. The woodstove is not lit. Nobody has introduced the girl and me, so, in a moment after KC has headed home to her family and when Yangjin is helping Nawang's mother cook, I say hello.

"Namaste, Tashi Delek. What is your name?" I phrase the question in Logé. The girl answers hesitantly.

"Bhuti," she whispers.

"What class are you in?" I ask, assuming that she is not only from Ghiling but also enrolled in the community school. This institution receives both state and foreign support and was started by a Tibetan refugee who came to live in the village after his family fled over the border in the 1960s.

The girl's face scrunches. She seems embarrassed and stops talking. I switch to Nepali. "Do you go to school in Kathmandu?"

"Pokhara." She turns back to her phone.

The girl and I sit in silence for a while. In the quiet, I am brought back to an encounter from several days earlier, in a hamlet north of Monthang. Yangjin and I had gone to interview a grandmother for our reproductive history work. The grandmother's narrative proved interesting, but it was dwarfed by meeting her daughter and granddaughter. The daughter had made her way to Germany. She works at a hotel, has learned German, and aspires to become an accountant. This woman's daughter, a pre-teen with an ink-black bob and a pout, was born in Germany. The girl's father did not seem to be present, and it was unclear if he was from Mustang, Germany, or elsewhere. This girl spoke clear English, no Logé, and only a handful of Nepali words. Her mother tongue, such as it was, was *Deutsch*. She seemed bored and lonely, stuck in a house with people who claimed her but to whom she had little connection. As with the girl across from me now, her phone was her portal, albeit a frustrating one, to a lifeworld elsewhere, otherwise. When I asked her how she was finding Mustang, her response was swift: "I can't wait to go home."

Yangjin comes in bearing trays of snacks. The shy girl leaps up and heads out of the room. I give Yangjin a look, as if to say, *What is her story?*

"*Didi*, it is a very sad situation," Yangjin answers, in English, which she presumes the girl cannot understand. "She is from Ghiling, but she was sent to a Korean Christian school in Pokhara when she was very young. Now her sponsorship has ended, and she has been sent back here. But she doesn't feel comfortable."

"She doesn't seem to understand Nepali or Logé well," I say, referring to the small splices of language we tried speaking with each other.

"No. Just from being in Pokhara she has some Nepali, but she can't speak much Logé or Tibetan. The school was supposed to be English medium, but I think she learned more Korean than anything else. She has trouble talking with her family."

"What will she do?" I ask. "What is her family's situation?"

"They are poor. Some challenge with the father," Yangjin motions as if she is drinking, by which she means, most likely, that the girl's dad is an alcoholic.

"What will she do now? What class is she in? She looks big."

"I think class six or seven. She will probably have to start lower, wherever she ends up."

I had heard of other similar experiences—sponsors abandoning their charges or having their own life circumstances change such that sponsorship became impossible. I was also aware of the increasing phenomenon across the northern Himalaya of children being recruited to Christian schools, some of which were more focused on evangelism than education. I understood that cultural and economic connections between Nepal and Korea were growing stronger, but I had not considered the possibility that a young person could be receiving an education *in Nepal* that would leave her so vulnerable to cultural alienation.

"I think someone is trying to find her a new sponsor to go to Dhaulagiri," continues Yangjin, referring to the main boarding school in Jomsom. "But I am not sure. She is like a foreigner in her own village."

At once consonant with and distinct from this young girl's story, I am reminded of a man from Samar, now in his mid-twenties and living in Kathmandu. He was sponsored by a Christian school. "My family blamed me for my education," he said. He did not initially identify with Christianity as a faith but rather accepted it as a means of getting educated. However, the stigma he faced from his family because he went to a Christian school pushed him toward this religion. "They didn't really care for me as a son, like the pastor's family did." The young man described how he returned to his village after completing his SLC, but village life proved interpersonally impossible. Hoping to continue his education in computer science, he returned to Kathmandu and tried to get support for further secular education from the pastor, but the pastor said he would only support this young man if he attended a Bible college. This engendered yet another crisis of identity and life strategy. He ended up at the religious college, with a scholarship, and received additional support from people associated with the Summer

Institute of Linguistics, with whom he now does translation. For him, language was far from lost—indeed it became part of a livelihood strategy—but education and its social effects produced fracture, a certain kind of internal exile.

## SUMMER CAMP AND SOCIAL STATUS

Chimi is passionate about early childhood education. She studied it as an undergraduate at a liberal arts school in the American Midwest. She has worked at preschools and daycares, and she has recently secured a full-time position at an independent, progressive school in Manhattan. Chimi aspires to further education, but these days she is focused on balancing the demands of her job and her family (siblings in New York, aging parents in Nepal) and planning for Himalayan summer camp. Before she landed the job at the private school, she had hoped to run a home daycare out of her spacious apartment in Jackson Heights, but "the building was not up to code for disability access. Welcome to New York!" She explains all of this as we sit in her living room, sipping an American version of Nepali fresh lemon sodas.

"How are plans for the summer camp coming?" I ask. Chimi has decided to use the month of vacation from her regular job to run a day camp for Himalayan youth.

"It has been a lot of work to organize, and also to try and convince the parents that it is worth it, but we have about twenty kids signed up, and I think we will get some more." Chimi's motivation is to provide a fun experience that not only fosters a sense of cultural pride in young Himalayan New Yorkers but also exposes them to different ways of knowing themselves.

It is late spring 2017, and the summer camp is scheduled to start in a couple of months. Her roommate and cousin, Mentok, a young woman who has just received her master's degree from an Ivy League institution, will help to run the camp.

"We're going to do art classes and some Tibetan," says Mentok. "We'll take the kids on field trips. We'll spend some time each day doing meditation but also exercise and other kinds of adventures. Restaurants. The Sherpa monastery. Things like that."

"I hope we can do this type of camp for some years," Chimi adds, "but my dream is to bring kids from here back to Nepal. Like *summer camp* and *study abroad* together." By the following summer, in 2018, this dream had become a reality—even though it only brought kids to Kathmandu.

Chimi's enthusiasm is infectious. By virtue of their presence but also by their actions, she and her cousin are in ideal positions to help these young kids navigate the waters of cultural belonging, American assimilation, and academic achievement that they themselves had to figure out without much guidance, albeit with a level of emotional and financial support from their families that is rare. Akin to many other immigrant communities, the pressure to be economically successful among people from Mustang is often greater than the drive to pursue an intellectual passion or to take an unfamiliar academic path.

I think about Nawang, who worked sixty hours a week at two menial jobs while he completed his associate degree. He achieved this goal despite the fact that most in his family did not understand why he would want to go to college. Particularly as the eldest son, with a widowed mother, it was understood that his primary responsibility was to earn money. With encouragement from me and others, he was accepted to a prestigious private New York university, only to watch his hopes of earning a bachelor's degree from this institution dashed as he realized that his financial aid package was insufficient to afford tuition and that he was unwilling to go into debt, given the other financial burdens he shouldered.

Such realities can combine with serious questions about the value of education—what it can do for you in the long run. This concern can become amplified with time or circumstance. Among all the extended families I know, few parents have really supported their children's desires for advanced study. Chimi and her cousin come from a branch of the Loba elite who have been willing to support their children's intellectual goals. This, of course, is distinct yet again from truly *accepting* the ways that U.S. college educations have changed their children's perspectives.

"I hope the kids appreciate all you are planning," I say, knowing that neither Chimi nor her cousin are being paid to run this camp. The tuition costs will be just enough to cover rental space and activity fees.

Chimi, ever positive, responds, "I know they will. They are so smart. But many of them are pretty confused about their identity, or how to relate to their parents, or what they might be able to achieve." As we speak, we move between Nepali and English, Logé around the edges.

The front door opens and in walks Pasang, one of Chimi's siblings and a young man who recently earned his bachelor's degree in the U.S. and is poised to start a PhD. Among the generation of Mustang people from their mid-twenties to mid-thirties, few have received U.S.-based higher education that is not framed as "practical." I know many young women, for instance, who have pursued nursing; others have studied accounting, computer science, or engineering. But few have chosen to study a "pure" academic field, like this young man's interest in social science. We've never met, but he's heard of me. "We have your book," he says, pointing toward a small bookshelf near the front door. I see a copy of my first book about Mustang, *Horses Like Lightning*.

"I read it!" says Mentok, chiding her cousin. "It was fun because it was filled with stories about all these people I know but from a time when I was off at school." All three of them had been educated at boarding schools in the mid-1990s, when I was living in Mustang.

"What was it like when you first went to school?" I ask.

"I loved it," Chimi answers. "Sure, we missed our parents, but we all took care of each other. It was hard but we learned a lot."

Mentok demurs. "I had a good school experience, but I really missed home. At the same time, I could sort of feel Mustang slipping away somehow. The times I went back, I felt, what do you say, *nostalgia*. But I also noticed how hard everybody had to work."

"School was okay for me," Pasang adds. He spent eleven years at Dhaulagiri Boarding School in Jomsom. "I agree that we took care of each other, and some of us had relatives around. But that's not the same as growing up with your parents and siblings." This comment reminds me of something a mother in Tsarang once said to me, about her two children: "Dasang and his sister have never lived together," she said, "but they know each other by Facebook."

Pasang continues to talk about his Jomsom days. "The thing I struggled with was the Thakali kids. They would tell us that we smelled. That we were stupid."

"I've heard similar things from people who went to Tibetan schools in Kathmandu or India," I respond. "Calling Loba kids dirty or stupid because they came from a village. Either way, it seems there was potential for feeling ashamed of where you come from."

Mentok adds, "Yes, there was a lot of *micro-aggression*." I pause, considering this melding of concepts—of culture and language, politics and positionality—into the seamless form of a Nepali-to-English code-switching sentence.

"In boarding school, I began to understand about *power*," Pasang says. "When I was little, my uncle would visit. He would bring snacks and pocket money. I loved those visits. It made me feel special. People would ask me who my father was, but I already understood enough about *social status* to talk about my uncle instead, since he is the king's nephew. Then they would give me respect."

"Going to school, and especially coming to America, has been good in so many ways," says Chimi. "It opened our minds. But we can still be *hypocritical.*" Pasang and Mentok nod. "Even though we are living across the world, people still pay attention to caste. If we *hang out* here with someone from Chorak, people gossip." The Chorak neighborhood of Monthang is located by the riverside. Chorak families are considered less "pure" by virtue of lineage and vocation. They are butchers, blacksmiths, musicians.

"In Mustang, social life can be difficult," Pasang says. "There are problems in many communities. But Monthang is the only place where we *physically remove* people from the main environment because of who they are, who their ancestors were. It is *segregation.* I feel ashamed of this."

"Yes," Chimi agrees. "In American school, we learn about Martin Luther King. But *discrimination* is still a big problem. We learn that outside of school."

# PART III

# SUBSISTENCE AND STRATEGY

People are trapped in history, and history is trapped in them.

—JAMES BALDWIN, *NOTES OF A NATIVE SON*

FOR PEOPLE FROM MUSTANG, CYCLES OF MIGRATION AND FORMS of mobility intertwine with identity. Still, borders matter. As culturally Tibetan people and citizens of Nepal, those from Mustang have been marginalized in a country that became a multiparty democracy only in 1990 and that was, until 2008, the modern world's only Hindu kingdom. Lo claims vibrant artistic and cultural institutions known across the Tibetan-speaking world. But to high-caste Hindu majority culture in Nepal, Mustang is fashioned as what anthropologist Anna Tsing might call an "out of the way place" of backwards, beef-eating, beer-drinking Buddhists. Even so, as a "hidden Himalayan kingdom," it remains a place on display.

Before the Chinese annexation of Tibet, Loba moved their animals seasonally, north onto the Tibetan plains. The closing of the Nepal/China border in 1960 reoriented people toward lowland pastures as well as to urban Nepal and India. In the 1980s, Nepali law shifted, creating the possibility for its citizens, including those from Mustang, to receive passports and work as wage laborers abroad—beyond what could be accessed through Nepal's open border with India. Migration patterns eventually gravitated toward New York. The *khora* of migration between Nepal and New York has everything to do with borders and with Tibetan proximity.

People from Mustang are enmeshed in complex dynamics of citizenship that involve the Nepali nation-state, U.S. immigration policy, and the global circulation of Tibetanness: cultural and symbolic capital that can spring from stereotypes about this region of the world. Through the *khora* of migration, people from Mustang can become yoked to the Chinese occupation of Tibet, even as their family histories are rooted in Nepal. This is a complex linking, at once strategic and deeply felt. Still, paradoxes of local, national, and international forms of belonging—of claiming and being claimed—abound. As these paradoxes play out, sometimes the ends of kinship unravel and must be remade; other times they are cut or are rendered invisible.

The short story, "Paper and Being," explores the relationship between those from Mustang and their Tibetan neighbors, over two centuries. Eventually, it becomes a story about America. This tale, told through the social lives of documents, is about making a living and claiming kin. Through land deeds and *nagarikta*, visas and green cards, citizenship and belonging are understood to be at once delimited by such artifacts and transcendent of them.

"Bringing Home the Trade," the ethnographic chapter, shows how the *khora* of migration between Nepal and New York is at once a novel and enduring strategy and how being "Himalayan" is, and is not, the same as being Nepali, American, or a native of Mustang. Beyond identity, economic expectations run high in households. Remittances are anticipated. The specter of returning to village life prompts narratives of failure and nostalgia, by turns. It takes creativity and confidence to bring trade back to Mustang instead of migrating out of Mustang as a way of being successful. Even so, family members support one another. Personal sacrifice endures, and the circulation of capital between people and through time makes life possible. "Living" means something different in America. Money is useful, but cash cannot untangle the knotted ends of kinship that bind older and younger generations. That requires the work of people.

# PAPER AND BEING

CONSIDER TREES AS THE BEGINNING, IN THIS NEARLY TREELESS place. Consider written testimony the beginning, in this oath-bound land where what is voiced, and what remains unvoiced, often matters most. People live in spaces between the warp and weft of words. Belonging is not uniform, but it is pressed into shape, recalling the fibers that run through sheets of handmade paper, pliant yet strong. Still, identity travels. Manuscripts that document domestic arrangements and community norms are written and revised. Traces of family history are wrapped in an offering scarf. They rest inside a dented tin trunk, under a second-hand mattress, in a cramped duplex, in a densely populated neighborhood, in a city that holds a cup of stories, overflowing.

## WILL AND WITNESS

*Lokta* paper is thin in places, bulky in others. Tendrils of bark imbed into pulpy sheets of pounded fiber. Over the years, rats have nibbled the deckled edges of this testament, but the document's fine Tibetan cursive remains legible.

Dated the tenth day of the second month of the Wood Pig year (1875), this document determines a relationship of inheritance between two brothers. Their names are Tashi Wangdu and Temba Sherab. Although Tashi Wangdu is older, he has remained unmarried and childless, whereas Temba Sherab has an heir. The two brothers have agreed that Temba Sherab's eldest son will inherit their family's estate and that the property—house, fields, grazing rights—will not be divided.

The testament begins with a homage to the gods, but it also acknowledges "the precious master of the law, the lord over men." The text presents Tashi Wangdu's position on matters of life, death, and land. "At the time of death," the agreement reads, "my property shall be passed on to the eldest son of my brother." The testament further stipulates that, should Tashi Wangdu rescind and leave this estate to someone else, a fine of 500 rupees shall be paid by elder to younger brother or his son, along with a fine of 300 rupees to the local arbiter of disputes. Likewise, if the younger Temba Sherab should seize this property himself or divide this household, he shall pay the same fine. The document is signed by both brothers. The village headman and the representative of the tax office bear witness to this inheritance agreement, signing their names at the bottom.

Written when the burgeoning nation of Nepal was but a century old, after the Nepal-Tibet War of 1855–56, the agreement speaks to a form of civil religion based on household and community relations. As with the spoken pledges that seal local relations of governance and authority, this written document outlines a code of moral conduct as much as it presents a legal frame for rightful action.

The estate in question includes fertile fields, ample pasture, and a large house in Tshognam. This settlement is part of the Shöyul, a place south of Lo, where people speak Seké, a language distinct from the Tibetan variants of surrounding communities, in a region that will, in time, become Mustang District.

Fifteen years after this agreement was drafted, upon the death of Tashi Wangdu, a man named Ngawang Chöden took possession of this estate. He was the eldest living son of Temba Sherab and, given the weight of written evidence, he was his uncle Tashi Wangdu's sole heir.

INHERITANCE DISPUTE

Ngawang Chöden's household also came to include a woman that his children and his wife, Dechen Angmo, called *ani* Yeshi Dolkar. To name her as a paternal aunt was accurate. However, how she became so, and whose child she was, remained unspoken, veiled, even though elder villagers knew who her father was. Yeshi Dolkar was the illegitimate daughter of Tashi Wangdu. This elder brother had not, after all, been childless—even as he might have wished to deny it.

Ngawang Chöden was what one might call "simple," a condition that those who knew him well said he had carried since he was young. In contrast, his devoted wife attributed this slowness to a fall he took off a horse, during the Dachang archery festival the year before they were married. Ngawang Chöden and Dechen Angmo raised their three children in the home that had once belonged to his uncle, a home where his father and mother had also spent their days and taken their final breaths. Now Ngawang

Chöden and Dechen Angmo were growing old themselves. They had secured husbands for their two daughters and a wife for their son. He would carry on as head of household, anchoring lineage to place. *Ani* Yeshi Dolkar had lived with them since their children were young, but she had not been raised in this village.

Realizing that Tashi Wangdu would not take responsibility for a daughter forged in passion but out of wedlock, the unfortunate woman who was Yeshi Dolkar's mother had weaned the girl early and sent her away to be raised in the house of her brother, Lhundrup Gyaltsen. He had married into a respectable family in Chongkhor, a hamlet that lay just over the Muya Pass, in the valley that housed a sacred site known in the Hindu lowlands as Muktinath, "Place of Liberation."

Yeshi Dolkar grew to love her uncle as a father, but Lhundrup Gyaltsen's wife harbored jealousy and resentment for this additional mouth to feed. Yeshi Dolkar worked hard. She was quick with a sickle in the fields, adept at milking cows. She was beautiful. When the girl was still flat-chested, a friend of Lhundrup Gyaltsen's approached him about taking Yeshi Dolkar as a bride for his son. They agreed to postpone the consummation of this marriage until Yeshi Dolkar was seventeen, but it had been arranged.

One could say that Yeshi Dolkar married up. She forged a home with a commoner—someone of neither noble birth nor low status but whose simple, well-established household helped her escape the stigma of her illegitimate birth and the begrudging hospitality of her aunt. The household's fields were rocky, and their home was small, but Yeshi Dolkar and her husband trusted each other. They farmed together and looked after each other. She bore one son and one daughter who lived past infancy. The family was, by all accounts, happy.

But happiness is fleeting, like that moment in early summer when willow catkins blanket the ground in snowy tufts.

By the time Yeshi Dolkar had lived four decades, her husband and son had both died, and her daughter had been married off. Her husband had succumbed to a disease brought on by a *lu*, the serpent spirit who lived in the village spring. Her son had been killed in a feud that erupted down in Dzong Samba—the "new fort" that would one day become "Jomsom." Without a husband or a living son, Yeshi Dolkar could not keep the home and fields in Chongkhor. Instead, they were claimed by her husband's younger brother and his family. Unmoored and alone, Yeshi Dolkar thought about moving back into the household of her uncle Lhundrup Gyaltsen, where she had been raised. But by this time her uncle had passed on, and his wife, who had never liked Yeshi Dolkar, was even more unwelcoming. As a widow with no child to care for her and nothing tying her to Chongkhor, she decided to move back to the village where she was born—indeed into the household that had once denied her existence. Ngawang Chöden knew that Yeshi Dolkar was his cousin-sister. Coming to know the full story of her life, but not to speak of it, was a sign of maturity. And so, although they never voiced the reasons for their reunification, Ngawang Chöden and Dechen Angmo took in *ani* Yeshi Dolkar. She became a loving aunt to their children. That was, until Yeshi Dolkar could foresee that her *actual* grandson, her son's son, would have nothing unless she tried to claim the property of Tashi Wangdu, her biological father.

As the inheritance dispute unfolded, the house in which Yeshi Dolkar, Ngawang Chöden, and Dechen Angmo had lived peacefully became a place of contention. On the eighth day of the seventh month of the Wood Rat year (1924), this inheritance dispute was settled, a judgment meted out by the headman and three others of high social standing. The document read:

> Whether one cuts away the top and has the turnip, or one cuts away the turnip at the bottom and has the leaves, the named heir of Tashi Wangdu should have this house from the prayer flags on down and from the foundations up and shall retain the fields known as Rakhog and Ngarla. But two fertile fields, along with one *dzi*, two corals, and one turquoise, shall be given to the woman named Yeshi Dolkar.

The once-unified estate was split into two uneven parts. Still, it was something—a seed of recognition. Ngawang Chöden and Dechen Angmo would never in their hearts accept this outcome. Dechen Angmo would blame her husband for his slow mind, his gullibility to Yeshi Dolkar's intelligence, as the reason behind what, to them, was an unsatisfactory settlement.

The document did not state that Yeshi Dolkar was Tashi Wangdu's daughter, but it didn't need to. The paper was ratified by the King of Lo, with a fine set at 500 rupees for any of the parties to the settlement saying anything contentious about this outcome.

LAND DEED

On prodding from his wife, Ngawang Chöden traveled to Lo Monthang where he requested an audience with the king. The local ruler took pity on

his situation: the spousal ire, the lost property. The king did not fine Ngawang Chöden for questioning the settlement, but the inheritance judgment
remained in place.

Gyurme Angyal, Yeshi Dolkar's great, great grandson, knew nothing of
this history until he discovered the inheritance dispute document within
the family papers—a bundle wrapped in cloth and sealed with wax, tucked
away in the shrine room. It was now about sixty-five years since that decision had been made. Gyurme Angyal had been born in the year of the Wood
Snake (1965). He knew that his grandfather had come back to Tshognam
from another village and that he had raised his family here, building a home
at one edge of the settlement, where both Gyurme Angyal's father and he
himself had been born. But other details remained unclear, until now.

Gyurme Angyal's mother had been a Tibetan. This was true in the strict
sense of modern borders rather than—as was the case for himself—in the
diaphanous way that a fabric of belonging is woven from the strands of culture, language, and topography, onto which political boundaries are over-
lain. No. She was Tibetan in the sense that her family had fled the violent
upheavals of the 1950s. Nomads by trade, they had moved from the western
Tibetan province of Ngari and crossed into Mustang in 1960. Their family
arranged with the villagers of Tangye that they could pitch their yak hair
tents and keep animals on the high pastures. They shepherded their own
flocks as well as sheep and goats owned by locals in exchange for a share of
milk, wool, and some measures of grain. Her family lived a quiet life, close
to the bone. Daily rhythms remained familiar, even if the ground to which
they staked their future had shifted radically in a few years.

Gyurme Angyal was twenty-five when he first read the inheritance dispute document and the earlier agreement between his great, great, great
grandfather and that man's brother. By this time, Gyurme Angyal was married with an infant child, but he possessed no birth certificate. This was
common for men of his generation, born at home, but it posed a challenge
if he hoped to procure a Nepali government-issued *nagarikta*, a citizenship
card. This document meant little in the village but, ironically, it was a
requirement for leaving Mustang. For Gyurme Angyal to receive such a document he needed to prove to officials at the district offices that his connection to this corner of Mustang was authentic, that this territory was his
birthright.

Gyurme Angyal had actually gone looking for a land deed that he would
use as proof to file an application for his *nagarikta* when he found the paper
trail of this inheritance dispute. In stumbling upon the papers, Gyurme

Angyal discovered a part of his family's past that he had not previously under-stood. As he held this sheaf of papers in his hand, he was grateful for the hours of tutorials in reading Tibetan that his father had dedicated to him. Without these, he would not have been able to decipher this trace of kinship.

Gyurme Angyal wondered what sort of woman Yeshi Dolkar had been. The fragments of evidence pointed toward someone strong willed and clever, not unlike his wife.

The land deed itself was a simple affair. Stamped in red and annotated in blue and black ink, the paper affirmed the names and dimensions of fields and recorded the payment of taxes in Devanagari script. It listed Gyurme Angyal's father and grandfather. It named him as inheritor of the property so described.

## NAGARIKTA

Although the land deed privileged Gyurme Angyal, the household also belonged to his younger brother, Nyima Tsering. They were both married to Pema Dolkar. Like marrying one's cross-cousin, polyandry was not uncommon. Both strategies of alliance presented ways for families to pro-tect property and make a living in multiple ways.

When, several months later, Nyima Tsering went to Jomsom to revise his own *nagarikta*, he produced that same land deed, along with other papers showing his history of schooling. He did not speak of the wife he shared with his brother.

Nyima Tsering had an old *nagarikta*, but the problem was this: his name on that document and various other pieces of evidence were spelled differ-ently. His initial *nagarikta* listed "Nema Chiring," following his school rec-ords, which read Raju (alias Nema Chiring). This conformed to the standard Panchayat-era habit of giving *bhote* school children Hindu names, on the presumption that schoolmasters would not be able to pronounce their real names and that this act of assimilation into the Nepali mainstream would help these students later in life.

The land deed listed "Nima Chering," a close approximation in Devana-gari to how this young man's name would be written in Tibetan script. All of these versions of Nyima Tsering's name were capped off with the surname "Gurung," although Nyima Tsering and his people lived quite far from other Nepalis who had been given this cognomen. (Notably, these people called themselves "Tamu" in their own language.) Such details of identity were often lost in translation between Nepali citizens and the state that claimed them.

The spelling irregularities proved difficult to resolve. Nyima Tsering worked his way to a resolution by moving up the chain of command, first meeting the peon at the gate, then discussing the matter with the chief district officer's secretary, and finally persuading the government officer himself. Nyima Tsering spoke fluent, if accented, Nepali. Although he had only received a fifth-grade education in the village government school, those years of instruction had prepared him for a lifetime of navigating the Nepali bureaucracy. He filled out the form, listing his name, the district and ward of his birth, his residential details, the name of his father, and his manufactured birthdate. (When he asked his mother about the circumstances of his birth, she recalled his animal year without hesitation and that it had been late winter. "Snow sat heavy on the roof," she said.) These details translated into a date: February 28, 1970. It stilled the turbidities of time.

Nyima Tsering handed over a small black-and-white photo of himself, taken the previous winter when he was passing through Kathmandu on his way to trade in India. After all the paperwork was signed and stamped and the requisite fees paid, he waited. Several days later, Nyima Tsering emerged from this convoluted process with a new *nagarikta*, this time with his name spelled as it was on the land deed.

Nyima Tsering left the district office with his laminated *nagarikta*. He was vaguely aware that in other countries you simply had to be born in a place to be granted the right to belong. Here, it was an effortful process, an active verb. But even if you have a paper that grants a certain form of state recognition and, with that, certain possibilities to claim pride of place, you may still feel unwelcome—boxed in, if not foreign, even in your birthplace.

PASSPORT

Not long after Nyima Tsering had his *nagarikta* sorted out, he returned to Jomsom, this time to apply for a passport. His elder brother was the one who had really grown to love their wife, the one who felt more settled into village life. Although Gyurme Angyal and Nyima Tsering would be called "big father" and "little father," respectively, by the children Pema Dolkar bore, all the adults involved knew it was Gyurme Angyal's seed that was being passed on. Nyima Tsering felt comfortable in their joint home but also, in the most intimate ways, like an outsider.

By 1992, the year Nyima Tsering turned twenty-two, he felt he had to leave the village. Two years earlier, the *jan andolan*, or People's Movement, transformed the country from an absolute monarchy to a constitutional democracy. To some, Nepal felt newly hopeful. Political parties became legal. Ethnic minorities and *dalit* "untouchables" began to mobilize. But this also marked a time of radical transition in Nepal's economy, as it was in so many other places in the swiftly globalizing world, into an era of new forms of dependency, including on cash.

Nyima Tsering could hear Pema Dolkar's voice in his head. "Fields and animals and some earnings from trade in the winter used to be enough. But now everything is *ále*," she said, using the local term for money. "A field won't pay boarding school fees. It won't cover the costs of pencils and uniforms. It won't pay for rice or cooking oil."

Nyima Tsering listened to the list of complaints from the woman who was, nominally, his wife. He was not alone in feeling that to make any real money you needed to leave the country. Others were trying for work visas to Korea, Malaysia, Japan. Labor agencies arranged the papers. He understood these migrations to be temporary—sometimes migrants were even called "temporary people" in their host countries—but this was acceptable. He could imagine working hard and saving to buy a plot of land in Kathmandu or Pokhara. Nyima Tsering had little to lose by going abroad.

The olive-colored Nepali passport felt good in his hands, with its crisp edges, its protective plastic sleeve. There was weight to it. Compared with the photo on his *nagarikta*, he looked older in his passport. As on his *nagarikta*, the passport listed his approximate birthday. It was a date he would accept. Gyurme Angyal was listed as next of kin. There was no evidence in this document that he was married.

Like so many others—his cousin-brothers, his lowland countrymen— Nyima Tsering relied on middlemen skilled in the art of skimming a living off the top of pools of aspiration to make the rest of his papers. In the days leading up to his departure for Seoul, Nyima Tsering took to pulling out the passport and staring at the visa that had been stamped into it. This document meant he could work legally in Korea for a period of three years. The Korean lettering seemed at once beautiful and strange, like a children's drawing, with its circles and sharp angles.

Nyima Tsering had heard from others who had already migrated about the urban manual labor that awaited him in Korea, even though he did not know the specifics of what he would do. When he landed in Seoul, shell-shocked and exhausted after a thirty-hour journey—including ten hours spent either trying to sleep or playing cards with fellow Nepalis in the Hong Kong transit lounge—he felt dizzy and queasy.

The years in Korea passed in a haze of steel, scaffolding, and troubled sleep. He was young and fairly strong, but his kidneys ached in the wintertime, and his knees began to give way, buckling at inopportune moments. His occasional days off presented times to get drunk and get a bit more sleep. Sometimes he accompanied fellow Nepali men, including two cousin-brothers from Mustang, to Seoul's red-light district. Loneliness clung to them like the women they visited: cloying, desperate. The rest of the time involved survival: ten hours a day on construction sites around the manifesting modern city.

Years from now, when he would live in the one-bedroom walk-up in Brooklyn, a place he again shared with men from his village, he would wax nostalgic about those days when he helped to construct the edifices of a new Asian Tiger. "At least they have machines to do some of the hardest work. I was scared at first in Korea, but I managed. In the village, all we had were our two hands, our backs, these legs," he would say, patting his arthritic knees.

Nyima Tsering and his buddies had only a handful of Korean phrases between them. They worked with other South Asians: Indians, Bangladeshis, Tamils. They could have found much to complain about, but at least the food was spicy, and they ate rice once a day. They were young. Three years did not seem interminable. By Korean standards, the cash they saved was fairly minimal, but it would go far in Nepal.

Thirty-six months later, Nyima Tsering returned to Kathmandu. It was a dusty day in April 1996. He carried $2,000 strapped to his waist in a money belt and had sent an equivalent amount through various channels to someone from his village who had a bank account. This was more cash than his family had ever seen at one time, more than double the income raised during the best of years selling clothes in roadside stalls in Assam during the winter.

Four years after his return, Nyima Tsering tried his luck again at going abroad. This time his target destination was not Korea but a place called *Amrika*, the U.S. of A. While other Nepalis were beginning to flow into what would become a tidal wave of wage labor to the Gulf States and Malaysia, he and his people had their foot in the door to America, in disproportionate numbers to their population in Nepal. All manner of rumor about how visas could be procured surrounded the fortress that was the United States Embassy in Kathmandu.

Nyima Tsering had invested his Korean earnings wisely. He bought a *ropani* of land in Pokhara, with Gyurme Angyal's blessing, and he had begun to build a modest house. However, after realizing that he might be able to make it to America, he paused construction and instead cast his lot into a *dukhor* that would help him pay the costs of passage to New York.

To be clear, before deciding to leave for New York, he had spent four long years in Nepal: four years marked by the full-scale escalation of a civil war that had been a mere discontented murmur when Nyima Tsering first returned from Korea; four years in which he also witnessed his elder brother's decline. A checkup at a hospital in Kathmandu revealed that Gyurme Angyal was infected with the Hepatitis B virus—likely from birth. Now, many years and drinks later, his liver was failing. Nyima Tsering did not know how much longer his brother would live. His personal resolve to "try for America," as the saying went, was deepened by family obligation. He could see the trajectory: medical bills, school fees for his brother's children, affording some degree of comfort for the woman who was, by cultural assessment, his wife, but for whom he had felt, up to this point, little affection.

## VISA

Nyima Tsering and Pema Dolkar slept together in the months before Gyurme Angyal's death. Their lovemaking surprised them both, a tender gift of bodies in the midst of dark, uncertain times.

Some months prior, Gyurme Angyal and Pema Dolkar had taken a small apartment in Chabhil, close to a private hospital in Kathmandu. Their children were in boarding school. Gyurme Angyal's sickness meant that they could now see their children on the weekend.

Nyima Tsering stayed with his brother and their wife for some weeks before he left for New York. Gyurme Angyal floated in and out of consciousness. When he was able, he prayed. Pema Dolkar's limbs and heart ached from the exhaustion of caretaking. For his part, Nyima Tsering already felt the weight—leaden, invisible—that had begun to descend on his shoulders. Electrical load-shedding left them in the dark and fetid stillness of a sick household. They went up to the roof and slipped into each other after the bedpans had been emptied, after the school uniforms had been washed. Only a thin foam mattress lay between the couple and the cool concrete roof, itself unforgiving on Nyima Tsering's knees.

A few days later, in early May 2001, Nyima Tsering was called for his visa interview. The process, like the U.S. embassy's architecture, seemed designed for intimidation. There were armed marines, layers of steel, concrete, and glass. But the consular officer smiled.

"You are from Mustang!" the officer exclaimed. "I really must go there before I'm reassigned. How magical it must be to live in a walled city. Like going back to medieval times." Nyima Tsering just nodded. The woman was overstepping, but it was the end of the day. What had been a pinched and sour expression seemed to relax into kindness as soon as he mentioned Mustang, this "Himalayan kingdom," as she called it. The officer spoke of the pictures she'd seen of the region. "They say it is just like Tibet—little Tibet!" She waxed sentimental about this landscape she had not visited but that looked a bit like the place she was from—somewhere in America called *Yu-Tah*.

The small bit of English that Nyima Tsering spoke was helpful, as was evidence of his Korean work visa and the fact that he had abided by the terms of that document. He explained that he would be visiting Americans whom he had befriended while he served as their guide and translator on their trek through Mustang. This story, combined with a decent bank balance (thanks to the *dukhor*) and the land deeds from his village and from Pokhara, provided sufficient verification for the consular officer. A six-month visitor visa was stamped into his passport. He booked a ticket to New York the next day.

On the morning of June 1, 2001, as Nyima Tsering tried to sleep in his cramped economy class seat, as he watched an animated movie about a great, gentle green monster named Shrek and ate chunks of desiccated chicken, Nepal's Crown Prince Dipendra gunned down his family at the Narayanhiti Palace in Kathmandu.

When Nyima Tsering landed at JFK Airport, he did not fully understand what the immigration officer said to him, but it was something about the King and Queen of Nepal. Nyima Tsering smiled and nodded. "Yes, king is good. Maoists not so good. Just like America, I don't like communisms," he had offered, hoping to stave off the need for further conversation. This seemed to have amused his interlocutor. He was shuttled on. But when Nyima Tsering met one of his friends outside baggage claim, the man looked stunned. He explained the situation urgently in a jumble of Seké, local Tibetan, and Nepali. Intrigue and conspiracy theories surrounded the murder-suicide of Nepal's royal family. "His brother and sister-in-law's bodies are still wearing marigolds. They have not even burned," said Nyima Tsering's friend, "but that brother Gyanendra is already grabbing for power."

Nyima Tsering clutched the luggage cart for balance. The *kathag* he still wore, a gesture of good luck and safe travels given him by Pema Dolkar before departure, clung to his sweaty neck. He swallowed hard, pushing down a bilious urge. Not that he had much affection for the Nepali royal family, but the news shocked him. The country that had issued him a passport and granted him citizenship if not belonging seemed to be descending into chaos.

As with his initial months in Korea, Nyima Tsering's first months in New York blurred. Every day he would line up along the curb of a wide street in Brooklyn and wait for work. This labor was all aggregated under the category of "construction," but it involved everything from scaling scaffolding in Midtown Manhattan to hauling downed trees in the backyards of wealthy white people in Connecticut. Nyima Tsering was paid in cash. As he had done in Seoul, he kept his wealth under his mattress—or, rather, the mattress he shared with several other Mustang men who worked night shifts.

In late August, Nyima Tsering received the phone call. Pema Dolkar sobbed on the other end of the line. "Your brother has died," she sputtered, and without pause, "In six months, I will have a child." Suffering and joy in one mouthful of news. His brother released from pain. A new being brought into this strange and broken world. His child, their child, would be born around the lunar new year.

"Should I come back?" Nyima Tsering asked Pema Dolkar. He was still paying off the *dukhor* that funded his journey.

"Are you joking? We need all you can send. For the funeral, then for everything else. No. Stay. I can manage. It is the only way to pay for the children's education. Maybe someday I can come there and work too." This seemed, to both of them, like a fantastic improbability, but Pema Dolkar said it anyway.

Nyima Tsering hung up the phone and cried. Wangdu, one of the other villagers with whom he lived, was home to comfort him.

"You have to try and make papers," Wangdu said, after some time. "I know a lawyer who can help." Wangdu had been in the States for about six months longer than Nyima Tsering. He had ten family members back in Nepal depending on him. The choice to stay in America or return to Nepal did not seem like a choice at all.

"The first thing you need is a *deb jangu*," continued Wangdu, referring to a Green Book issued by the Tibetan government in exile. "Trust me. It is the best way." Nyima Tsering thought about how one green document could lead to another.

Nyima Tsering was able to imagine sending one of his brother's children—or maybe even the child who would be his—to a Tibetan school in India or Kathmandu. Many others from Mustang had done just that.

In such a school, they would get a good education, mostly for free. They would learn to read and write in Tibetan. This all seemed plausible, important even. As news of his brother's death in Nepal sank in, he began to understand that he needed to be Tibetan in order to become American.

## GREEN CARD

But what, exactly, was this becoming? Was it about language? After all, his mother had been a Tibetan. He spoke some words of the nomad Tibetan of his maternal grandparents along with Seké and local Tibetan dialect—not to mention Nepali, Hindi, some Korean, and some English. Was it a location? In many ways, and at different times in history, this land now known as Mustang had been part of western Tibetan kingdoms. Tithes had flowed between Lo and Lhasa. Still, time, politics, and distinct forms of suffering and loss remained matters to resolve.

Nyima Tsering recalled the sting that came with being a *bhote* in what was, at that time, a troubled Hindu state under the thumb of the One China policy. Boudha and Swayambhu were becoming more swollen by the year with gilded monasteries built with the largesse of foreign sponsors and exile Tibetan money. In some Nepali circles, this bred resentment. Nepali tourism depended heavily on the image of its mountainous environments and religious monuments, waiting to be discovered by trekkers and spiritual seekers. This was especially true of Mustang. Yet to celebrate the Dalai Lama's birthday publicly or to demonstrate for Tibetan independence outside the Chinese embassy in Kathmandu could still turn a young man from Mustang into a bloody mess. It was soft power against state sovereignty, and the situation seemed to be getting worse. Thinking about these issues assuaged Nyima Tsering's conscience. He hired a Nepali lawyer and began working on the papers.

Then came September 11, 2001. That day seemed to Nyima Tsering like the end of the world. After the first tower was struck, he walked with some of his friends up the hill of Greenpoint Cemetery, staring in disbelief as flames of steel and ash blanketed the Manhattan skyline. He was used to instability in Nepal. But this was violence of another order.

The Nepali lawyer assured him that because he was "not a Muslim, even if you are brown," he would still be able to proceed with his case, although it might be slowed considerably.

"Don't worry," he said. "We got the paperwork started. This is all that matters."

In the months that followed, Nyima Tsering felt lucky, such as it was, that to the few non-immigrant Americans with whom he interacted, the word "Tibetan" conjured images of a smiling Buddhist monk who had won the Nobel Peace Prize, whereas "China" bespoke human rights abuses, Communism, and conspicuous consumption. (Never mind that each item in his kitchen and most of his clothes, whether acquired in a Kathmandu kiosk or a strip mall in New Jersey, had been made in China.) Of course, this didn't stop people from calling him "Chink" or "Fuckingmexican" when the F train platform became a rush hour cauldron of workaday ire. Nepal—as a concept, as a country—meant next to nothing to most of the people he encountered daily. Of course, people knew Mt. Everest. Some had even heard about that love-crazed prince who had recently gunned down his family. But few could firmly locate Nepal on their mental map of the world.

Over the next eight years, Nyima Tsering lived and worked in an immigration *bardo*, an in-between state tethering the end of one paper-life and rebirth in another. Nyima Tsering kept his passport and *nagarikta* tucked away. "Those other papers that tie you to property in Nepal," the lawyer instructed, "just keep them safe somewhere. Who knows? Maybe the old barley field will be worth something, someday," he laughed.

Nyima Tsering thought of Pema Dolkar, thought of her with a hoe in one hand and a thermos of tea in the other, heading out to irrigate and weed such a field. She and the other village women sang as they worked, stopping between rows to catch their breaths. Paisley scarves covered their heads, caught their sweat.

Not unlike the journey from one human lifetime to the next, the immigration *bardo* took its toll on Nyima Tsering. It was a place of ghosts and specters, of attachment, delusion, and desire. He recalled the high-altitude herding that marked his childhood. He remembered his mother's stories about escaping over the mountains from Tibet into Lo and the quavering cadence of his maternal grandmother's voice. He unearthed the discrimination and police profiling to which he had been subject in Kathmandu. He remembered a Tibetan friend who had been beaten near to death by Nepali police. These recollections allowed for a slippage of experience, a grafting of self onto other. Words on paper became a path out of one version of the past into what felt like a more certain future.

As the years went by, construction labor wore on Nyima Tsering but grew steadier, more lucrative. He became skilled at masonry, and, for someone who grew up without electricity, he was a natural at wiring homes. He eventually found a good job with a contractor in Queens, a kind Punjabi. He worked alongside a few others from Mustang, several Sherpa, and a hand-ful of men from North India. He had a social security number. He paid taxes. He settled his initial visa debt and, faithfully, sent as much money as he could back to Pema Dolkar and the children in Nepal.

The children—all of them were his, now more than ever. Little Phurwa Tashi, his biological son, cemented this connection. That boy was seven, starting school. They met each other on Skype. Phurwa Tashi's elder sisters had passed their SLC exams. One had dreams of studying in America.

On the day that his green card arrived, Nyima Tsering had worked twelve hours at a kitchen renovation job in Red Hook. His hands were raw and chafed from tile grout. His knees ached, as usual. Still, he ripped open the envelope. There, in shimmering holographic majesty, was his Legal Perma-nent Residence (LPR) identification. The Statue of Liberty shone behind his own name. It listed his surname, still Gurung, and his given name, as he had fought so long ago to have it spelled. His birthday remained that same February day. Under "country of birth," it listed the People's Republic of China. Nyima Tsering sighed, a deep exhale of fulfillment tinged with res-ignation. This seemed to be the way of things.

In time, Nyima Tsering filed paperwork to bring Pema Dolkar and the children to join him in New York. Fortunately, no paternity test was required, as it would come to be in some cases in future years. How would he have unraveled the logic of fraternal polyandry on the application for family reunification visas? The death of his brother had simplified things. It stung to realize this, as he sat in his lawyer's office once again, wrangling the com-plexities of living onto the blank spaces of a government form. To all but Phurwa Tashi, he was still "little father," but he was their father nonetheless.

What of those fields back in Tshognam and the house his ancestors had built?

When Pema Dolkar and the children left Nepal for New York, the family installed a distant cousin as caretaker. Nyima Tsering retained the deeds. One field had been given over to an apple orchard, whose harvest fetched a handsome price each fall. Other fields lay fallow, including the ones for which Yeshi Dolkar had fought so hard, long ago.

# BRINGING HOME THE TRADE

Karma and Yungdung's home sits on a plot of land at the upper edge of the village, overlooking stands of poplar and willow and, in summer, a cabbage patch. This modest structure has been built into a vertical landscape. The roof is crowned with stacks of firewood and a clutch of solar panels. It sits level with an open-air stall in which horses are tethered and fed and cows can be milked. A stone wall, taller than a man, buttresses this bit of flat land and frames the entrance to the house: a kitchen, a dining room, two bedrooms, and several smaller spaces used for storage. Below this main floor sits a room where Karma distills her *arak*. This rammed earth structure held up by poplar beams has a stilt-like sensibility, though it is sturdy.

The wooden front door is glossy and bright, painted in a color that, since the earthquakes of 2015, I now see as tarpaulin blue. Below and to the left of this threshold, again held up by a bank of stone, is another flat area, the *ulza*. Sometimes used for threshing, it now serves as an entrance to the dining room of a small hotel built beside the home. "Welcome to the Full Moon Lodge," a wooden signboard announces, swaying against the whitewashed structure. The lodge has several large bedrooms, a tiled bathroom with commode and shower, and a small patio, where sun-ripened tomatoes dry atop a plastic table and geraniums sprout from old paint cans.

A stream, which feeds the village's irrigation canals, borders their property. For years, this modest flow served as Karma's kitchen sink: the place where her calloused hands, inured against cold, would scrub the filmy residue of lentils from the belly of a pressure cooker with ash from the hearth and a coarse blot of wool.

Over the years, Karma's kitchen has been remade, recasting the footprint of domesticity, if not the boundaries of home. Now she has a proper stainless-steel basin into which water flows from a tap. Where once the walls were washed nightly with mud, now a backsplash of cornflower and white tiles runs in an "L" around the room and frames a double window. Strips of rust-colored Formica mirror this shape, creating a countertop. Wooden cabinets border the tiles, making space for mugs and plates, hiding the gas cylinder that fuels a two-burner stove. An upright refrigerator marks the division between kitchen and living room. It is a place to store meat and vegetables, even though electricity pulses in and out like the cell phone signal. Karma's traditional clay stove, complete with a metal pipe chimney, rests cold and quiet in the corner.

As I sit on a stool waiting for Karma to return home from her fields on a late summer day in 2014, I consider each of these domestic transformations as another sort of harvest, this one of cash. These aesthetic changes index the *khora* of migration, marking Yungdung's years spent abroad, first in Korea and then in the U.S.

I think about how these turnings are situated within enduring cycles of seasonal migration and what is called *tshong gyug*, bringing home the trade. This concept helps to situate Mustang's place in histories of trans-Himalayan traders, including the centuries-old patterns of exchange across high Asia: lowland grains for upland salt, tea for horses, and much more. Specifically, *tshong gyug* describes a livelihood strategy that was built on navigating the cultural worlds between upland Tibetan sensibilities, the Sanskritized culture of Nepal's middle hills, and cities in north India. Without being too functionalist about it, this pattern of mobility is an effort to square the ecological constraints of Mustang's high-altitude environment with the need to support households, monasteries, and other cultural institutions. It captures the idea that to make it in Mustang economically, you must use its position as a geologic thoroughfare to your advantage. People and things travel the length of the Kali Gandaki, by foot, by mule train, by horse, by vehicle. It is not an easy passage, but it is possible—at times even lucrative.

*Tshong gyug* has also served as a synonym for the time around the lunar new year when people from Mustang return to their villages after a winter of commodity exchange. One element of this practice is known as *rikhor*, a strategy that involves buying cheap items in bulk and then selling them for a small profit elsewhere, such as the bazaar town of Beni in neighboring Myagdi District or in Pokhara, Kathmandu, and elsewhere. In addition to reselling goods at a markup, *rikhor* can involve hawking Mustang-specific products such as *dzimbu*, dried wild chive, to southern markets. The purchase and resale of winter clothing in places like Assam and Lucknow have also come to be identified with one particular commodity: sweaters. To "go for *sweater*" means to engage in this type of exchange.

Some of these cash-generating seasonal migrations are built—literally—from the bodies of animals: sheep and goats raised on the pastures of Tibet or Lo are then trafficked through the district each autumn to feed the sacrificial feasts of Dashain, Nepal's most celebrated Hindu festival. But bringing home the trade also reflects desires to consume other commodities—salt, sugar, cooking oil, gas stoves, televisions, mobile phones—and to generate symbolic and social capital as well as economic returns. As these forms of exchange continue today, many people bemoan the decline in profitability of *rikhor*, although they still appreciate the ways that this practice allows them to escape the harshest months of Mustang winter. This obligation to bring home the trade has now also come to signal the remittance flow between New York and Nepal.

Yungdung has already made tea and is working on lunch by the time Karma returns from their fields. Due to the years Yungdung spent as a line cook in Chinese restaurants in the tristate area, they now bicker over who gets to cook.

I feel sun and sweat on Karma's shoulders as we embrace. Two years have passed since my last visit. All the Facebook greetings sent through her daughter and the occasional crackling phone call are no substitute for being here. Lines have deepened across the full moon of her face, but she remains beautiful.

"Yungdung's knees have been causing him pain again," says Karma, as explanation for why she was alone in the fields. "The *drumbu* lights up like a fire sometimes," she continues, speaking of her husband's rheumatism. "Last week he couldn't even get out of bed." This information spills out in lieu of small talk. Yungdung moves across the wood floor with a creaky, bow-legged stoicism.

"This week is better," he says, speaking quickly and with some shyness as he serves up his special chow mein. "No chili," he nods toward the plates. "Her ulcer is acting up." In this dance of hospitality, Karma reaches for the plastic jar of *martsa*, knowing that I enjoy the bite of local chili powder, Sichuan pepper, and mint pulverized into a paste.

Yungdung hands us our plates before grabbing some pills, popping one into his mouth and handing one to Karma. "*Pressure*," he says. "We both have it." Hypertension threads through their lives as it does for so many others of the salt butter tea persuasion. This old married couple doles out care in blister packs of Indian-made generics stuffed into small plastic bags and hung from the window ledge, near a thermos of black tea, so as not to forget this daily ritual.

"Now all we do is remind each other about the medicines we have to take." Karma says this with a laugh, but the exchange is dusted in seriousness. Frustration smolders just below the surface in my friend. We eat in relative silence, with compliments to the chef.

Yungdung stacks the dishes in the sink and takes his leave. Karma and I sit together in the rays of sun and dust that fan from the open doorway.

"So, how are you?" I ask. "You seem upset."

"What to do?" Karma begins to unleash. "My husband went away for many years and then came back with useless legs, without making papers, without enough money to buy land and build a house in Kathmandu or Pokhara. Half of this village is in New York. People send money. But after more than twenty years of his coming and going, all we have is this old house, a little hotel with rooms that are too big to make a profit, and sons who won't get married!"

Like many men of his generation, Yungdung came of age as a householder through the seasonal rhythms of the sweater trade in India. Down in the winter, after harvest. Up in the long shadow of lunar new year, saddlebags heavy with rice, powdered milk, turmeric, a bit of cash for school fees and medicines. His first foray into wage labor abroad came in the 1980s, when he spent time in Korea. I met this family during the lull between Yungdung's cycles of exporting himself for work. When news came, in the early 2000s, that he'd made it to the United States, I was not surprised. We visited each other occasionally during the long decade he spent picking up construction jobs or chopping vegetables in Asian greasy spoons. He'd shared a third-floor walk-up in Brooklyn with a handful of men from the village. On their day off, they would drink Budweiser, watch television, and play cards. The rest of the time, life passed to the rhythm of manual labor and exhausted sleep, with little of the seasonal respites and cultural trappings of village life. Karma once called her husband's first few years in New York "volunteer time" because it had taken that long to earn back the cost of his passage to America.

Yungdung was one of the few people from Mustang I knew who had chosen to return home, of his own accord, with significant savings but without a green card. When I asked him about this decision, his answer was simple: "I missed being here. We all need cash but what good is money if you're dead?"

Yungdung had been home for a number of years now. People considered the hotel he'd built a good investment. It was the first in this village, itself located off the main trekking trail but also off the motor road and, as a result, growing more popular with trekkers who wanted to experience Mustang without gulping diesel fuel. But had Yungdung been of a younger generation, he would have certainly been chided as a failure by more people than just his wife. His lack of papers would have signaled an inability to manage the *khora* of migration, to keep the wheel spinning forward for his kin. And, ironically, what marked him and others as successful a generation ago— going to Korea, working in bottled water factories or sweatshops that produced jeans and leather jackets, and returning after a few years with money to invest locally—was now read as failure.

Both about sixty, Karma and Yungdung have three children, two sons and a daughter. Their eldest son is in his mid-thirties. With a basic formal education earned at a boarding school in India, he also knows village rituals. A filmmaker and an accomplished autodidact, he has spent time abroad but not in the hardscrabble manner of his father. Karma has given up on this son doing anything that people here would recognize as conventionally valuable. "He is so smart, but money falls through his pockets," Karma says. "I'll be happy if he can just take care of himself when we are old." She admires his ambition, but, "like a wild horse," he cannot control it. This leaves her bitter.

At the time of this visit, their middle son is in the village, but he would rather be anywhere else. He helps around the house a little and makes the occasional motorcycle run up to Muktinath to see a girlfriend his mother is aware of but chooses to ignore. By the next time I visit, in 2016, he will be a year into a three-year contract labor position in Japan with several other local young men. "I really don't know why he is there," Karma will say. "They're just earning enough to eat instant noodles. They could do that in Nepal!" This son, too, seems an unlikely prospect on which to hinge their old age. By 2019, he will be married to a young woman with ties to New York.

The couple's daughter has her mother's countenance and her father's wit. At the time of this visit, she is completing a bachelor's degree. Several years on from this, she will be employed by an educational organization in Mustang. "The girl is good around the house, unlike her brothers." Karma rests her hands in her lap. We lean in close, as if time and distance might be bridged by the narrow space between our bodies. "But she seems lonely. She doesn't want to go to New York, but maybe she should. I don't know."

"And marriage?" I ask.

"I will never force her to go as a *nama*," answers Karma. "Not like it was for me. What is the point of her studying if she is just going to have her mother's life? That is like tossing money into a river." Karma stares down at her fingers. "She comes home when she can and helps us, but it is not enough. Sometime soon we'll either have to give up our animals and fields or give up the hotel. We can't keep doing both."

In asking after others in the village, I learn that most of the elders, including Karma and Yungdung, are no longer drinking or have curbed their intake severely. This place has been shot through with so many early deaths, the result of liver failure and other forms of alcohol-as-disease. "We have to stay healthy because who will be here to take care of us?" Karma quips, adding that she still sells the distilled homebrew for which this village is famous.

"Remember that son Minduk gave birth to that winter long ago, when you were here?"

"I remember."

"Well, that boy is now building a hotel with money his father and brothers sent from New York. Down by their old house. You probably saw the bags of cement and the *rongba* workers when you came up through the village, past the walnut tree."

I recall that this young man's "big father" left for America when Minduk was pregnant. Two decades later, he remains in Brooklyn. One of his elder sons, now returned from New York with papers to facilitate the physical *khora* of migration, is managing the construction. The younger brother whose birth I witnessed will run the hotel when it is completed.

"They'll probably get all the business that we get now." Jealousy puckers the corners of Karma's mouth. She seems melancholy, anxious. "Nobody will see us up here at the edge of the village."

Karma can run this household with her eyes closed. This task has been made easier by water taps and cooking gas, a bank account. Still, she questions the logic of everything: the logic of departure, the logic of return, the logic of fields, the logic of family. Here, now, the ends of kinship unravel and re-form into a snarled bundle of expectation and anxiety.

I show Karma pictures of my recent trip to Lo: the new hotels going up in Monthang, the reconstructed monastery in Namgyal, the customs check post near the Kora La, a pass that marks Mustang's border with Tibet. Her face brightens. We speak of how things used to be, when bringing home the trade was a more circumscribed choreography of barter and belonging, not these architectures of desire that stretch across the world.

"I remember making trips up to the border for the *tshongra*, trade fairs, with my elder brother and sister when I was fifteen or sixteen," she says. "It was so open, like the palm of a hand. Not a stone in sight."

## SENSES OF CONNECTION

Many years earlier, on a frigid day in January 1998, I meet Dorje outside FAO Schwartz, the upscale toy store that once anchored the southeastern edge of Central Park in New York City.

Dorje is new to New York. He works at a restaurant in Manhattan and lives in Brooklyn. We had spoken in Nepali on the phone before our rendezvous, trying to figure out a place to meet. After some discussion, we had realized we both knew the store with "expensive toys for children" near the "big park."

Dorje and I have never met, but I know his elder brother well. His mother has sent me from Mustang with a cloth sack of *tsampa* from his natal village, along with a plastic bag filled with chili powder mixed with *yerma*, Sichuan pepper. I am meant to deliver the care package.

We meet outside the toy store. It is sleeting. We take shelter in a local deli and order coffee, his with sugar, mine with milk. At twenty-four, I am newly returned to the States after three years of living in Nepal. Dorje is a few years younger than me. He is one of the first people from Mustang to arrive in New York.

As Dorje and I chat, nestled within the steel and concrete canyons of New York, I remember Mustang's fluted cliffs, its caverns and gorges. As Dorje describes his restaurant work and his daily commute by subway, I am reminded of the sheep and goats that snake across Mustang hillsides, turning sparse grasslands into human sustenance: meat, milk, wool.

"How are you finding it, here in New York?" I ask.

"Everything is different," Dorje answers. "Air. Water. Food. Life."

"And the work?"

"I chop vegetables and wash dishes," Dorje answers. He had never cooked a meal or washed a dish in his life before coming to America. "I am doing women's work."

One of Dorje's cousin-brothers, another in this first wave of migration, has gotten a job at a sushi restaurant, he tells me. From the landlocked trans-Himalaya, where shrimp are known as *bu*, bugs, and eating fish is karmically wasteful, to a sushi restaurant. We laugh.

Dorje is living with two other Nepalis, neither from Mustang, both of whom he'd known at boarding school in Kalimpong. "We work hard—twelve, fourteen hours—but we are making good money. It helps our families."

As we talk, Dorje's presentation becomes stronger, more confident. And so, I am surprised at his reaction when I open my backpack. The smells of home spill out. I hand him the packages from his mother: chili powder in a recycled Nestle Everyday milk bag, a red cotton sack sewn closed with thread and bulging with roasted barley flour like a plump persimmon. Dorje casts down his eyes. Tears well up.

I have underestimated the power of the senses. A mother draws her son close, retying these loose ends of kinship through her act of care. They find connection, even in absence.

## LIVING

Wangdu and I meet in the garden of the Kathmandu Guest House, a tourist institution in the heart of the tourist institution that is Thamel. It is the summer of 2016, and we have not seen each other in person for several years, although we've kept up through mutual friends and the occasional Skype chat. We are both getting older. Crow's feet rim our eyes. However, to see Wangdu, with his ponytail, his warm smile, and his swagger, brings me back to a younger version of myself. "*Si-na-la*," he calls in greeting, a sweet approximation of my name in Tibetan accent. I push back the wrought iron garden chair and give him a hug. This is not a culturally appropriate greeting, but Wangdu has resided in at least five countries and has lived well over nine lives. He can handle a hug, and our affection for each other is genuine. We sit down among the jacaranda and birds of paradise, the North Face–clad trekkers and the upper-class Kathmanduites, and order fresh lemon sodas. Over the next hour, we find joy in sharing stories.

When it comes to bringing home the trade, Wangdu is the exception rather than the rule. He has worked in a chicken slaughterhouse in a mid-Atlantic state and helped to write scholarly works on Mustang. He's been a lama and a line cook. What has been, for others, a slog through many different forms of manual labor—from unmechanized agriculture in Mustang to work on construction sites or in restaurants in New York—has been for Wangdu a series of difficult yet interesting possibilities for laboring hard and living fully. He owns a house in Kathmandu and is now a permanent resident of a European country. He has a complicated family network for whom he cares. This man has succeeded in maintaining various forms of community obligation while at the same time losing neither his sense of humor nor his perspective. He grins when he speaks of impermanence.

As we sip our lemon sodas, Wangdu pulls out his wallet and removes a scrap of paper. "This wallet has been many places, but I still have your old address in here." He removes an ancient business card of mine, one that I had designed during my Fulbright year in Mustang, with the Tibetan word for "horse" written in the corner. On the back of this card, which must date from 1995, is the Oxford address where Ken and I lived in the early aughts and where Wangdu, too, had spent some time.

"That is like a ticket for time travel," I say.

"When I was working in some awful place, it was nice to look at. I remembered how you loved horses. I remembered my horse," he muses. "And then Oxford. When I see the name of that street, I remember how much you had to pay for rent!" he jokes. "When you were a poor student with no money."

Now it is my turn to laugh. "True. Our house in Vermont is much nicer than that underground apartment," I say, speaking of the one-bedroom basement flat in which we had lived. "A much better deal. Maybe we are getting smarter with age."

Wangdu stops short. "You live in *Ber-Mont*? I thought New York."

"No, we lived in New York when I was studying for my PhD, but now we live in Vermont. Next to New Hampshire, where my university is." Just as Wangdu knows that my daughter is now more woman than girl, he knows that I am a college professor, but he has not kept track of our family's precise movements.

"New Hampshire? *Granite State. Live free and die.* So many trees and not much else. I stayed there for about two years!"

"When?" I ask, astounded.

"After the chicken factory. Before my second time in Europe." I realize that this was about half a decade before I started my position at Dartmouth.

"No, really? Where in New Hampshire?"

"Lebanon."

"Lebanon is very close to my house."

"Peking Tokyo." Wangdu's response leaves me confused. Was he also saying that he'd lived in China and Japan in between the New Hampshire and Oxford? *It could have happened*, I think to myself. Wangdu sees my puzzlement and adds, "White River Junction. Hanover. Wilder. These are all close to you?"

"Yes!" I nearly jump out of my chair. "But what about Peking and Tokyo?"

"No, not Peking *and* Tokyo. *Peking Tokyo.* It is a restaurant."

I flash to a dingy red sign above a two-story brick and concrete structure on the edge of the Lebanon town green. It is a sign I have seen hundreds of times, a sign I drive past at least three days each week, located as it is beside the ballet studio where my daughter has danced since she was three. I have never gone inside the restaurant. I say as much to Wangdu, my head spinning.

"I went there for *living*. Stayed for a while and earned pretty good money. My English didn't improve much, but that is where I learned Chinese! It was much better than the chicken factory. Some others from Mustang worked there too. I helped them get jobs."

Wangdu calls this period of working in a Chinese restaurant and sushi bar in rural New Hampshire "living." This is, and is not, a euphemism. This English word punctuates a Mustang migrant sensibility about home and away, work and rest, the rhythms of weeks or months, and the sacrifices made to bring home the trade. Usually it refers to a "live-in" arrangement in which a person is put up in simple quarters provided by a restaurant or lives in a family's home as a nanny or housekeeper for most of the week.

"Living" does not discriminate on the basis of gender. I have known old married men, young unmarried women, and everyone in between to practice "living." It is understood as an opportunity to save more money than you might otherwise, if you shared an apartment in Brooklyn or Queens with family or fellow villagers, but it can be viewed as less desirable than a decent-paying job (nails, non-residential childcare, work in a grocery store, Manhattan restaurant or hotel, driving a taxi) that allows for the possibility of coming home at the end of the day and, in so doing, maintaining more of a culturally consonant and fulfilling domestic life.

In other words, "living" confers less social capital though sometimes more savings. At times, people from Mustang have used it as a strategy to pay off the debt associated with procuring visas in as few years as possible. But it can also signify a different order of hardship, depending on the sleeping quarters in question, a boss's expectations, the degree of isolation. Sometimes "living" locations are just a short train away from New York. Other times, they are hours, worlds, away on a Greyhound or Peter Pan bus. Those who are "living" pulse in and out of Mustang–New York life, particularly in the years before social media platforms began to build new virtual networks of connection and care between people, threading together the ends of kinship in new ways.

## COST-BENEFIT ANALYSIS

My initial shock in learning that Wangdu had spent significant time near the place I now call home gave way to reassurance. The fact that I had ended up at Dartmouth began to make a new sort of karmic sense. Given this, I should not have been surprised when, while sitting in the Dartmouth College Library on a frigid April day in 2018, I reread notes from a phone conversation I'd had with another friend, dated June 17, 2002. The first line reads, *Gyaltsen living ma gaayo. Lebanon, NH.* In Nepali, this young man had "gone to living" in the same place as Wangdu.

Gyaltsen is a handful of years younger than me, a generation younger than Wangdu. Whereas Wangdu comes from Baragaon, Gyaltsen hails from Lo. As I read the notes of this conversation, I realize that a third man, from yet another area of Mustang, was with Gyaltsen in New Hampshire during these early years of the *khora* of migration. These men all shared a connection to founding members of the New York–Mustang *kyidug*, a community social service organization. As it was initially conceived, all of the culturally Tibetan people of Mustang living in New York were encompassed by this group. Later it would split into factions, one representing Lo and the other focused on Baragaon.

As I keep reading these notes, I recall the trip I took to visit Gyaltsen in New Hampshire. I drove there from Ithaca, New York. When we spoke on the phone before this trip, Gyaltsen had instructed, "When you call the restaurant, ask for 'Rubin' okay, *didi*?" This was in the days before cell phones were ubiquitous. I would need to go through the boss at Peking Tokyo to reach Gyaltsen.

"Okay, but why 'Rubin'?"

"That is what the Chinese boss calls me. He thinks it is easier to say than 'Gyaltsen.'"

"That could be a Latino name," I said. "Why did a Chinese guy choose it?"

"Yes, sort of Mexican, but it is also close to 'Rabindra,' which is the name the Nepali schoolmasters gave me when I went to Jomsom. That is the name on my passport." Gyaltsen paused before continuing. "Sometimes people in New York thought I was from Mexico anyway. White Americans think anyone with dark hair and dark eyes who works in a restaurant is from there, isn't it?"

"It can be that way, Gyaltsen. It can be."

A few weeks after our phone call, Gyaltsen and I met in what I recall as a roadside café and that I now realize was probably the Lebanon Diner, a place that serves up my daughter's favorite chocolate milkshake. Our meeting focused on matters of love and family obligation, financial aspirations and debt, American and Nepali politics. Gyaltsen seemed unmoored. He had fallen hard for a woman from Colorado whom he'd met while leading a trek. The relationship seemed as impossible as it was alluring. Our meeting occurred months after September 11, 2001, and the royal massacre in Nepal in June that same year. Nepal had descended into a state of emergency as the civil war escalated. The larger world, too, seemed newly on edge.

Gyaltsen admitted to loneliness, but he said he was happy to be out of New York. Recalling that fateful day, which he calls "911," he explained, "I was in my restaurant, not far from the towers. I saw them fall. People came running into our restaurant with blood on their faces and so much shock. Nobody could understand what was happening." We spoke about one man from Mustang who worked in a restaurant at the bottom of one of the towers. He was okay but had been unable to communicate with his family, and, for hours that stretched out like days, many in the New York Mustang community feared the worst.

"Things have gotten bad in America," I said, not sure what else to offer.

"Yes, and also in Nepal. Many killings by *Maobadi*, *Khaubadi*, police, army." Maobadi are Nepali Maoists, and Khaubadi is a play on the Nepali verb "to eat" and refers to bandits who used the political upheaval of the Maoist era to steal, loot, and survive.

"But Mustang is okay?"

"Mustang is okay because the army and police are not letting any *rongba* up past Kag," he answered. I noted that an old checkpost town, a place of cultural and geographic confluence, has retained its meaning.

"With them gone, how is the agricultural work getting done?" I asked. Even as early as 2002, labor shortages prompted by out-migration meant that locals throughout Mustang began relying on seasonal lowland laborers to help plant and harvest fields.

"Some people are planting less, keeping fewer animals. . . . People in our villages are lazy. Always looking out for themselves or ways to make easy money. They don't want to do work if they can hire a *rongba* to do it."

"But you are all working hard here," I responded. Many people who have gone "living," like Gyaltsen, worked twelve-hour shifts or longer. Some slept on stockroom floors.

"That is different. *Dollar rupee different.*"

True enough. A common refrain from field notes: *What I make in a month in New York it would take me a year to earn in Nepal.* But, still, the contrasts of "living" with the ostensibly less alienated nature of work-life in Mustang reminds me that it is not so much labor itself but rather the perceived nature of work's reward, the visibility or invisibility of the worst parts of this human slog in the eyes of others, that matters more.

In rereading these notes, in considering the whole Rubin-Gyaltsen situation and contemplating the politics of racialized identity and immigration they signal, I am also reminded of another moment in Mustang-American experiences with "living." That same year, 2002, an entrepreneur from Baragaon who had already done very well for himself in New York was trying to recruit dozens of Mustang men to work agricultural fields in California—a contract labor arrangement for which each person *would have to pay* Rs. 16 *lakh*, or about US$20,000 at that time, for the privilege of the guest worker permit that this position would provide. Now, as then, I sit with the knowledge that people whose own land is being farmed by lowland Nepali laborers, if farmed at all, would consider paying for the opportunity to work legally in the toxic salad bowl and strawberry fields of central California. I consider that they would have also likely "passed" for some kind of indigenous person from Latin America in the process—albeit without necessarily understanding the risks and the cultural baggage that such misrecognition signals.

Rigid social hierarchies and the propensity to undermine the success of others—what is referred to in Nepali as *khutta tanne*, "pulling [others] down by their legs"—remain a social norm in Mustang and one that many people feel migration helps them to escape. Common, too, is a sense of jealousy linked to pride and the capacity to see only what you don't have. As one local entrepreneur and politician from Monthang described it to me, "Almost 100 percent of people are *proudy*. Only 2 percent are not *proudy*. 'Instead of thinking about your own hardships, your source of worry is seeing other people's happiness,'" he said, quoting a Nepali proverb.

As demeaning and demanding as "living" may be, some argue that it can produce the economic capital to create the conditions for new symbolic and social capital, both as an immigrant and for family back in Nepal, in ways that would never be possible without migration. Even so, some from Mustang critique this form of labor, equating it to "being an American *coolie*," a derogatory Nepali word for someone who carries loads for a living. Add to this another field note refrain: *If you are going to work that hard, you should build your own place, not another people's country.* The value of hard cash in exchange for hard labor confronts the value of home and territory as a place worthy of toil and sacrifice.

Forms of effort link time and place: farming and herding in spring, summer, and fall; the sweater trade after harvest, through winter; return and repeat. The fact that a man might be willing to chop vegetables and wash dishes in Lebanon, New Hampshire, but would not perform such work in Mustang is not a contradiction. Rational Man lives in a wider world, of gender and power, of constraint and aspiration. Exchange rates proffer an undeniable calculus of cost and benefit.

Beyond this, "living" can mitigate the pressure to participate in Mustang social and economic expectations during the early years of migration, when, as one person put it, "All I did was chop vegetables, mop the floor, eat rice, and sleep like a dead man." Yet "living" can become its own *bardo*, the liminal state between lifetimes.

## THE EX-MONK JEEP MAFIA

It is early autumn and high tourist season in Mustang, 2014. Monsoon has given way to open skies. Billowing cumulus clouds cast earthly shadows that echo shade. Dust is everywhere. The motorable road in Mustang has birthed a new kind of politics, one of fossil fuels and right-of-way, driving schedules, landslide repair, and ticket tariffs.

Since an ongoing dispute between drivers from Tshug and those from Tsele has yet to be resolved, we walk the distance between these two villages. We sling our backpacks on at the Tshug jeep depot, wrap our heads in scarves against the wind, and walk toward the Mustang Gate. At this spot, the mighty Kali Gandaki contracts from fingers to fist, its flow forced through a narrow arc punched through a sedimentary cliff of ochre rock. The river runs high. We cross a metal bridge—made for feet but passable for hooves as well as motorcycle and mountain bike tires. Three jeeps are parked on the far side of the river. One is getting a bath. Its stiff metal doors yawn open. A young man with a K-pop hairdo and sun-bleached "I ♥ Nepal" T-shirt is wiping down the back window. It seems a futile act, bespeaking pride and desperation, by turns. Another young man reclines on the hood of his vehicle, eyes closed.

"Anyone going up?" Nawang calls out. There are six of us, two foreigners and four locals. We hope that one of these jeeps will ferry us to Tsele, where we will buy tickets for the local jeep service to Ghiling. No answer. Nawang tries again, closer this time to the napping driver. "Hey, you going up?" The driver stirs but just enough to wave his hand and signal "no."

"Not our shift," the other driver answers. The rag in his hand is soaked in river water. "Besides, we can't cut you a ticket down here. You have to walk up."

Usually generous and good-natured, Nawang grumbles as we begin the vertical climb from the riverside to the village. "They're just waiting for that big tourist group behind us because they'll be able to charge them three thousand rupees for a ten-minute ride!"

We arrive, sweaty and with grit in our teeth, at the trekking lodge that doubles as the jeep counter. I buy Cokes and Orange Fanta for the group. We run our heads under the village water tap and wipe off the dust, now mud, from our faces. Nawang heads off to buy our passage to Ghiling. He returns a few minutes later clutching a thin, pink piece of paper, our collective ticket.

"They wouldn't sell us seats on the afternoon local," he says. "They made us book a private jeep. Said they only had room for three more people on the local, but really it is because they know we are with two foreigners," Nawang motions to me and my student, Hannah, who has accompanied me on this trip to Lo. "With more tourists coming just behind, they can charge what they want."

Nawang looks agitated for a moment but then breaks into a smile. "But it is okay. They tried to charge Rs. 8,000. Then I started talking to the boy behind the counter. I thought I knew his face. And, you know what? He was in the same class as my younger brother. His parents sent him to Penor Rinpoche's monastery when he was twelve. Now he is twenty-two and an ex-monk, *dralog*. So, anyway, we started talking, and he charged us five thousand only."

"Half the drivers are *dralog*," Kunzom responds. Given the work she has been doing to build a new community school in Ghami, she navigates this stretch of Mustang highway often. Kunzom does not suffer fools, and she has had to negotiate continuously to get building supplies and provisions up valley. "Fucking *dralog* mafia," she mutters. "They spend the first part of their lives earning merit, and the second part of their lives swindling people out of money!"

"But, *didi*, how else are they going to make a living?" Nawang responds. His initial agitation has melted away, and he has gotten curious about this situation—its economic and social implications. Although he's lived in New York for the better part of a decade, Nawang remains attuned to life in Mustang.

"Sure, they need to make money. And I don't really care if they leave the monastery. Half of them were sent off by their parents as soon as they could wipe their own behinds. Most don't know where they belong, but they've ended up back here. At least they got some education," she says, her voice softening.

"That ticket seller told me that most of the drivers have also tried, and failed, to go out," Nawang adds, "out" being a euphemism for migration abroad. "He has two sisters in New York and a cousin in France. More are going to France these days. He tried twice to get a visa for the U.S. and failed. Now he'll drive for others until he can afford his own jeep or save enough money to build a house in Pokhara. After all those years in India, he doesn't really feel good in the mountains."

"That's what happens when you get the abroad *virus*, and you don't get the visa injection," says Kunzom. "You feel sick wherever you are."


PRAYER FLAGS

On a steamy July afternoon in 2016, I am driving down Northern Boulevard in Queens with three young Mustang-Americans. We've got the windows down, and we're looking for lunch. Tenzin, a student at a private university in New York, suggests the Dawa Café.

"They've got great *sha paglep*," she says, speaking of a traditional Tibetan dish of fried dough stuffed with meat, "or you can get goat cheese and garlic scape frittata. Hipster brunch on one side of the menu, ethnic food on the other," Tenzin smirks. Her sense of irony runs clean like the trickle of sweat down my back. This café has entered into a growing economic niche in New York: boho Himalayan chic.

Nawang navigates. His thumbs massage directions from Google Maps. "Right! Right!" he exclaims.

"Does this look like a Kathmandu taxi?" I tease, quickly changing lanes.

Chukyi laughs. Unlike my other two passengers, we've just met each other. This young woman was born in Mustang and, after a rather remarkable educational journey, is entering her senior year at a prestigious New England liberal arts college. As we drive toward the restaurant, Chukyi speaks in a language described as *ra ma lug*, "neither goat nor sheep." She mixes Nepali and English, standard Tibetan and Logé.

"I really hate answering the question, 'Where are you from?'" she says. "Mustang is too specific. Just saying Nepal never feels right, maybe because

I've been in America for so long." Chukyi came to New York at the start of middle school. "Usually I just say I'm Tibetan, but I get a funny feeling in my stomach."

Tenzin nods. She has been in the U.S. since she was three. "I tried going to Students for a Free Tibet meeting once," she shares, "but I felt like a poser."

"Sometimes I just say I'm from the Himalaya," Chukyi continues. "Usually that satisfies people. They think of Everest or Buddhism or whatever. But it's not really a country."

"It might not be a country, but it worked to get city government to pay attention," Nawang comments, referencing a recent event sponsored by the New York City mayor's office. "Everyone felt welcome at the Himalayan Town Hall." This event was a remarkable gathering of people from Nepal, Bhutan, North India, China, and exile Tibet encountering local political leaders and social service organizations, including those that had been created by fellow immigrants. The Himalayan Town Hall made a sometimes-invisible community visible, strengthening a network of support within the "sanctuary city" of New York.

Whether walking through Diversity Plaza in Queens, exploring Brooklyn blocks with their health food stores that sell organic *tsampa* and Himalayan salt, or touring the Rubin Museum in Manhattan, Himalayan- and Tibetan-inspired institutions and experiences are evident in New York. In the fall of 2016, Mayor Bill de Blasio visited the Amdo Kitchen *momo* truck in Jackson Heights, delighting in dumplings during his Nosh the Vote campaign—an effort to marry multiculturalism and "foodie" appreciation to political agency.

According to the Mayor's Office of Immigrant Affairs, approximately 30,000 people make up Himalayan New York. This is a tiny drop in the proverbial bucket of the city's Asian immigrants. Nawang once told me that when a Queens councilmember was asked, in 2013, about how he envisioned serving his Himalayan constituents, the elected official responded by saying that he didn't realize there were people from that part of the world in Queens. This, despite the fact that the old church around the corner from his office had been transformed into a Sherpa monastery and community center.

What creates this visible invisibility? In part, it stems from Himalayan New Yorkers' positions as "flexible citizens." In her ethnography *Flexible Citizenship*, anthropologist Aihwa Ong uses this phrase to describe the "cultural logics of capitalist accumulation, travel, and displacements that induce subjects to respond fluidly and opportunistically to changing political-economic conditions."

Ong is speaking about twentieth-century East Asian cosmopolitans. For twenty-first-century Himalayan New Yorkers, the "flexibility" bears out less in terms of elite access to power within and across national boundaries and more toward a sociopolitical dexterity among people whose cultural and religious allegiances, language abilities, political leanings, and forms of documentation all point toward complex identities, at once connected to specific nation-states and existing beyond or outside them. In New York, as is sometimes the case in Nepal, the term "Himalayan" can become a vaguely depoliticized substitute for "Tibetan." In other contexts, it points toward Nepali-speaking Bhutanese refugees, Ladakhi, Thakali, Sherpa, Bhutia, Loba, and all manner of people bearing the surname Gurung. This flexibility—if we want to call it that—can include forms of belonging defined by the act of refusing citizenship or by taking on the citizenship of a stateless nation, as Carole McGranahan documents for exile Tibetans and Audra Simpson details in relation to Mohawk Indigenous communities on both sides of the U.S.-Canada border. It can be instantiated through strategic and heartfelt ritual enactments of ethnicity aimed at various audiences (asylum judges, local bureaucrats, fellow community members, national governing bodies) in the hopes of securing rights—to land and property, to language and self-determination, as Sara Shneiderman and Tina Shrestha explore. Or it can manifest by becoming "paper citizens" in multiple locales, as Kamal Sadiq describes.

"There is the café," says Nawang, pointing down a quiet, tree-lined block. "See the strollers outside. And the prayer flags."

"Prayer flags," Tenzin muses. "Maybe that is what we need instead of any sort of national flag. Everyone can agree on that."

This may be true, I think. But just as a *nagarikta* cannot account for the complexity of Himalayan identity, nor can the U.S. Census or Department of Homeland Security records. Each signals something important about how people navigate the *khora* of migration. Flexible identities are borne out of necessity and desire, pride and ambition, by turns. However, the intimate terrain of belonging can be more tentative than documents acknowledge. What does it mean, for instance, to speak multiple languages—standard Tibetan and Logé, Nepali, Hindi, English—but none of them fluently? To hold citizenship or legal residence in several countries but to struggle with what "home" means? To have who you are and where you come from at once exoticized and obscured?

And what of these strings of *lung ta*, rainbow-colored flags known as "windhorse," here on a New York City street? These woodblock-printed pieces of colored cotton are themselves symbolic of groundedness and movement, by turns. Each color represents an element: earth, air, water, fire, and space. As prayers are released from the flags into the atmosphere, they know nothing of borders and boundaries, even as they speak of luck and health, prosperity and the sanctity of Buddha's teachings. These flags ride the wind, galloping across currents of aspiration on their journey skyward, their journey home.

## CASH CROPS

Wind and dust are the pervasive elements, but we decide to walk. In mid-September 2016, Kunzom, Yangjin, and I are making our way north to Lo. We will only get as far as Kag today. We've entrusted our bags to the proprietor of Yac Donalds (yes, *Yac Donalds*), who races ahead in his pickup truck. The vehicle has a green plate, which signals its place in the hierarchy of local transportation: a private car, one connected to a business. We watch clouds of ancient river silt balloon from behind the Toyota, then disappear.

Walking slowly, an hour later we reach the junction where the Kali Gandaki meets the Panda Khola. Just beyond the walled-in poplar nursery at this confluence is Nhunzin's tea shop.

"*Hello, darling!*" Kunzom calls out as we walk through Nhunzin's courtyard and into the shop. "Do you have something for our thirst?" Kunzom had been raving about Nhunzin's apple cider for the last half hour.

"Come, sit. I'll heat it up for you," Nhunzin welcomes. This young entrepreneur from Kag is round faced and quiet. I can tell that she appreciates Kunzom's ebullience, even as it makes her blush.

The inside of this tea shop is tidy. It is made of poplar and pine, both newly hewn. Yellow and cream-colored *kathag* have been hung from the low rafters, which have themselves been dabbed with butter for good luck—willing a strong beginning to this new business venture. The smooth flesh of the poplar mirrors the silky texture of the old-style offering scarves, whereas the knotted, brassy pine reminds me of the new, synthetic *kathag*, made in China, bought in bulk.

Nhunzin sets down three espresso cups, imprinted with the Illy logo, into which she has poured a steaming brew. The cider smells faintly of cinnamon. We sip and savor.

Apples became a staple cash crop in the region decades ago, thanks to the horticultural genius and vision of Pasang Sherpa, a man who worked as a research assistant for the famous Tibetologist, David Snellgrove, before studying agronomy in France and later settling in lower Mustang. Apples have been juiced, dried, distilled, and made into pies, fritters, and pancakes for decades. The motor road now means lowered transport costs. Notwithstanding landslides, Fuji and Gala, Honeycrisp and Red Delicious can arrive at southern markets still smelling of the mountains.

"How is the business going?" Kunzom asks.

"Pretty good. I am experimenting with some new teas." I learn that this local entrepreneur has two master's degrees, both in agricultural science, one of which she earned abroad. She has spent time in Kathmandu but has decided to return home and start this enterprise. Nhunzin seems introverted but also a savvy businesswoman. "I know that I'll only make so much from this little shop, but there are markets in Kathmandu and, eventually, I want to try for *export.*" Instead of bringing home the trade, she is bringing the trade home.

Nhunzin clears away our cups and brings out her next offering, a refreshing mix of apple and sea buckthorn juice. This little red berry (*Hippophae rhamnoides*) grows wild on the hillsides of the Muktinath Valley and other sites throughout Mustang. It is packed with vitamin C and is an ingredient in Tibetan medicines. But it has more recently been turned into another cash crop, with cuttings and plantations being overseen by the women of Dzar, the village where Kunzom was born. In places like Finland, sea buckthorn is distilled into facial serums and other high-end cosmetics. Here, the juice concentrate is bottled and sold mostly to trekkers and pilgrims.

"The Dzar mothers' group says that the juice is good for two years," Nhunzin explains, "but I am not so sure. It might taste okay, but I've heard that the medical benefit for *immune system* goes away after about a year."

This little shop brims with produce, both cultivated and wild crafted. In addition to the apple products, Nhunzin bottles and markets local apricot oil as a skin and hair tonic. Barley grass is drying on the table. It will be ground into tea powder. She credits a relative living in Japan with this idea. She dries wild thyme and caraway seed that grow at the edges of fields. Himalayan chrysanthemum flowers are drying in woven baskets. These, too, will be turned into tea.

"It is difficult to *scale up,*" Nhunzin explains. "I don't want to be like those Chinese and Indian companies who just use everything from the environment to make a profit. I think people will pay more for these products."

"She doesn't grow her own apples," Kunzom says, turning to me. "But she does *value added.*" The cinnamon, the citrusy bite of sea buckthorn, are her inventions.

As we chat, taking rest from wind and sun, I think about another young female agricultural entrepreneur, who decided to export Mustang buckwheat to France. I do not know the details of how she managed this venture, but I imagine Mustang buckwheat flour in Paris natural food markets, where instead of filling the bellies of villagers with thick buckwheat paste, this grain will now please a different palate, reborn as *crêpe*.

When I ask people about the economic future of Mustang, they tend to cite the apple boom—never mind long-term questions about water supplies and climate change. Some have suggested that this district could be refashioned as an "organic zone," where local crops are sent down to feed growing cosmopolitan populations, both foreign and domestic, who are rightfully fearful of pesticides and GMOs. Of course, I can't lose sight of the paradox that, as this happens, these local products may well become less affordable for locals. Like lamb and wine in New Zealand, this has already begun happening with Mustang apples. This, too, against the tide of heavily processed, packaged, and preserved "food" coming up from the lowlands and, with even greater force, streaming over the border from China: MSG-laden instant noodles, Lhasa Beer and liquor, candies in the shape of rockets, Coca-Cola.

I also think about how cash itself has taken over—not only as a necessary form of exchange but as a proxy for what used to sustain social relations. Throughout Mustang, people bemoan the monetization of everything. With more cash flowing in, partly from remittances, "money has become the new religion," as a Loba man now living in Pokhara put it. Many have noted the decline in the trading partner relationships called *netsang* in favor of cash exchanges for goods and services, even between people who are connected by these bonds of fictive kinship, reciprocity, and social obligation. The voices of several men from Lo speak to this sensibility:

> Nowadays people are thinking only about earning cash. Economically, people are better off, but they are never satisfied. They used to be satisfied with a *lakh*. Now, if they have a *lakh*, they want a *crore*. It goes on like this. People are going abroad because they think if we can earn one *lakh* here, then in America we can earn one *crore*. They don't think about how this changes society.

> Before, we used to go to Lo, bringing rice from Pokhara, just to be paid in buckwheat paste and Tibetan salt. Now, a *lakh* is nothing. People waste that on one night of drinking and dice.

In New York, people from Mustang have turned the traditional social institution of rotating credit systems, *dukhor*, into a method for generating the capital needed to purchase homes, buy livery vehicles, start businesses. People today speak of the pressure to "do a *dukhor*, get a mortgage." I consider how this term itself links time, *du*, to a sense of the cyclical and taking turns, signified by *khor*. This economic strategy distills the cultural ideal that one can accomplish far more when acting collectively. It also keeps people at once socially and economically bound to one another through these formal mechanisms of economic returns. Still, the pressure to succeed and to measure that success against the material circumstances of others—to keep up with the Bistas and the Thakuris (Mustang's versions of the "Joneses")— remains great. *Dukhor* are often grounded in kinship. They foster the *khora* of migration by circulating cash that, in turn, facilitates the movement of people between Nepal and New York. It is a system at once transactional and intimate, obligatory and loving.

On the one hand, I am amazed at the economic virtuosity of Mustang people, the ways that they have succeeded not only in migrating but also in using their own social systems toward realizing a distinctly American notion of advancement: "making money out of money, making money out of air," as one young man from the Muktinath Valley, now a real estate agent in Queens, put it. This seems, well, entirely befitting of a New York state of mind. On the other hand, I think about the social transformations that these shifts have engendered. When speaking of this love affair with cash, a middle-aged man from Tsarang summarized, "Before, people used to have an entirely different value system, with land and property at the center. Now it is all about running after cash, trying to grab wealth from the sky, with fields and houses empty."

In the wake of that stark assessment, I am left thinking about how *léka* means work or labor, but at labor's root is *lé*, karmic action.

# PART IV

# WOMEN AND MEN

I know there is no straight road
No straight road in this world
Only a giant labyrinth
Of intersecting crossroads

—FEDERICO GARCÍA LORCA, "FLOATING BRIDGES"

KINSHIP LIVES AT THE CROSSROADS OF BIOLOGICAL AND SOCIAL
reproduction. It links women and men. In Mustang, as elsewhere, to marry

and have children are the mandates of householders. The circumstances of marriages and the social bonds created through matchmaking have at once changed and remained constant through the *khora* of migration. Movement recasts alliance and descent. Still, parents dig in their heels. Children comply, unless they rebel.

Anthropologists have long framed kinship as the foundation of belonging, identity, and rights—at once cultural and legal. Kinship travels. And yet *how* kinship travels can be complicated by new dynamics of mobility and attendant expectations about what unions are meant to accomplish, near and far. The *khora* of migration facilitates betrothal and betrayal, love and longing. In this and other ways, Mustang reflects what anthropologist Michael Herzfeld has called "the village in the world and the world in the village."

In the short story, "Night Visitors," Jigme is the eldest son in a family who needs a *nama*, a daughter-in-law. He is uncertain: of himself, of what love means, and of what marriage has to do with affection. He struggles to name an acceptable bride and, when he does, he wonders what sorts of happiness and suffering this choice will produce.

"At the Threshold of This Life," the ethnographic chapter, takes its title from a Loba wedding song, *Tse Go La*. Like marriages themselves, each of these words holds multiple meanings: of life and lifespan, of doors and thresholds, of mountain passes and the soul. This chapter begins with a wedding ceremony that occurs in New York but that reinscribes family connections in Lo. Different forms of relationship are considered: love and arranged marriages, monks who become householders, polyandrous and cross-cousin matrimony. We glimpse the nuances of sex and gender in ways that do not necessarily conform to social norms. Finally, this chapter asks how parents back in Nepal wrestle with the possibility that their children will not return, that home is being built elsewhere.

# NIGHT VISITORS

JIGME STARED DOWN AT HIS PHONE, TRYING TO CHOOSE AN appropriate emoji. He had dialed her number but, thankfully, Pema did not answer. Now it was his duty to send her a message—a message, improbably, of love.

Jigme's trekking group had already walked eight hours that day. Most of the Americans as well as the rest of the Nepali staff were now nursing blisters and drinking sweet black tea out of stainless-steel mugs beside their camp, near the edge of Rara Lake. But Jigme could not sit still. He needed to find cell phone reception. More than that, he needed a quiet place to think.

Somewhere along the trail his phone had picked up a weak signal—just enough for a text from his younger brother to crack the shell of disconnectivity he'd built around himself since leaving Kathmandu.

The text message was imperfect in tone and content but one sent, Jigme had to believe, with affection. "Bro, Agi say call to Pema." This was followed by an emoticon of the eponymous yellow smiley face with a gun to its head. This was his brother's way of slicing through excuses but also recognizing Jigme's ambivalence, his fear. Pema would be Jigme's *nama*. He needed to call her.

Jigme walked toward the lake. His feet parted the strands of grass that ringed the shore, and he began to move, tracing the contours of this azure pool of water in a clockwise direction. One of the porters told him that he'd gotten a phone signal on a ridge north of where they'd set up camp. "I went to take a shit," the porter said, "and a text came through from my cousin in Doha." Jigme reached the top of this bluff and plunked down on a lichen-coated stone. His jeans bore the markings of this sort of travel—travel he had chosen, for now, as a way of making a living. The faded denim bore spots of tea from breakfast two days ago, a splash of yellow *dal* wiped across his thigh, dust at the ankles, and a belt buckle a notch tighter after a week on the road. All the glucose biscuits in the world could not keep him from shrinking when he walked his rural country.

At least he knew his country, though, unlike so many of his age-mates who were now cooking Kung Pao chicken off the New Jersey Turnpike or doing nails in Manhattan. After a childhood that included being uprooted from Mustang at the age of seven and installed in a Tibetan boarding school in Kalimpong, he had spent half a decade in Kathmandu, languorous and despondent, listening to turgid Brahmin professors lecture in moldy halls about the workings of "commerce"—a subject that seemed a universe away from his uncles doing business deals in Assam. After passing his bachelor of business administration exams, he waited nearly a year for his official results and diploma. During this time, he was denied a U.S. visa once, and he did not have the wherewithal to try again. And so, Jigme found his way into the trekking business. His family needed the money, and he needed to *do* something.

Through boarding school connections, Jigme had convinced a Sherpa former classmate of his to hire him as a guide for a company that specialized in medical tourism: connecting foreign and Nepali doctors who provided ephemeral care to the rural poor living in some of Nepal's most remote and picturesque places. Jigme had mixed feelings about the whole enterprise—trying to conjure health in a landscape so much more complicated than pills and capsules—but he enjoyed the doctors' self-possession, their sense of purpose. It fed him a diet of certainty, like a nutrient his body lacked. And with the job came the opportunity to train as a health assistant, a course of study that felt more reliable than the vagaries of commerce.

This year, Jigme had returned to his village, Tsarang, for harvest. He loved the moments when summer turned toward autumn in Lo, when the lively click of grasshoppers transitioned to the whoop of cranes heading south, when sweet peas were plucked from vines, and buckwheat flowers peaked in their pink fluorescence. And he knew that his parents needed the help, even though his hands were unaccustomed to farming. His palms bled and calloused after a week of cutting grass, but as he worked alongside his mother, he felt lighter than he had in a long time.

As he was getting ready to leave Tsarang for this trek to Rara Lake, his mother and father sat him down.

"It is time. *Lonak*, the inauspicious year, will end soon. We need a *nama*," said his mother. She needed help in the household. Anyone who looked at the family hearth could tell this was so. Pots of milk curdled to rancid pools before they could be turned to yogurt. Carpets remained unshaken. Yesterday's dinner became tomorrow's breakfast a bit too often. As Jigme's mother settled into middle age, she had developed a brittleness, at once hard and fragile, that Jigme had not remembered as a child. It was as if the changes in her family and village had caused a bitter taste to settle on her tongue.

"With both your sisters gone as brides and now mothers themselves, and with your cousins off to America, this house needs a *nama*." She voiced what his father would not: that his marriage was not about him. He knew this to be true and yet, somehow, he had spent the better part of the last year convinced that there would be another way. Hire laborers. Plant fewer fields. Let his younger brother—the one who actually *had* a girlfriend—marry first. But that was matter out of place.

"Son, who would you choose?" his father asked. Jigme had not been prepared for this possibility. He stammered. His father took a long sip of tea, a film of butter settling across his upper lip, before he spoke again.

"I will deliver the *kathag* to whichever family you think would bring you a good-hearted bride." Jigme's father was tall, robust. Some would describe him as burly. But to Jigme, he had always seemed gentle, even small.

Jigme was being given an opportunity to direct his fate, but he could think of nothing to say, no one to name.

His father sighed. "I know you tell me not to pressure you, but this is the way of things. I had three children by the time I was your age," he said. Jigme was twenty-seven.

Jigme felt dizzy. *Who to name? Who to name?* His head spun. The Wheel of Life, of relations and probable partners, became like a blur of WeChat moments or Instagram posts of beautiful young women striking poses beside the *stupa* at Boudha or the Empire State Building. He could choose none of these people.

Without thinking he said, "Pema Yangzom."

His mother shot her husband a look. His father seemed only partially relieved. "Are you sure about this choice?" he asked. "She is from a good family. She would make a proper match. But she is well educated. She lives in Kathmandu. She may expect something else from us than we can give. Do you know her?"

Again, Jigme's head reeled. He respected Pema Yangzom, liked her even, but they had only exchanged a few words face-to-face. She was several years older than him. Unlike so many of their generation, she had leveraged education into a new set of possibilities in Nepal, refusing to decamp to New York. She worked for an NGO and helped a cousin run an apple business. But that was about all he knew about her.

"Yes," Jigme lied. "We've met in restaurants in Kathmandu, and we chat online. She is good-hearted." As Jigme continued to speak, he astonished himself. He spun this fantasy into form. He was not sure why he had chosen Pema. She was not the first person he could think of, but she didn't register as insincere or pretentious. She seemed to know who she was. Perhaps her sense of direction would make up for his listlessness.

"But can she work?" his mother asked.

Jigme's father answered. "If this is the *nama* our son would like to choose, then we will figure out the rest. Besides, if she wants to earn a salary, then we can use that money to hire help."

"A hired lowlander who doesn't speak our language is not the same thing as a good daughter-in-law," Jigme's mother refuted.

"She has a good mother," Jigme's father added. "I am sure she can work."

In the days between sweet pea and barley harvests, Jigme's father rode off to visit Pema Yangzom's father, bearing the appropriate gifts. The young woman's family did not seem to balk at the ask, but nor were they solicitous. Jigme, of course, was not present for this moment. Neither was Pema Yangzom. But the rumors began to fly soon thereafter that the engagement had been formalized and that a wedding would take place the following year.

Jigme could not sleep in the days after this formal encounter between families. He thought of Pema Yangzom, imagining her ire and sympathizing with her fear. He had left Tsarang as quietly as possible, ignoring his father's instructions to contact Pema when he reached Kathmandu. He couldn't yet face her, this woman to whom he had pledged his life.

Now, on this bluff above Rara Lake, he stared down at his phone and scrolled through screens of manufactured emotions, trying to pick one to send, along with a few simple words.

"Hey, Jigme! I didn't think anyone else would be up here." An American voice broke the silence. Jigme enjoyed this young doctor from St. Paul, Minnesota. Matt. Young, blond haired, blue eyed. Perfect teeth. He spoke of a wife and a "child on the way." *On the way from where?* Jigme wondered.

"I heard there might be cell reception up here," said Matt.

"Yes. I got three bars."

"Cool. Gonna call the missus."

"Okay, Matt. I was just sending a message to a friend. I'm leaving now." Jigme flushed with embarrassment.

"A friend, Jigme, or, you know, a *friend*?"

"What do you mean?" Jigme feigned ignorance, not wanting to talk about his situation with anyone, least of all Matt.

"A *girlfriend*. That special someone."

"No, not like that. Just friend."

"Have you ever been in love, Jigme?" This question caught him short. He did not respond at first but just stared down at his sneakers. Matt asked again. "Well, have you?"

In that moment, the earth seemed to part. Jigme fell into his memories.

Jigme remembered his cousin, older than him by two decades but a cousin nonetheless, who famously broke his leg while trying to climb into his lover's house in the dark. They called this *ulu bulu*, night crawling, a way of fighting loneliness and boredom, of exploring bodies and, on occasion, making babies. At its best, it resolved attraction and settled into a relationship. Sometimes elopements were plotted and households were imagined in the half-light of dawn, before the braying of donkeys, the long, wistful moans of cows, the liquid melody of tea being churned.

At its worst, this practice of stealthy sexuality seemed violent to Jigme. Although he would not admit it to his age-mates, he could feel the sense of terror that could surround such encounters for women, particularly if the young man who crawled into her bed was someone she did not want, even though her mother may have left the door open.

It was decades ago when his cousin broke his leg. That was a time in the village when there were fewer lights and evening distractions. No solar panels. No television. No Facebook or Viber. This was a time when used D batteries would sit on windowsills beside potted marigolds, their owners convinced that exposure to high-altitude sun would help them recharge so that they might fuel a flimsy aluminum torch for a few more hours. Maybe *ulu bulu* was easier or felt more natural then. He wondered how his people practiced *ulu bulu* in New York. It was difficult to imagine sneaking into houses past deadbolts and security cameras in the tenement apartments his friends had described.

Jigme thought back to a conversation he'd had with his friends at boarding school in Kalimpong. "*Ulu* is when it goes in. *Bulu* is when it comes out," some of the boys joked. At this pubescent moment, they were just trying to wrap their heads around the mechanics of it all.

Love. How to disentangle that word from the sensation of sticky adolescence in a narrow cot, of discovering desire between one's palms?

Love. What to do with the memories of Tsewang?

As Jigme sat on that bluff staring down at Rara's waters, he felt as if Tsewang were sitting beside him, a warm hand resting on his thigh. He recalled that moment during final examinations in class ten when they found each other. Tentative, behind the row of *mani* stones toward the edge of town. Just two boys, playing around. Sinful in so many ways. But beautiful. He had never before been blanketed by such human warmth, such trust. The closeness was much more than a mirroring, a proximity to self. It had been generous.

Jigme knew that Matt was waiting for an answer, but he took his time, scratched the ground with his foot. He thought at that moment about the helicopter that had plunged into this lake in 2001, burying in these cool waters some of the last remaining members of the Nepali royal family after many others had been gunned down in the "unimaginable incident" in which Crown Prince Dipendra went on a shooting spree, killing his parents and seven other relatives before shooting himself. This gun-crazed, narcotic-fueled rampage was also about love and marriage, or so the story went. Jigme felt like he was being cornered into his future.

And then there were the tales he'd heard from classmates who came from the Muktinath Valley, where bride stealing had been a sanctioned form of betrothal. Stories about mothers and aunties being captured and literally dragged away, crying, on horseback. At that moment, he felt like he could again understand something of their pain and resignation—the ache that was sometimes the price of belonging.

*Jigme* meant "fearless." His name was an echo of some other person, not the person he felt he was.

None of this was entirely new to him, though. He had been engaged once before. The breakup had happened about two years ago now, but it still stung. His parents had chosen Bhuti. There had been no asking him for suggestions then. They made the arrangements swiftly, and Bhuti moved in with the family that winter, with a formal wedding ceremony planned for the following summer.

Bhuti was nice enough, pretty, a year or two younger than Jigme. But she seemed more mature and had more experience in matters of the heart. She commanded attention from his father in a way that made his mother uncomfortable. But never mind, she had been chosen. During the frigid winter months in Kathmandu, when concrete hurt everyone's bones and coughs settled in like dense valley fog, they slept together. There had been some privacy, tucked into a double bed in a room otherwise used for storage. But the privacy only extended as far as the physical room. Jigme's mother had made it clear that she not only wanted a daughter-in-law but that she also expected a child.

Jigme could have chalked up his inability to consummate their engagement to nerves. Bhuti was not a virgin. She had left a boyfriend for this engagement. He knew she cared about this other person. She did not hide her affection, nor did she mask her own acquiescence at the decision to respect her parents' wishes and accept the offer of engagement from Jigme's family. Bhuti was a dutiful daughter. *Mikha*, gossip, was a feral horse—wild, strong-willed, unpredictable. She had agreed to the marriage and set aside her lover.

In these intimate moments, Bhuti had confided in Jigme about the medicines she'd taken to avoid getting pregnant, the ones she hid from her mother, and about what sex is supposed to feel like. She had been gentle with him at first. But Bhuti's body was like a giant boulder cast onto a trail from a landslide—an unmovable obstacle, something he would need to figure out how to work around.

Nights passed. The chill of Kathmandu winter began to lift. Losar came and went. Jigme groped tentatively, trying to find some way to give her pleasure. Bhuti responded, but her fingers did nothing to rouse him. One night, she rolled over, exasperated. "If you can't figure out how to be a husband, I might just go back to Jangchup," she said, speaking of her lover. He didn't take the threat seriously. After all, it would bring shame on both their families. But, in the end, after what must have felt to Bhuti like months of interminable nights, that is exactly what she did. Never mind the shame. That too would pass, with time.

"Jigme? Yoo-hoo? Where did you go? You seem to be daydreaming." Matt brought him back to the present.

"Oh, sorry," he said. "No. No, I have never been in love." He was still thinking about that word. About Tsewang and Bhuti and Pema. Despite the years of English medium schooling, he had no language to describe what he felt.

He looked down at his phone and settled on a digital sticker. It was a boy on his knees, sending little heart balloons to a girl in a cloud of sparkles. Would this do? He tapped the emoticon and pressed send.

# AT THE THRESHOLD OF THIS LIFE

The wedding announcement came by mail, a thick gold lamé envelope lined in red. The card inside felicitated in English and Tibetan, with phrases as ornate as the lettering. Nyima and Dorje were getting married. I was one of nearly seven hundred guests invited to this event in March 2015.

The wedding party was to occur at a Manhattan venue known as the Armenian Hall. Unlike the Burmese Hall in Queens, which the community sometimes rents for other events—itself not much more than a finished basement with folding tables and a built-in stage—the Armenian Hall is grand. Chandeliers, a dramatic staircase, fancy bathrooms. I had last been there for a Losar party some years before. I recalled the Nigerian security guards and the massive oil paintings depicting the Armenian diaspora on the walls. For that event, the stage was given over to a giant banner with Losar greetings in Nepali and Tibetan, against the backdrop of a slightly blurry reproduction of Lo Monthang. For a wedding party, the stage would turn into a shrine, complete with a portrait of the Dalai Lama and Sakya Gomang Rinpoche and a low divan on which Nyima and Dorje would sit for hours, alongside representatives of their families: a place to be praised, blessed, and buried in *kathag* before the formalities would give way to disco.

This *changsa*, an "exchange of beer" ceremony that marks a marriage, has been a long time coming. Nyima and Dorje were betrothed several years ago and already have a two-year-old daughter. However, a series of family deaths postponed this celebration. It is improper to celebrate the formal linking of households in a year also marked by death.

On the afternoon of the wedding, I dress in a *chuba* and the Mustang style of woven apron and head out from a friend's place in the East Village. Although the wedding party won't begin until this evening, I am expected at Dorje's sister's place in Queens, the home into which Nyima will now move as a *nama*. There, the more private rituals, at once religious and sartorial, are taking place. At Grand Central, I discover that the 7 train is out of commission, so I walk back outside in this ethnic outfit, feeling self-conscious, to find a taxi.

The taxi driver is a Sherpa. "Namaste," he says, without missing a beat. "Where are you going?" I explain, in Nepali, that I'm going to my *mithini's* daughter's wedding. A *mithini*, or *rokmo* in Logé, is a fictive sister. We are halfway through the Midtown Tunnel when he turns off the meter. "Just pay me what you think," he says. I learn that he had been a trekking guide before coming to New York. He's been to Mustang many times.

The taxi driver drops me off on a side street in front of a brick duplex not far from Queens Boulevard. I have been here once before, when Dorje's brother Lobsang was visiting from Nepal. Lobsang is an old friend, and that was a quiet moment of conversation and reconnection. Now, the house is raucous. A landslide of shoes spills out over the threshold.

Women rush around, trying to find the right pins for their *chuba* and straightening the men's fur-lined hats. Kunzom's elder sister is at the helm in the kitchen. She smiles and greets me, her hands dishing out *dresil*, festive rice pudding, as fast as she can. The two bathrooms in this single-family home have been marked with "Ladies" and "Gents" signs. One of Nyima's two younger sisters hardly acknowledges me as we pass in the hallway. I wonder what she thinks of this "auntie" with a connection to her homeland, itself a place where she has spent very little time.

The living room is lined in wood paneling. This, combined with the eight-foot ceilings, makes me feel as if we are on a ship together, sailing through seas at once familiar and new. It is an apt metaphor for the immigrant experience.

While the women cluster in the kitchen, most of the men are seated around the living room. The lack of alcohol is noticeable. Everyone is clear eyed—sober and felicitous, for now. I wonder how this moment might have played out differently had the wedding been in Mustang. I say hello to those I know, including two members of the Lo royal family who have come from Nepal for this wedding. This arranged partnership links two branches of Mustang nobility. The presence of these elite men lends the occasion a majestic air.

Such knottings bespeak the ends of kinship. Old ropes, newly tied, linking biology to social alliance in ways that keep status intact. The extended family into which Nyima is marrying owns this four-bedroom house. They also own a mansion nestled up against the hills beyond Swayambhu in Kathmandu, and they are the inheritors of one of the palaces in Lo. In other words, they have done well when it comes to real estate.

Throughout the whirl of activity at the groom's house, little Sangmo, Nyima and Dorje's toddler, spins around in her fuchsia *chuba* like a sprite. She is passed between various aunts and cousins, sometimes crying for her mother. Aside from the Newari videographer and his crew, I am the only person not from Mustang in the place. I search for Nyima and her mother, Dolma. The bride is sequestered in a bedroom, her mother in attendance. Nyima looks radiant. Dolma offers me a warm embrace.

"Sangmo will have a memory of her mother's wedding," says Nyima. Her tone seems joyful yet tinged with embarrassment. Although the bride was raised in a household governed by strict Loba norms, and although all are proud of this union, I wonder if, in her years of working for white American families as babysitter, some other normative sensibility has lodged— one that recalls an old playground rhyme: *First comes love, then comes marriage, then comes the baby in the baby carriage.*

One of the groom's sisters helps Nyima dress. "How do you do this?" Nyima asks, laughing and fumbling with Tibetan boots, a form of cultural regalia that she has never worn.

"You look so young," says Nyima's sister-in-law. "What is your animal year?"

"Snake. In Western years, I am twenty-five. But in our years, I'm twenty-seven," Nyima responds. "My mother was twenty-five when she got married too."

"I was twenty-five when I married Ken," I offer.

"Really?" Nyima looks surprised. "Is that unusual for foreigners?" she says. We both laugh when she calls me *chikya*, foreigner, because I am not— and yet still sort of am—a foreigner here.

"Yes. Most of my close friends didn't get married until they were at least thirty," I answer.

"But you didn't have Aida until later, right?" asks Nyima.

"I was almost thirty-one," I answer, as I help Nyima fasten necklaces of turquoise, coral, and pearl.

"You must have taken medicine," says Nyima, speaking of birth control. I nod, and, although there is no reason for it, we each blush.

"And you only have one child?" the sister-in-law interjects.

"*Chika rang chik*, one and only one," I say, holding up a finger.

"*Nyingjé*," she says. "How lonely for her. For us, one is not enough. But now, more than three is too many."

I walk back upstairs and am greeted by a princess of Lo. Raised in Kathmandu, she is now attending university in the American South. The young woman's raven hair falls in ringlets down her back. Her lips are glossy and full. She clutches a Michael Kors bag. Her hot pink *chuba* is made of raw silk, offset by a cobalt blouse. She seems to float above the room: expected to be there but also somewhat out of place. She chats in English-Nepali with a cousin. They speak about college courses and majors, Nepali phrases peppered with "like" and "um" and "totally." Meanwhile, in the next room, the ritual singing has begun. Dorje and Nyima are dressed and seated in their places of honor. Their demeanor is composed.

Another member of the royal family comes up to me. "I think it has been twenty years since I've seen you, but I still remember. You were riding a black horse."

I feel that day in my bones. A thunderstorm was approaching. I was riding Lobsang's gelding alone. The horse was struggling against me, feeling that strangeness of an unfamiliar rider, perhaps even of gender. This young man and I had ridden together for a while. Earlier, during my first extended stay in Mustang, he flirted with me in his antique shop in Monthang and spoke of his desire to leave Nepal. Now he owns a gas station in Jersey City.

Gyaltsen, the young man I visited in New Hampshire in 2002, joins our conversation. Like all of us, he looks older, handsome in a slate fedora, carrying his three-year-old son. "Do you still ride horses?" he asks.

"When I can," I answer. The love I carry for horses is also an ache.

"She used to spend so much time with my father," Gyaltsen says to the other man. Gyaltsen's father is an expert horseman from whom I learned a lot when I was younger.

I mill around and find Yeshi Sangmo, the niece of an *amchi* with whom I've worked closely and someone trained as a Tibetan doctor herself. We hug, happy to see each other. She nannies for a living. Meanwhile, her two-year-old son lives with her mother-in-law in Kathmandu. I ask if she misses practicing medicine. Her answer is by turns despondent and practical. "I do miss it. But I had the chance to learn scriptures," she says, "to become literate in Tibetan, to benefit people. I still see patients sometimes, when they come to me."

By the time rituals are completed, it is well past the 7:30 p.m. start time for the party listed on the invitation, and we are still in Queens. I ask

Dorje's brother how we'll all get to the Armenian Hall on the Lower East Side. "Chartered bus," he answers. Soon thereafter, we are funneling out of the house into a tourist coach, complete with intercom and funny driver, decorated in *kathag* and auspicious symbols. As we leave the house, *chang* is offered, and women sing wedding songs. I joke with Dolma that instead of the bride's family arriving in a long train of horses for this wedding, we are all taking one giant metal animal to the site of celebration. Elder men in the groom's party end up in another car because the bus is overflowing. There are people in the aisles and on laps.

I sit in the very back of the bus with a young woman named Kunga. I know her father, a member of the royal family of Lo, but I have not met her before this evening. She admits that this is the first Loba wedding she has ever attended. We speak most comfortably in English.

"My parents have struggled so hard to give me and my siblings incredible opportunities for education. But it also means that I don't really know my culture—or I am just starting to learn it now. I went to boarding school in India from the time I was very young. I have never been to Mustang. It is strange to be learning about it at this point in my life, and here." Kunga came to the U.S. for college where she studied biomedical sciences. She is now working in data analysis and considering a PhD in neuroscience.

"My parents really want me to go on in medicine, so I took a lot of pre-med classes, but then I had to take an anatomy class, and it was just too hard cutting into a body. I knew that was not for me." Her admission evokes many thoughts: of the sanctity of a body's wholeness in some religious traditions, of the ritual dismemberment and feeding of bodies to vultures in the Tibetan practice of sky burial, of what "medicine" means across culture.

"I'm interested in neuro and psychiatry," she adds, "but this type of science is harder for my parents to understand. You know, the mental things." It is clear that she wants their approval for her life choices.

"There are many different ways to practice medicine," I say. "Focusing on mental health might be harder for your parents to accept, but it could be really helpful to the community." I think about the child of another friend who spiraled into serious mental illness, and the pain and stigma his behavior engendered, the difficulty in communicating to immigrant health services local categories of disease or the relationship between body and mind in Tibetan Buddhism.

"Are your parents pressuring you to marry?" I ask. We are, after all, in the middle of an arranged marriage ceremony of a young woman not unlike Kunga, if Kunga had not left Nepal for education.

"Not at this point. My mother does remind me that it is marrying time, that I am the right age. But since I have an elder sister, there is less pressure on me. She is working in London, where she also went to school. She really has no interest in getting married. So, I don't have to worry. For now."

We pull up in front of the Armenian Hall and file out into the night. Formal blessings are overseen by the abbot of Namgyal monastery. He has been here seeing donors and giving teachings, but the timing of this wedding is not a coincidence—just as the moment of the betrothal announcement had been coordinated between lamas in Nepal and the family in New York. Nyima and Dorje are blessed with butter and consecrated water. Tibetan trumpets sound into the Manhattan night. Marriage song spirals skyward.

We walk in and down the staircase, past images of another people's diaspora, into the main hall. Moving slowly in this sea of bodies, I notice patterns of resemblance: the long, thin face of one branch of the royal family recast across dozens of young men in baggy jeans; the freckles and bright eyes of a Baragaon lineage reflected in a group of female cousins, each made up with fake eyelashes and perfect eyeliner; the oval face and prominent Buddha ears of yet another family tree scattered through the crowd; the high cheekbones, large head, and chiseled jaws of Lo nobility leading the procession. DNA is more than a double helix. It is a rope of relatedness. Here, too, are the ends of kinship.

The evening winds on. It is a long road of speeches, fried snacks, and cultural performance. At one point, Chimi, another well-educated cousin of Nyima's, is compelled to speak. She is unmarried and in her mid-thirties, noticeably so. In the voice of a strong tenor, one that several generations back would have called loudly from rooftops, she says, "I would like to say something about this wonderful couple. But first I have to ask some questions. How many of you are in a love marriage?" A murmur waves through the crowd, and a few tentative hands go up. She repeats the question, in English and Nepali, and a few more hands raise. Then she asks, "How many of you are in *arranged marriage*?" Same thing. Only a few hands go up.

"Now I want you to think about what it would be like to have not known your wife or husband before you got engaged. I could not imagine that. But that is what it was like for this couple, before their families made arrangements."

What Chimi says is true. There is a significant age difference between the bride and groom. Dorje left Nepal for New York in 1997; Nyima didn't arrive until 2011. The woman on the stage continues, "And now look at them.

They are such a beautiful couple and family. They are honoring our culture by the choices they are making."

I'm fascinated by this oratory. It affirms the importance of romantic love and the possibility of finding such love through an arranged marriage. Even so, her words valorize a social institution that she herself cannot imagine being part of, even as it is a practice she admires. Just as she sees trust and "heart understanding" in this couple, she also recognizes the power to reproduce certain forms of culture through marriage. Still, like an open secret, this speech points toward the shifting terrain of matrimony, not only in America but also in Nepal, where love that ends in a mutual agreement to form a household—*phorong-morong* in local parlance and what might be called a "common law" marriage elsewhere—is becoming the norm, particularly for people from less elite families.

As I listen to Chimi praise Nyima and Dorje, I hear a chorus of opinions from people I have interviewed about marriage. "Falling in love is a waste of time," said one twenty-something educator. "Love affairs are something we do in hostels or during college life, but these don't lead to marriage." A middle-aged man from Baragaon opined, "Arranged marriage is practical. It helps society. If a girl marries a Bahun or Chetri or even a Sherpa for love, then she is lost to their world. *Love* or *arrange*, everyone will have more respect if they are both from Mustang. If someone marries a foreigner, they don't care for their people." This is countered by a young woman from Baragaon: "Sometimes I think that I will marry someone from my own place, but when I see the ways village people can behave, I think that being married to a *rongba* would be fine. A foreigner, maybe even better." An unmarried and successful woman entrepreneur shares, "I saw so much conflict in marriage. I decided I wanted to stay single and take care of my parents. It was my decision. Many people came asking for my hand, but I didn't want to get married." An ex-monk in his sixties says, "I was first a monk. Then my father called me back to the household, and I got married with my brother. But then I eloped with another woman. Now I don't have a needle to my name from my old house, but my heart-mind is peaceful."

Although Chimi doesn't speak of this, I consider how Nyima and Dorje's marriage also reflects an *ani-ashang*, or cross-cousin, logic of union. They are distant cousins. Patrilineal bone, *rü*, does not cross, but they are still in relation. In Central Tibet, such an arrangement could be considered incestuous, but it is a preferred approach to marriage across much of the Himalaya. As with fraternal polyandry, it can help to accrue, secure, and preserve power and property. But what this practice means for people from

Mustang is changing too. I recall a conversation from 2012, with an older woman from Ghiling: "We used to think *ani-ashang* was best, but now we wonder. We used to know who everyone was, but with so many people leaving, it is more difficult to know lineage for certain. My son has told me about *gene*. I am curious about that."

Chimi's speech also reminds me that while marriage might include intimacy, it is not just an intimate act but rather one that emerges through collective ritual action, toward the maintenance of a particular form of being human together. Ever the anthropologist, I sketch kinship diagrams in my head as she speaks. It helps me visualize just how strategic this marriage is, how it fits within the other choices the bride's and groom's families have made. Dorje's elder brother, Lobsang, married a woman from a high-status Baragaon family and, in so doing, repeated a pattern of alliance that could be Shakespearean, were it not rooted in Mustang.

It is 12:30 a.m. by the time dinner is served.

We make the transition from feast and culture show to formal ceremony. Lobsang gets up to give a speech. This man usually presents with a lot of Mustang machismo. But now he shakes as he speaks, nervous and moved. "Even here in this city far away from Mustang, we are still keeping our culture alive," he begins. "We can see it in the ways that the young people are dancing and in how our language is being used here, the stories we are telling and the songs we are singing," he says. "Did you know that there are about four thousand languages in the world, but one is dying every day? We cannot let that happen to our own language." I think about Kunga and how on the bus ride earlier she admitted that she's been exposed to more Logé in New York than ever before in her life.

Then, as a way of further illustrating that a wedding is never just about the couple in question, and that a wedding occurring in New York is never *only* occurring in New York, Lobsang adds a note of gratitude for those who have donated funds in honor of this auspicious event to his village. "I am proud that from New York there has come 25 *lakh* to support the mothers' group. This makes me proud." This is a significant amount of money—more than US$25,000. And this is just from one event.

Among the many things I notice this evening, one is the sense that people are doing well here. Despite the fourteen-hour days at nail salons and visa debt, a sense of possibility pervades. I see the sister of a friend, a woman who has had a very difficult life. It has been years since we've visited. She looks healthy—what people from Mustang would call *gyakpa*, "fat," but as a compliment. She talks about her babysitting job and how much she enjoys being here. "The work is difficult, but it is nothing like what we did in Lo, the agricultural labor, dealing with village struggles." Indeed, she looks about a decade younger than the last time I saw her and, even with the weight, lighter. Migration can be liberating, particularly for those on the bottom of a socioeconomic hierarchy. This is part of what makes the *khora* of migration also a quintessentially American story, bootstraps and all.

During the formal *kathag*-giving moment, guests file onto the stage to place scarves at the foot of the Dalai Lama's image and then to Dorje, Nyima, and Dorje's sister who is the designated attendant. It is with her that guests also deposit envelopes of cash—the proverbial nest egg. This ritual takes an hour and a half. A quick calculation indicates that more than three thousand *kathag* have been offered. By the end of the evening, they will be gathered up in garbage bags, plastic stuffed like a Michelin Man of merit.

As the other guests and I pass time together, I feel myself firmly rooted in the social slot of householder. No longer an apparition—a young, unmarried female spending time with older men who know about medicine and horses—I am now a full person, by virtue of my own marriage and motherhood. I am part of the space that Nyima and Dorje are moving into: of intimacy and obligation, of providence and care.

And yet I am also a specter. While welcomed and integrated into this scene, I remain a foreigner-not-foreigner who has a connection to the place that binds us all but that few of the younger generations know directly. I share these feelings with Dolma at some point this evening. "You *are* Mustang, so having you here is also like being in Mustang," she answers. This is a sweet thing for her to say, even as it is untrue.

As I stand in line to offer my *kathag* and envelope to the new couple, I learn that I am standing behind Yangjin's sister. We have only ever seen each other in pictures, but recognition comes like a camera flash. I tell her that I had such a wonderful time several months earlier at her family homes in Tshoshar and Marang. A look of wonder and confusion passes over her, as if she has seen a ghost.

The Loba emcee calls a "first dance." However, unlike this practice at American weddings, in which the spotlight is on the bride and groom, here it is a moment of what anthropologist Victor Turner would call *communitas*: a state where all members of a community share a common experience that unite them in particular ways, often as an inversion of social norms. Members of the bride's and groom's families head to the floor. Dolma pulls me up, and we move together. It reminds me of the night, so many years ago, when in the half-light of her home in Lo, in the presence of some in this room, we became a certain kind of sister to each other.

Some minutes later, Dolma and Nyima fall into a beautiful, bittersweet embrace. They cry in acknowledgment that this reconfiguration of households is now complete: a mother has, in a sense, lost a daughter. Formality dissolves into the simple act of loving and being loved, of care and longing. They hold each other beyond the specificities of time and place, even as they are enfolded, like their brocade gowns, within the fabric of culture.

As evening pushes toward morning, a kind of joy unfolds that seems distinct from the similar ritual moment in Mustang. All the elements of a traditional wedding ceremony have taken place. But a sense of sweet abandon pervades—emotion that seems less possible in Nepal. I watch a middle-aged husband and wife dance together under the disco ball. They move not within the regimented confines of village melody but as their bodies feel like it, to the rhythm of contemporary Nepali, Tibetan, and American pop tunes. One kind of mobility—the capacity to migrate—has allowed another kind of movement—a sense of playfulness and self-expression—to emerge.

### THE BEST HUSBANDS

The first time I saw Wangyal in New York, it was difficult to recognize him. As he walked up behind me, his deep voice was familiar. "Eh, are you lost? This isn't Mustang." I turned around, under the subway tracks on Roosevelt Avenue, and encountered a householder: jeans, sweatshirt, a thick head of hair. But when this ex-monk smiled, his long face parted by dimples, I saw my teacher and my friend. "Come, let's have tea," he said.

A scholar of Mustang history and a monk in the Sakya tradition, Wangyal had been an attendant to the late Chopgye Trichen Rinpoche, himself connected to the royal family of Lo. But Wangyal was also the middle son of a very poor family. Political change and economic possibility felt out of reach for him in Nepal. When he got the opportunity to come to the U.S., he took it. That was nearly twenty years ago. As we sat that day in 2002, drinking milk tea in a Jackson Heights restaurant, I asked Wangyal if he still considered himself a monk. I cringe, in retrospect, at the awkwardness of my question, but I recall Wangyal's graceful answer. "The day starts and ends for me the same. I sit, I read *peja*, I make offerings. What does it matter the clothes I wear?"

When I met Khandro, the woman who would become Wangyal's wife, I could tell that Wangyal was embarrassed. They were living together, along with Khandro's two cousins, in a flat in Elmhurst. They did not speak of each other as married, but she moved around him with a cherished sense of comportment that gave them away.

The next time I visited Wangyal and Khandro, she was visibly pregnant. "*Dralog* make the best husbands," Khandro said, as she lumbered around, preparing for her shift at a nail salon. "They are educated and kind, and they even know how to wash their own clothes!" We both laughed. "Some say that if a woman gets together with a *dralog*, then his sin transfers to her, but I don't believe it."

When I spent time with Wangyal in 2017, he held his adolescent son in his arms with affection. The boy was in the seventh grade, roughly the same age as my daughter, with a quirky smile and his father's dimples. He spoke mostly in English. Wangyal's mother-in-law sat on the couch across from us, spinning an upright prayer wheel. She was the better part of blind, but her hearing was good. "Who is that *chikya* who can speak?" she asked of the room and by which she meant speak *her* language.

"This is Rinzin Wangmo," Wangyal answered, using my Tibetan name. "She was once my student." As we talked, Wangyal shared news about the New York Mustang Association's aspirations to buy real estate for a community center in Queens, his involvement in running language and culture classes on his day off, the fact that he was sometimes called to do religious rituals for people. "Even *dralog* can be useful here," he said.

Wangyal scrolled through a social media forum on Mustang's religion and history that he helps to moderate. He held out his phone so that I could scan my QC code and join this virtual community.

"When we met, I was the scholar and you were the student," he mused. "Now you have a PhD, and I fill shelves with organic groceries all day long. What happened?"

"You are still a scholar," I responded. "And I am still learning."

## SKETCHES OF MATRIMONY AND ITS OTHERS

The young man exudes the entitlement of someone whose mother brought him tea in bed for his entire childhood. He has never been to Mustang, but he claims his culturally Tibetan heritage when it is convenient, like when he learns that the owner of the coffee shop where he is training as a barista "*loves* the Dalai Lama." I ask him if he, now in his early twenties, has any interest in marriage. He laughs. "Girlfriends are okay. But I just want to live my own life."

The old *ngakpa* is a master of astrological calculations. Today, though, he calculates the dwindling population of his village, including members of this place now in New York, against the population of unmarried men. "We have ninety-four people left. It used to be ninety-six, but two died last year, and there were no births. Among these, there are twenty unmarried men. If they all married and had two children, we would have a future."

Like the archery festival and midsummer harvest rituals, the annual soccer tournaments have become a venue for flirting, trysts. In villages with cellular signal, WeChat and Facebook help to facilitate liaisons. But people worry about the proliferation of *nyelu*, illegitimate children. A friend tells me, "Parents of daughters are now asking for *security deposit* of 1 *lakh* if a young man starts dating a daughter." People learned this phrase from negotiating with landlords in New York and put it to use in Mustang. She explains that this arrangement provides financial security against raising a child alone. "It is protection. Like *condom*, but different."

People say that the owner of a particular hotel is "like a woman." He is married and has children, but he carries himself with effeminate flair. He is beautiful, keeps his hair long. I find myself wondering what he would look like in drag and what coming out in Mustang might mean.

I spend the afternoon in a Baragaon village making *momo* with a person who is dressed as a woman but whose long neck is marked by an Adam's apple. This person lives, through the sociality of language, in feminine pronouns. She was born in this village and remains unmarried. Like other unmarried women, she sometimes does the work of men: trading, traveling. But she also does the work of women: caring for elders, tending to domestic life.

When a Baragaon noblewoman was literally dragged away at eighteen by her spouse-to-be and his posse on horseback, she was terrified. The first years proved hard, but she settled in eventually. Still, she calls this practice of bride capture "backwards" and wishes this cultural institution gone. She speaks of mothers' groups and women's rights. "Now people can report to the police, but there is still social pressure. If a girl is captured into marriage and then tries to leave, people call her unclean."

A man in his fifties tells a *sasum* story. "When I was six, my mother passed away. My sister was already sent away as a *nama*. We only had my father, brother, and me. We needed a woman in the house, so my father arranged it. By that time, I was twelve, my brother was fifteen, and our wife was eighteen. We didn't like her, but we bore one daughter. After several years, she returned to her home. We gave her property for the daughter, and we divorced. But now we are again a polyandrous family. My brother and I are married to one woman. This is a *love marriage*." I wonder, as he shares this narrative with me, how this second wife defines love.

The *amchi*, now sixtyish, tells me of his erstwhile lover, not the woman he married. Like others of his generation, marriage was a necessity, born of family circumstance and the need for labor. His admission reminds me of stories I've heard from his contemporaries: of drunken husbands and wicked stepmothers, of illness and betrayal and forbearance, of all the reasons why marital bonds form and all the reasons why they fray. "The younger people think marriage should be like a Bollywood film. This is an illusion."

A young man from Baragaon had a Tibetan girlfriend. He really liked this girl and told his parents. He thought they would be happy. Wouldn't marrying a Tibetan be a good thing? But they disapproved. He left the Tibetan and tried to find a local bride from Mustang. He succeeded, but he fell for a lower status person. Again, his parents rebuked his choice of girl, village, and family—even though they were all living in New York. The father threatened to disown him. The mother threatened suicide. People say that the young man lost his mind after these events. He still lives with his parents.

Nawang shares the story of a love affair gone awry. It is not his story, but he tells it anyway. The relationship began heady, filled with promises and affection. After the woman left for New York, the couple struggled with long-distance love—a love that the young woman's parents did not condone. Eventually, the couple's genuine commitment to each other was thwarted after the woman received her green card because her family needed the money that a "paper marriage" would fetch. Her immigration status was now a commodity: a fund that could pay for her mother's gall bladder operation and relieve family debt. The paper marriage did not undo the couple. Rather, a true proposal from a Loba family living in Kathmandu whose son was an accountant in New York did in the relationship. Although the woman didn't know the Loba accountant, her parents felt it was a better match than her long-distance love.

"It is so hard to plan a future, when marriage proposals can come not just from other villages but from across the world," says Nawang. "Marriage has always been about money, but now it is also like a *savings account*." He goes on speaking in Nepali peppered with English sentiments: *tragic*, *challenge, hidden love.* "We are the *transit* generation," he concludes. "Between one way of being together and the next."

SPECTERS OF RETURN

The trail that leads up from the Kali Gandaki toward the Muktinath Valley wends past the hamlet of Khinga and into the village of Dzar. This path is hemmed in by stone walls on one side and the slope of a mountain on the other. Through the 1980s and 1990s, teahouses mushroomed along the trail. Some of these lodges were built of rammed earth; others were cast in cement. Petrified loaves of German bakery bread imported from Pokhara and dusty Snickers bars lined marigold-festooned windows. All boasted apple pancakes on their menus. Between April and November, these lodges welcomed a generous stream of trekkers. While several of these teahouses also functioned as homes, family households usually lay elsewhere, near the patchworks of barley, wheat, and buckwheat that blanketed the valley's palm.

In those days, the trail was wide enough to accommodate horses, cows, and human traffic—but not abreast. Glacial runoff, when combined with summer rain, could turn parts of the path into bogs capable of sucking off horseshoes and hiking boots. Fog could linger on this side of the valley, even as sun streamed over the mountains and glinted off the roofs of Muktinath temples. Over the years, the path has widened to a road, accommodating tractors, motorcycles, and minibuses. Since the summer of 2017, it has run as a smooth ribbon of bitumen pitch, straight up from Kag. Some call this development.

One late September day in 2016, Kunzom, Yangjin, and I head down from Dzar toward Tsultrim and Rinzin's apple orchard and farmhouse to join them for lunch. "Let's go through the fields instead of the road," Kunzom suggests. She's just uprooted three plump turnips from her neighbor's garden, wrung the necks of their leaves, and handed one each to Yangjin and me. "Sweetest around. Here, like this." Her fingers work skin from flesh, peeling back the spindly root, making petals out of purple cellulose, turning the turnip into a lotus, before she bites in. "We used to do this as kids," she says, holding the stump. "Mustang popsicle!" Her laugh leads us through a buckwheat field.

We've only been in Dzar for twenty-four hours, but I can already sense Kunzom's ambivalence, the emotional wringing of hands that being here presents for her. This is the place where she was born and spent her early childhood, the place where her father and several of her older siblings died, the place where ancestral responsibilities endure and houses have fallen into disrepair. Her family was the first to start a lodge in Dzar. In its day, this hotel stood as an architectural wonder, with its bank of glass windows, its sheltered garden and tidy dormitory rooms. Now, it stands as a reminder of the pace of change. Stone walls need tending. Apples spill across the yard. For the past few years, one of Kunzom's cousins has been revitalizing the lodge, keeping the mice at bay.

Tsultrim and Rinzin used to run a hotel too, just over a footbridge and down the irrigation canal from Kunzom's family lodge. Now, they have given up the hotelier life, reducing the footprint of their household to several rooms in this establishment. The remaining rooms are rented to lowland Nepalis from the much poorer district of Rukum who help Tsultrim and Rinzin plant, harvest, and care for livestock. What was once a rather grand common room now sits empty, save the platters of *churpi* and apricots spread out on the dining tables, drying in indirect sun.

This home that once bore a hotel plaque is not Tsultrim's ancestral household. That structure is tucked farther into this village, where houses fit together like puzzle pieces, winding around an old palace fortress. Vertical stands of cloud-colored prayer flags, *darchog*, mark the rooflines in Dzar, each flag representing a household member. These *darchog* are a certain metric of belonging, but they no longer account for people who live here. Ghostly cotton, riding the wind, they honor ancestors as much as they have become specters of those who are away and who may not return. So many young people have left Dzar that it is more common when one meets someone here under forty to presume that they are visiting from New York, Paris, or Kathmandu than it is to imagine that they live here.

I have known Tsultrim and Rinzin's family for as long as I've been coming to Mustang. With his baritone resonance that crackles into a high-pitched guffaw, Tsultrim possesses a worldliness even as he, a descendent of Dzar's lineage of headmen, remains a manager of village tradition and a man of power. Rinzin moves with graceful countenance, her high forehead lending an aristocratic air to this woman who has often worked until the point of collapse. Despite the possibilities that it could have been otherwise, Tsultrim and Rinzin love each other with a palpable tenderness, like first snow.

Theirs had been an arranged marriage and, eventually, a polyandrous one. Rinzin had wed Tsultrim, but when Tsultrim became deathly ill with tuberculosis, the parents of both parties persuaded Rinzin to also marry

Tsepak, Tsultrim's younger brother. It was a way of guarding against the hardship that would come if Tsultrim were to die. Fortunately, Tsultrim recovered. The union with Tsepak took root in small ways, with regard to intimacy. It is safe to say that one child of five is biologically his. But Tsultrim remains head of household, and they are all one close-knit family. Tsepak was part of the first wave of Mustang migrants to New York in the late 1990s.

"Tsultrim and Rinzin seem to be spending more time at the farmhouse," I say as we walk along the raised edge of a field.

"Sometimes it is more peaceful out of the village," says Kunzom. "Plus, they've got a lot to look after down there. Hundreds of apple trees. The Jersey cows." These corpulent bovines are a recent import and, one could argue, not only a prestige item but also a direct response to the shrinking labor pool. On my last trip to Dzar, Rinzin had explained the logic as she stroked the hide of a calf. "These cows are big and lazy. Like Americans. They sit around and eat, and then they give a lot of milk. You don't need many people to take care of them. Mustang cows are scrawny, and you need to chase them up and down the mountains. Like Nepalis!"

As we walk, I think about Tsultrim's mother. Nearing ninety, *ibi* Singye's back bends like a question mark. Her wrists and waist are as thin as a child's. Along with Rinzin's hundred-year-old mother who still lives in Jomsom, and Kunzom's ninety-nine-year-old mother in Kathmandu, Singye is the last of a generation who remembers the days when going to the capital city was like crossing over into another world.

"They have good help," Yangjin says. "But they must wonder what will happen when they get old. Will any of their children come back?"

Tsultrim and Rinzin's progeny all live in the U.S. The eldest daughter, married with a child, is a nurse. The eldest son, now with two kids of his own, works for a successful Baragaon businessman in Brooklyn. The middle daughter, once betrothed to the Muktinath nunnery, escaped this fate in no small part due to her father's efforts, against the grain of village tradition. She is now also a nurse and an unmarried free spirit. The youngest daughter has joined the U.S. Army, and the youngest son is an engineer.

"I don't think they will come back," Kunzom replies. "I mean, can *you* imagine any of them becoming farmers?"

"No, but I can see them feeling guilty," I say.

"At least two of them followed their parents' wishes about marriage," Yangjin notes. She is the only sibling in her family to remain in Nepal and would find herself, within the year, betrothed. Tsultrim and Rinzin's elder son and daughter let their matches be made by parental negotiation. Each celebrated these unions in Nepal *and* New York. As these children stepped over the threshold into adult lives, they followed the form, if not the function, of what a Mustang marriage was supposed to be.

We near the edge of Tsultrim's property when Kunzom points down below.

"See that spot? Near the old apricot trees? That used to be my father's favorite place. He would spend days, weeks, down there in retreat, or sometimes just to get away from things—probably from my mom and all the kids! I loved spending time with him there." Kunzom is the youngest of thirteen children. The baby. The surprise that came when her mother was fifty. I imagine Kunzom's father playing with her as a grandparent might. "He would cook over an open fire and make plates out of stones. Everything seems more delicious when you eat off stone, with your hands."

We pass through the metal gate that marks the entrance to Tsultrim and Rinzin's apple orchard. The trees—more than three hundred of them—shine in shades of red and green, as if bedecked with jewels.

"Oh, *dzema la*, Mustang beauties! We're down here!" Tsultrim sounds a playful welcome. We find him lounging under a tree heavy with fruit. Once slim, he is still handsome, even though his belly has rounded over the years. Tsultrim gives me a bear hug, asks after my family.

"Come. Let me show you how things are growing." We've all been here before, but we indulge Tsultrim in this tour. He is wearing stained khaki pants and dress loafers, the soles worn thin. He clasps his hands behind his back as he walks. "Golden and Red Delicious. Gala. Fuji. Cortland. I've invested in more saplings this year. Some of them are doing well but others . . . I think we need to give them more love. And more Jersey cow shit." We all laugh.

Kunzom reaches up for a Golden Delicious. "Mustang apples may not be like *yartsa gunbu*," she says speaking of the *cordyceps* caterpillar fungus— aka Himalayan Viagra—that is worth more than its weight in gold, "but they are another way to make a lot of money," she says between bites.

"True," Tsultrim answers. "The price we can get per kilo has been increasing," he glances over his shoulder, toward the road, "because the cost of transportation is going down."

The last time I was here, two years ago, Tsultrim had looked up at the sky and shouted, as if to reach his eldest son across the seas, "Lhundup! This is your inheritance. It is waiting for you." This time, there was no such proclamation. Instead, Tsultrim says, "I'm setting this up so that it will be a good investment for someone."

"For Lhundup?" I ask.

"If he wants it. Or if any of the kids want it. Or someone else. I cannot predict." My friend is serious now. "But it will bring a good income. I've tried to make them something worth coming back for, but who knows—"

I think about the conversation we had the other night in Kag with a relative of Tsultrim's, as she held court in her home. This gorgeous noblewoman, whom I've had the privilege to watch age, was exhausted after working in her garden all day. She lounged on a platform bed, scratched her armpit with immodest alacrity, and declared, "The best ideas come from those who go out and then return. They lose their laziness abroad, and then come back appreciating how hard we work here. They carry in new ideas." She rubbed her arthritic hands. "When do young people ever see the work before then? They're off to boarding school before they learn to wipe snot from their noses. Problem is," she mused, tucking in her heels and leaning forward, "The ones who go hardly ever come back. And the ones who marry over there—forget it!"

We tour the remaining rows of Tsultrim's new saplings in silence. "Let's go see the Jersey cows," I suggest.

Rinzin is washing rainbow chard by the water spigot outside the farmhouse. She looks up and smiles. This time it is my turn to ask after her health. She's suffered from various problems recently. "Are you well?"

"I am well. Come inside. Eat."

We enter the new home. With its pitched roof and fancy bathrooms, it recalls a Swiss chalet. Tsultrim designed this structure to represent his imagination of an American farmhouse. I think that the pitched metal roof is a smart addition, given the ways that weather patterns are changing in Mustang. We sit on mattresses on the floor, drinking milk tea and chatting with Rinzin as she cooks up pumpkin curry and sautés chard. The pressure cooker whistles. Lunch is ready.

On a previous trip to Mustang, in 2014, I had found Rinzin presiding over the annual sea buckthorn harvest, working with her fellow village women to press and bottle this brambly berry into currency. The mothers' group gathered in the Dzar community house. They grumbled as they worked about how old they were getting, how little help they had. A sense of abandonment filled the hall, like vapor rising from the vats of sea buckthorn juice: pungent and overpowering. To this, Rinzin offered, "It is our right to tell our children to come back. Do they have no shame?" Others chided her, gently. "You know we can't control what they do."

Now, Rinzin serves up a feast in this sturdy house, built on uncertainty. We eat until our stomachs bulge and then take naps in the dappled shade of someone else's future.

# PART V

# LAND AND LINEAGE

Coolness: the sound of the bell as it leaves the bell.

Green leaves, white water, the barley yellowing.

—YOSA BUSON HAIKU, TRANSLATED BY W. S. MERWIN

These watchers locate in their repertory
mythic fragments of some kindred story
and draw them dripping out of memory's well.

—RACHEL HADAS, "THE CHORUS"

WHETHER IN NEPALI OR TIBETAN, PEOPLE SPEAK OF THE WORLDS THEY occupy in relation to their elements. The earth, air, and water of a place matter. They shape a sense of belonging, impacting the body and the heart-mind. To eat the food you cultivate or the animals you husband is one way to be well. Still, matters of economy shift the palate of desire and alter what it means to work. Consider what belonging to territory engenders—to claim it and have it claim you. As anthropologist Keith Basso learned from his Western Apache friends, wisdom sits in places. Land shapes people even as people shape the stories they tell and retell about the geographies of home. Still, the *khora* of migration makes and remakes connections between people and place, between physical and sacred geography, across international borders and less visible boundaries.

What happens when Earth asserts its primal power and places must be remade? The 2015 Nepal earthquakes were a reminder that our firmament itself is fluid, at times alive with movement. We might also consider more subtle moments of change: a tree is felled, a spring dries up, a storm blows in, snowfall silences and buries.

The short story, "Gods and Demons," tacks between Baragaon and Brooklyn. It describes how kinship endures and transforms the expectations of a father, Tamdin, and a son, Yutok, and how these connections are themselves tied to land and lineage. Their experiences show how the decision to migrate affects not only the people who stay behind but also the land itself. Migratory pathways between Mustang to New York are implicated in other patterns of movement within Nepal and between Nepal and the Gulf States. Trajectories intertwine, revealing inequalities and fostering new alliances between different kinds of Nepalis. This story also teaches us something about the nature of mind, the boundaries between illness and well-being, and what the body remembers.

"The Ground beneath Our Feet" invites discussions of development and displacement, mobility and the limitations on movement experienced by people from Mustang. Objects move, too, and oblige us to consider the trafficking of cultural heritage from Mustang into the wider world, including New York. Mustang's location along a geopolitically sensitive border, the recent discovery of uranium resources in Lo, and the region's "Third Pole" status in the Anthropocene means that the *khora* of migration is also being shaped by the forces of political ecology and climate change. What are the possibilities and the limits of growth—of sweet peas and rapeseed, of bridges and tunnels? When people pray, offering blessings to living landscapes in the hopes of good outcomes, what do the non-humans hear? How do gods of place respond to change?

# GODS AND DEMONS

Sangmo is a slight woman, but her voice carries. She leans out the window of the family home and shouts at her husband, "Come inside! Jamyang is calling!"

Tamdin places his hands on his knees and hoists himself upright. The aches in his joints feel infinite. He spits, as if to expel the pain. This old man weeding his field is also one of Mustang's most revered ritual specialists. The work of a priest is the work of a farmer. Both involve cultivation. Tamdin looks down at his knuckles as he rises. These knots of flesh and bone remind him of the gnarled stumps of poplar trees, places where old growth and new life meet.

"*Ya ya!*" he yells back to his wife, before turning to Ram, the lowland Nepali laborer by his side. "Younger son. Phone from America." He says these words in Nepali unadorned by tense and inflected with a high mountain accent.

Ram nods and returns to his weeding. Although only eighteen, this young man from down south in Myagdi District has been working fields and herding sheep and goats in Mustang for three years. He came to Dzong about a year ago, on a tip from a cousin who is a jeep driver in Tshug.

Ram is from a family of five children. His widowed mother lives in Beni Bazaar, where she runs a tea and snacks stand. Her husband was killed in the Maoist raid on Beni back in 2004 and, despite her entrepreneurial spirit, this widow struggles to support her children. For Ram and his elder siblings, becoming a migrant laborer was not optional. His *didi* waitresses at a Pakistani-run restaurant in Abu Dhabi. His *dai* acquired a guest worker visa for Qatar, where he now does construction. With money her older children send back, his mother keeps the two youngest children in simple meals and school uniforms. Ram listens to his brother's and sister's stories of hell-like heat and brutal bosses through the staccato thrum of internet calling apps. Both warn him against joining the throngs of Nepalis heading to the Gulf, but Ram has a difficult time imagining growing old in Mustang, farming other people's land, herding other people's sheep.

Ram wipes his hand across his forehead. His sweat-stained T-shirt reads "I Can't Afford to ♥ NY." He found the shirt in Pokhara, already faded by the sun in one of the clothing kiosks down by Mustang Chowk, near the cell phone fixers and the plumbing supply dealers. He does not read much English, but he knew enough to appreciate the irony. After several seasons of working in Mustang, Ram has grown accustomed to the displays of wealth up the Kali Gandaki—the million-rupee dowries, the glistening Pulsar motorcycles—all of which seem to be made possible by funds flowing back from New York. It grates on him. His mother owns only one nice *saree* and denies herself milk, saving it for the tea she serves others.

But Tamdin and Sangmo are kind. They feed him well and pay him decently, no doubt because two of their children are in New York.

Ram knows little of the Buddha *dharma*. The distinctions between branches of this faith as practiced in Mustang are lost on him, but he can tell that, despite Tamdin's quiet demeanor, the old man is powerful. He is a conjurer not unlike the *jhankri* from Ram's birth village. Still, Tamdin reads Tibetan scriptures each morning and evening—something the *jhankri* cannot do.

When Ram fell ill during his first weeks in Tamdin's household, sweat and nightmares overtaking him, he was treated with herbal powders that stuck to the roof of his mouth, with incense, bone soup, and prayer. Tamdin returned Ram to health, resetting his *la*, his life force, back into his body. Since then, Ram has worn the protective amulets given him by Tamdin. This is not his religion, but it is an act of care that he accepts.

Sangmo speaks very few words of Nepali, and Ram has yet to pick up more than the most basic words in local Tibetan. *Ále* is money. *Yöba* is food, especially rice. *Nyal* means rest or sleep. *Piza* is boy. They smile at each other a lot.

Even if Ram wants to make friends with others his age in the village, language and culture remain an obstacle. Most of the young people living in Dzong are actually from neighboring Dolpo, a place where land is rockier, passes are higher, growing seasons are shorter, and fewer people speak Nepali. What began as a flow of seasonal labor about a decade ago has turned into the full-scale leasing by local landlords of homes and fields to Dolpo families. Bled of its young and able-bodied constituents, the village has been transfused with new life from other places. Most of the original inhabitants who remain are people of Tamdin and Sangmo's generation.

Despite differences of age and culture, Ram and Tamdin get along. They chat as they work the fields or tidy up the old mud brick house.

"Our sons tell us not to plant fields anymore," Tamdin once said to Ram. "But what use is land if you don't cultivate it? They say it is too much work for old people. But what choice do they leave us?"

Tamdin's eldest and middle daughters married out of the village years ago. Although they live in nearby settlements, they are now beholden to their husbands' families. Their youngest daughter hitched her fate to a man twenty years her senior, a trader who made it big as a gold smuggler in Hong Kong. She long ago abandoned village life for Kathmandu, her kids tucked away in fancy boarding schools. Tamdin and Sangmo's two sons are in New York. Yutok, the oldest son, had been in Japan before he went off to New York, and before that he'd spent his youth in an Indian boarding school. The youngest son, Jamyang, had been educated in Kathmandu.

As Ram passed weeks and months in this household, he learned that Jamyang drives a taxi. "He is very clever. Passed SLC in first rank. Has good English," Tamdin explained. "Yutok works at a restaurant. Jamyang is clever, but Yutok has more wisdom."

Yutok was trained as a *ngakpa*, following the path of family lineage. After high school and before he got a visa to Japan, Yutok spent a few years in the village. "It was time for his *tsham*," said Tamdin. "For some of his retreat he was in the house, but he also stayed up in that cave over there," gesturing toward the cliffs that lined that Dzar-Dzong valley. "Three years, three months, three days. Like me, when I was younger." To Ram, the landscape looked so barren that he could not imagine spending deep time in such a place or, for that matter, being alone for so long.

"That must have been boring!" Ram exclaimed. That day, they were working to repair an irrigation channel, their hands caked in wet earth and grass.

Tamdin laughed, the weight of work lightened by this young person's presence. "During that time, I taught Yutok about our religion," Tamdin explained, his voice soft. "He knows the deities of this place. *Lu, tsen, sabdak, yul lha*. Where they live. In rocks and springs and mountains. What they like. What makes them angry."

"Gods in the rocks?" The idea that water could be holy or that protectors watched over certain places made sense to Ram, but Mustang's sacred geography baffled him.

"Yes. In the rocks and mountains, not just inside the temple."

Some weeks later, as they sat on the roof of Tamdin's home, watching Sangmo arrange *dzimbu* to dry in the sun, Ram ventured, "Do you think they will ever come home?"

"Now we have cash that we did not have before," Tamdin answered. "But what use is money without people? My sons should return to work the land of the place they were born." Sangmo listened to her husband but said nothing. Her hands moved across the filaments of *dzimbu*, touching a taste at once acrid and sweet.

Now, tired of weeding, Ram leans back against a stone wall and rests. He thinks about the framed photographs of Tamdin and Sangmo's children and grandchildren. They hang where mud brick meets roofline. Ram recalls the collage of fading portraits set beside the shrine in his mother's rented quarters in Beni. It seems to him that these pictures framed the end of something. Children stand frozen in time, iconic and abstract, like the stylized pantheons of Buddhist protectors, like the Hindu avatar for which he is named.

Time passes.

The sun shines straight above Ram's head, but Tamdin does not return to the fields after the phone call. Ram's stomach rumbles. Sangmo will have midday food prepared. He hopes for rice with buckwheat greens soaked in buttermilk or wet chili tinged with Sichuan pepper and fresh mint and buckwheat bread. He has grown fond of these flavors.

Ram sets down his sickle and heads home, such as it is.

When he arrives, he finds Tamdin with his head in his hands. Sangmo's salt and pepper hair, normally tied in a neat bun, has come undone. Tears run the course of her wrinkled cheeks. The hearth is cold.

Tamdin looks up, his eyes wide and sad. "Eldest son is sick. In hospital. In America."


MANHATTAN, SUMMER 2013

It can be described as a fire in the mind. Embers smolder, sometimes for years, and then ignite. It is also like drowning. Surface and depth comingle. Which way is up?

On this steaming July night, a dark-skinned man is drumming on an upturned plastic bucket. Afro-Caribbean rhythms pulse through the 14th Street subway station. The sound of percussion tightens Yutok's throat, triggering voices and visions. That makeshift drum may well have been a *damaru*, the two-headed instrument that Yutok learned to wield so long ago, from his father. The beat upends him.

Yutok finds himself in a place between memory and forgetting, between dread and pleasure, between pain and euphoria. It is as if the volume on the world has been turned up. He sees a stream of images, deities his father trained him to honor and appease, dancing in front of him in the flickering fluorescent light. Sharp aches pass across his kidneys. The top of his head tingles. He feels weightless and leaden at once.

He first experienced this smoldering in his mind as a teenager. He'd been in India, in secondary school, sitting in mathematics class. One of his classmates was drumming his pencil on the desk as he searched for the solution to a problem, his feet tapping against the side of the dented metal desk.

Usually, such fidgeting did not disturb Yutok, but for some reason that day he felt the rhythm as a quickening heartbeat, *ba-dung, ba-dung, ba-dung*. Was the sound coming from inside or outside his body? His head ached. He shut his eyes, but this brought no relief. When he opened his eyes, he saw a wrathful *yidam* dancing on the blackboard. He leapt out of his seat and addressed the deity. "Dorje Phurba, why have you come?"

Yutok had no idea that he'd said this aloud. His classmates turned and stared, but Yutok paid them no mind. Instead, he felt the heat from the ring of flame that surrounded the dancing deity, his three-bladed dagger turning gold, then silver, then copper in the light. Yutok felt a surge of bliss, but this soon dissolved into a sense of danger.

A palm on a shoulder. Was it his shoulder? He opened his eyes to see a friend and behind him their teacher. Yutok could make out what they were saying, but he felt as if they were speaking to him from down a long tunnel. Slowly the world came back into focus.

"Okay. I am okay. Water?" he managed to say. The teacher brought a thermos. Yutok's friend held fast to his hand. This touch felt comforting, but Yutok remained unsettled. Were these people, his friend and his teacher, there to help him? Or was Dorje Phurba protecting him? Suspicion became a dominant emotion.

"Let's find you a place to rest," his teacher said. Unlike some of the other teachers, this man was humane.

But was this kindness to be trusted? Could he drink the water he'd been offered? Yutok's head cracked and spun.

"I am just wondering about the answer," Yutok managed to say. Yutok felt himself getting angry, his mind like bare feet on hot stones. "And what have they put in that water? What makes it so cool and delicious?" Words came to him: *tortoise, venom, apricot.* Was he saying these words? Where were they coming from?

His teacher and his friend looked strange. Did they not see the possibility for harm? Could they not hear the rhythm of these sounds inside his head?

Then, nothing. The world grew dark.

The next thing Yutok remembered was waking up in his school's infirmary. He'd been sleeping hard, his hair matted to his forehead. He watched the ceiling fan. Everything seemed clear again.

Yutok's teacher was an ex-monk. As this young man lay catatonic on the infirmary cot, the teacher called a powerful local lama, a Nyingma master like Yutok's father. The lama performed a purification ritual and made supplications, calling on the lineage stretching back to the master Dorje Lingpa, trying to appease what had overtaken this young man. Dorje Phurba demanded as much.

It took two days of ritual and a visit from an Indian doctor who gave Yutok pills that left his mouth tasting of metal before the young man seemed to stabilize.

The school nurse called it an "episode."

Rumors flew around the school. His friends thought he'd tried hashish with one of the tourists who sometimes made it to this Himalayan foothill town—those dreadlocked, strung out white kids. Others said that maybe he was going to become a *lhapa*, an oracle, or that he was cracking under the pressure leading up to exams.

Yutok didn't know what to think. Whatever fiery wave had passed through him seemed to have subsided. He implored the headmaster not to send word to his parents about the episode. Still, Yutok felt as if he should tell his father about this someday. Whatever else might be happening, he knew that Dorje Phurba was an important *yidam* who protected their village.

In the months that followed, Yutok either slept so deeply that he felt weighted down by dreams, or he slept hardly at all. He made it through his exams on sweet tea and packets of instant noodles, his brain abuzz with sugar and cardamom, MSG and turmeric.

Several years passed before such a hallucination engulfed him again. This time it was in the seclusion of his *tsham*, and everything was different. Yutok had been back in the village for only a few months before beginning his retreat. In the months that followed, Yutok's muscles ached and then became accustomed to the fluid movements of daily prostrations. Only his father broke the human silence, leading him through instructions and empower-ments. They chanted scripture together. Although much of the retreat was spent in his family's shrine room, core months of practice passed alone in a mountain cave above the village.

There, Dorje Phurba and other deities came to him, after days of sitting and breathing quietly. He was visited by both peaceful and wrathful forms of these deities: a necklace of skulls gave way to wish-fulfilling jewels and beguiling gestures of supplication. In that moment, light and dark distin-guished themselves. That cave felt anything but confining. It was a womb. It birthed him. Although he was mostly alone, he felt his father beside him. Although he was often hungry, the handfuls of *tsampa* and thin tea, the buckwheat cakes his mother cooked and sent up with his father, wrapped in one of her scarves, were enough. When the force inside him morphed from peaceful to wrathful, he rode it.

Yutok stepped out onto the cave ledge, climbed around the backside to relieve himself, and stared up at Yak Gawa. This mountain face looked like a majestic beast, white glacial blaze across a black body of rock. He watched lammergeiers ride the wind.

Still, he would not call what he felt in those moments "control."

Now, in this fetid underground tunnel, under the fluorescent glow and grime of a Manhattan subway station at 2 a.m., after working a twelve-hour shift running $40 plates of pistachio-crusted cod and bowls of ginger-infused mussels to people who do not even notice he exists, in a city that has at once welcomed him and swallowed him whole, Yutok listens to the mesmeriz-ing percussion, that black man conjuring beauty from found objects, from that which this nation discards.

The next thing Yutok knows, he is in a clean, white room under a clean, white sheet. He shivers. His body aches. He inspects the person under this sheet with a detached curiosity. Bruises on wrists and thighs. Scrapes across kneecaps. A tangled gown. No underwear.

The next thought that enters his mind is about tip money. It had been a good night. Even as a table runner he'd made $400. Yutok pictures the res-taurant where he works, with its overstuffed leather booths, the bar flashed in copper. He feels the weight of three plates balanced along his forearm and recalls the beautiful Filipina hostess. They kissed each other as they clocked out for the evening. This was not their first kiss. He remembers walking toward the subway station, regretting that he did not suggest they spend what remained of the night together.

But what night? How long ago? As clearly as he recalls these details, he cannot place much else.

"Hello?" he calls out, hoisting himself upright on the narrow bed. "Hello?"

A few minutes later, the door opens and a thin man with kind eyes, close-cropped dark hair, and a goatee enters the room. He is dressed in green from head to toe and carries a clipboard.

"Welcome back to the world of the living," the man says. "Can you tell me your name?"

"Yutok. Yutok Gurung."

"Check. Now, what about your birthdate?"

Yutok pauses. It had been an inexact date in the first instance, but the answer comes spilling out, like an incantation. "March 15, 1984."

"Check," repeats the man. "Ides of March. Solid." He hums his next words—"Back to life, back to reality"—and then says, "You're probably not a Roman history buff. Probably don't even remember De La Soul." The hospital worker speaks these words to himself, but aloud. It is as if by referencing his own knowledge—of literature, of popular music, of life outside this hospital—he might escape some of the daily trauma-drama he manages.

Yutok looks confused. The man's face softens. "I'm sorry," says the worker, looking down at his clipboard, "Yutok." The man reaches out gently, taking Yutok's arm and wrapping a blood pressure cuff around it. "It has been a long night." The man pronounces his name *you-toke*, but it is still recognizable. Other Americans have done worse. "I'm glad you're feeling better. Meds seem to be working. Things got pretty rough there for a while." Yutok feels the cuff constrict, then loosen. This dense holding then letting go soothes him, as does the man's warm fingers on his skin.

"Can you tell me—" Yutok begins.

"What happened?" the man answers. "I'll let Dr. Rivera do that. He will be here in a moment. But let me get your brother. He's been so worried. He's slept out in the visitor lounge since Sunday."

"And today? What day is today?"

"Tuesday."

"And where?"

"Bellevue, man. Bellevue."

DZONG, SPRING 2014

Tamdin is called down to Kag to conduct a fire *puja* for a new hotel, the Mountain View Shangri La Mustang Resort. The names of these places seem to keep getting longer, he thinks, the construction more elaborate. They remind him of the pastel origami birds in the book Yutok brought home from Japan. All fold and flourish.

All the same, the hotel is owned by one of his wife's nephews, and his presence is required. The old *ngakpa* determined an auspicious date for the *puja* and called on the few remaining tantrists in the area to perform the ritual with him. Yeshi from Tiri will meet him in Kag. Takla will meet him in Dzar, and they will ride down together.

Tamdin is not looking forward to the journey. Not so long ago, he would have saddled up his horse and headed straight down the spine of the Dzar-Dzong valley. But he is old. The family's last horse was sold some months ago. He will take the bus, filled as it will be with Indian pilgrims complaining of cold, smelling of sandalwood and *ghee* after their *darshan* at Muktinath. Although nobody can deny the convenience of jeeps and buses, Tamdin does not like what the road has done to the land.

He will also take Ram. The boy has proven useful around the house, and even though he knows nothing of ritual practice, Ram can help move tables and gather dirt, sand, and twigs for the ritual. Tamdin braces himself for the work ahead. He anticipates the pinch in his back from wielding the *ngachen*, his mouth by turns parched and whetted with sips of tea, always too salty in this house. But the work of ritual is his vocation, so he wakes with the rooster and prepares.

Tamdin hitches up his cloak and reaches for the red backpack that his younger son had gifted him the previous year on his first trip back from New York, after marriage and a green card. "Real North *Face*, not North *Fake*," Jamyang said, seeming pleased with himself, but Tamdin had not understood the joke. He was grateful for the gift but more grateful still that this son managed a visit. At that point, it had been seven years.

Tamdin wraps up his *dorje* and *drilbu*, the thunderbolt scepter and bell, and places them in the backpack, along with his *damaru* and the long metal rod that opens up to a cup from which he will pour oil and brandish fire to bless the hotel, dispelling obstacles and ushering in prosperity. He handles his silver-plated thigh bone trumpet with care, covering it in a clean *kathag*. This old *ngakpa* enjoys the way these implements feel in his hands. They suit him. He places them into the backpack.

In holding these objects and considering their power, Tamdin thinks of Yutok. It has been three seasons since the phone call from Jamyang, that conversation in which brotherly secrets spilled out. Jamyang confessed that when Yutok had been in Japan, he had not been duped by his boss and given only a two-year work visa instead of the usual three but rather had been found naked and disoriented in a public park; that this led to a violent rage and apprehension by the police, resulting in jail and, eventually, deportation; that, after several years in New York, Yutok's mind had burst into flame again; about government hospitals, Jamyang's lost days of work, Yutok's weakened, tender state; about the doctor's words of causes and conditions that neither brother could fully comprehend.

In the most recent reports Tamdin received about Yutok, usually from Jamyang, he seemed to be doing better.

But what was "better"? Jamyang explained that his brother now had a stable job as a stock boy at a grocery store. Yutok called once or twice. He sounded calm. He mentioned the weather in New York and the way that, in autumn, the leaves turned colors like they did at home in Mustang. He did not mention the twenty pounds he had gained, weight that did not seem to come from rice. He did not mention the white-hot stigmata of his Medicaid-supplied anti-psychotics, pills he hid and swallowed dry.

Tamdin learns some of these details obliquely from Jamyang. He senses Yutok's struggle to find a way with gods and demons. In this, father and son are tethered by bone across the body of the sky.

Tamdin locates the ritual texts he will need for the fire *puja* and adds them to the backpack, along with colored string for the effigies he will sculpt and a handful of the root he will boil in butter to make the red pigment for *torma*, barley cake sacrifices painted the color of blood. He finds the stash of wool with which he likes to make wicks for butter lamps. The oil, butter, grains, flowers, dung, and other household items required for the ritual will come from his nephew's household.

"Household." What does this word mean anymore? Mountain View Shangri La Mustang Resort is no household, not in the traditional sense. Sure, the hotel owner has a stake in the happenings of Kag, its governance and its ritual calendar. Sure, the place belongs to a family with deep ties to this land. But the elders have all died, the inheriting generation has dispersed, and everything seems to be about money these days.

Has it always been like this? Tamdin wants to believe that the answer is no. Just like he wants to believe that the things those New York doctors say about his son, in a language he does not know, in a universe he sees only through idealized photographs and sanitized instant messages, are wrong. At the very least, this notion that a mind could be irrevocably broken, but that chemicals that make you fat and dull can also keep you well, does not align with his conceptions of mind or madness.

Tamdin does not usually feel the bilious combination of distress and resentment, but today it burns his belly. He scowls as he shakes Ram awake.

Sangmo rises, wordlessly, and makes tea.

## DZONG, SPRING 2015

Tamdin is on the roof of his home, resting in the midday sun, when the earthquake comes. It is sound but also feeling, roiling in the ground. The old tantrist sits up but then does not move. He is not sure what to do, but he knows this is *sa yom*, the shaking of the earth.

He looks at his watch—a shiny gold gift from Jamyang—and counts seconds. Twenty-six, twenty-seven, twenty-eight. He looks up, across the village. All the houses are moving, like the froth that rises when water boils in a pot. A minute passes before he remembers to breathe.

Even after these earthen waves stop rolling across roofs, Tamdin can see that the trees in his neighbor's apple orchard are still shaking. A strange wind blows from the north. At this time of day, it usually comes from the south.

Tamdin notices that the firewood, neatly stacked along the edge of his roof and those of his neighbors, is tumbling down. He remembers the *mantra—Dorje Sempa Sa Lem. Dorje Sempa Sa Lem. Dorje Sempa Sa Lem—* and voices it, asking this protector to hold down the ground.

Sangmo's wail pierces his prayers. He hears Ram calling from the courtyard, *ayo, ayo, ayo*. In Nepali, *ayo* is a lament. It expresses pain. But it also simply means *it has come*.

Down in Kathmandu, Dharahara Tower has collapsed, killing lovers and families out for a Saturday stroll. The *stupa* at Boudha and Swayambhu falter, golden spires and Buddha eyes askew. In Bhaktapur, temples buckle.

This is to say nothing of the homes and businesses that bury people in an instant, the church that caves in on a congregation during midday services. The avalanche that erases the village of Langtang with half the force of an atomic bomb.

Tamdin knows none of this, but his sense of trauma is acute: unsettled earth, untimely dead. He imagines that, in the weeks and months to come, people will speak of Kathmandu and hard-hit villages as a place overrun by ghosts. So many lives cut short, without one butter lamp, one prayer.

Tentatively, Tamdin rises and makes his way down the ladder to the main floor of the house, where he finds Sangmo curled in a corner, crying. The photos of their family—Jamyang, Yutok, their daughters, and one granddaughter—have fallen off their hooks. Picture glass has shattered across the low tables, mixing with a thermos of tea that has spilled on the floor. He picks up his wife and carries her outside.

After Tamdin steps across his threshold, he spits three times on the ground. This is a bodily impulse in sinful, unsettled moments.

"*Hajakpa*," Sangmo says. It is a first word beyond tears—a word that, in a sense, recognizes nefarious harm that oughtn't be named. Then she spits too.

That day, there are no cracks in their home, but in the coming days, long vertical lines appear. When Tamdin examines the village *gönpa*, he sees sky and roof together, like two palms almost touching.

It takes several days for phone calls from Jamyang and Yutok to come through from New York. When they do, Tamdin has few words. Yes, they are okay. Yes, the family home is damaged. No, nobody died here.

Tamdin learns from his sons, in New York, about the old wooden bridge in Jomsom. "We saw it on the computer. It folded into itself," Yutok explains, "like a hand making *namaste*." Tamdin worries, as he so often does, about Yutok's mind. It has been nearly two years since the hospital episode. Tamdin does not speak to Yutok about Sangmo's nightmares, her weakened state. Instead, he tells Yutok, "I am doing rituals for *sabdak* and *tsen*," entreating his son to do the same.

Jamyang reports that Ghiling and Namgyal, villages farther north in Lo, have suffered severe damage, as has the palace in Monthang. "The *kyidug* is raising money to send to Mustang and other places," says his younger son. Tamdin marvels that such news travels around the world to reach him back in Mustang.

For days after the first earthquake, Sangmo refuses to sleep inside. She still empties and fills the water offering bowls in the damaged shrine room. She still cooks in the hearth, although she has little appetite. "I keep hearing the sound of the earth tearing apart," she confides to Tamdin. "I feel like vomiting. Fear has swallowed me."

Others also sleep outside. As people begin to do the work of dismantling damaged structures so that they can rebuild, they talk about what happened. They name it.

"This is *sagul*," Tamdin hears his cousin explain to Ram, in her simple Nepali, into which local Tibetan is spliced. "The shaking of the earth is because of a kind of animal. Some say it is something like a goat, with a lot of fur. Others say it is a tortoise under the ground. Or an elephant. Some say it is a fish. Others say it is a pig."

"Does it have teeth?" Ram asks.

"Maybe it has big teeth," she answers. "It has long nails and a big long tail."

"Horns?"

"No, I don't think it has horns. Our earth sits on its back. When it shakes its body, limbs, or tail, the earth moves."

Ram also hears that earthquakes are caused by the waves of a sea, deep underground. He is not clear about which answer is true.

Three old men—Tamdin, his neighbor Dandrul, and Buchung, the village *amchi*—take turns helping one another to assess damage in the village. Someone from Jomsom comes to tell them that they can get some government assistance to rebuild and repair, but they do not believe this news. Others tell them that a Sakya Buddhist association will send money. This they believe.

They talk as they work. "We have had earthquakes before. My older brother was small for the last one. I was not yet born," says Dandrul.

Buchung adds, "If an earthquake comes after the harvest, it is a good sign. It shakes the wooden box where we keep our grains. It settles the grains and makes room for more. But," he continues, "if it comes when there are new shoots in the fields, like it did now, then we will not have a good harvest. Instead, it brings pests."

Tamdin thinks in other terms. "People are digging the earth so much, using dozers, petrol, all these things," he says. "By making new roads everywhere, we are disturbing *lu* and *sabdak*. We are giving up on growing food. Instead we just plant apples to make money. This angers the forces within the earth. They shake to wake us up."

Ram is helping to clear the monastery courtyard of rubble when he overhears the senior monk talking to several novices. "According to scientists, this event comes when rocks collide into each other, under the earth's skin." He speaks in Nepali because the young monks are all from elsewhere and are still learning Tibetan. Tragedy becomes catechism. "From a Buddhist point of view, the world rests on Sipa Khorlo, the Wheel of Life, the one we can see on the walls of our monasteries. The body of that animal, *sagul*, that old people speak of is really the Wheel of Life. It is as people say. It is a kind of animal, but it also comes due to human behavior. The effects of *karma*. Everything we create."

Some days later, Ram walks over to Rani Powa to buy some supplies for the household. Tamdin has given him some money for a bowl of instant noodles and tea. There are no tourists now, and so nobody stops him from occupying a table at the Laliguras Hotel. He orders lunch and sits, chatting with the hotel manager.

"Where were you when the earthquake came?" Ram asks.

"I was near my family's old house," he answers, gesturing over his shoulder toward the settlement of Purang. "I had ridden my motorcycle down there, and I was putting oil on my chain. But then my bike began to wobble. The stone walls that line our fields tumbled down. It felt like the world shook for five minutes. Just before the earthquake, I noticed cows and horses running up and down, here and there. Then shaking started. The animals knew before people. They always do."

BROOKLYN, SUMMER 2015

In the aftermath of the earthquakes, Yutok has a hard time turning away from social media. Like so many other Nepalis, he is worried for his family. But he is also fascinated by the ways people talk about these events. How they try to explain. As if that would help the ones who died. He captures screenshots of these posts and reads them many times.

Beneath land there is big ocean. Water moves here and there. There is no space for *sagul* to breathe. It moves to breathe. This creates waves which shake the land. It is something like the child in the mother's womb, before birth.

It is due to tectonic plate. Some old people believe that it is a fish that the world sits on, or some sort of ghost. But that is wrong. It all depends on plate. It is because Nepal is inside the Indian plate and the Tibetan plate. If they are joined properly, then earth is fine. I learned this working in Korea.

Earth is like flame which was parted from sun, once upon a time. Even though the outer temperature of earth is now less, the inner flame and heat have not yet finished. That vapor from the inner flame is still coming out. When this vapor comes out, earth shakes. Like a pressure cooker when steam comes out.

Some say it is like the shell of an egg. We are the shell, and the earthquake is the liquid inside of the egg.

It is earth doing a somersault.

These days people care too much about this *rinpoche* or that *rinpoche*. This causes disharmony. We have so much envy, anger, such short tempers. We are unsatisfied. It must be for this reason that Nepal experiences such suffering.

It is not just in Nepal. These things happen all over the world. Some say it is because people are sinful. There are sins all over the world, so I cannot say that it happened because of sin.

What do you expect? It is *kaliyug*. We live in degenerate times. Guru Rinpoche predicted. Maybe this year the gods will lose to the demons.

For several months, under the heat and light of New York summer, Yutok does as his father asks. He makes offerings. He appeases deities of place from a distance.

BROOKLYN, SUMMER 2017

On a June morning, Yutok rises earlier than usual. He has told his friend Tashi that he can take the first shift at the Whole Foods greenhouse where they work. Tashi's aunt, the woman who raised him, is going through chemotherapy for stomach cancer, and it is Tashi's turn to accompany her to treatment.

Yutok sits up in bed and performs his quiet morning *puja*: a whispered tumble of prayer, the pulsing snap of fingers. At the end, he sounds a long-life prayer for Tashi's aunt, though this is not part of his usual practice. Yutok then slips a prescription bottle out from underneath his pillow and takes his medicine.

It has been four years since his stay in the psychiatric unit at Bellevue Hospital and months since he last tried to forego either his medications or his sessions with Dr. Rivera—this man he has come to trust, despite the cultural differences between them. To his credit, Dr. Rivera has learned to listen to Yutok. Their meetings are not about re-upping the Rx and the quick exit. They have feeling.

During one of their first outpatient appointments, after the drama of that harrowing hospital admission, Dr. Rivera shared fragments of his own story.

An immigrant who escaped war-torn El Salvador, he is the eldest of five siblings and the only one to make it through Mexico and eventually across the border, under the guardianship of his mother's sister. "I almost died, during the crossing." He explained that he spent his adolescence working his way up North America's eastern edge to *Nueva York*, where he "somehow made it through high school," then went on to college and medical school. "Columbia. Sinai." Yutok did not know these places. He wondered if they were schools or countries.

"And your parents?" Yutok asked. "Brothers and sisters?"

"Never saw them again," the doctor replied, looking long and lovingly at this fellow brown-skinned immigrant man. His honesty was arresting.

"When I was working in Japan, I became lost mind there. They put me into a cell by myself. Just a few days. But it made me wild, like a . . ." Yutok paused to remember the English word. "Like a jackal." He flashed on an image of that tawny, howling creature calling out to the Himalayan night. This bit of his truth was an offering, in return for the doctor's story. Yutok thought about the cave where he completed his retreat and how, even in the loneliest of moments, he still rested with the majesty of stars.

Last year, when Yutok's mother, Sangmo, died of pneumonia during the winter spent in Kathmandu, after the earthquakes weakened her, Dr. Rivera held his crying patient in his arms. Jamyang returned to Nepal to perform the acts an eldest son should because Yutok could not leave, given his pending travel documents. He could not return to see his dying mother. Dr. Rivera recognized in himself Yutok's grief and anger. It was, if not transference, then a mirroring.

Dr. Rivera was not a priest like Yutok's father, but he could still produce in Yutok a feeling of protection, of being protected. Yutok despised his medicines, even with the various shifts in dose and regimen—what Dr. Rivera called "fine tuning" and what Yutok experienced as shapeshifting sizes, colors, and aftertastes of pills. Yet his respect for this man who had shown him no judgment but only care exceeded his capacity to disobey. He took the pills, one might say, religiously. He prayed over the medicines every morning. He visualized them resting in the open palm of his *yidam*, peaceful in form.

Yutok finishes his *puja*. The rest of the apartment sleeps. Yutok's cousin-brother, Rapsang, breathes heavily, as if he is blowing out a candle. Sherab, another villager from Dzong and a roommate, is curled up on a Tibetan carpet that doubles as bed and couch, two 16-ounce Pabst Blue Ribbon cans on the floor beside him. Rapsang and Sherab work at Whole Foods too.

Sherab got Yutok the job there about a year ago, and Yutok, in turn, helped Tashi do the same.

Yutok remembers how Sherab described this situation. "The bosses love Tibetans," Sherab said. "Or people they think are Tibetan. They say we are *neat-and-clean*. They think we treat all their expensive, organic vegetables with loving kindness!" Sometimes Sherab drinks too much, but Yutok enjoys his sense of humor.

Yutok and Tashi started out as stock boys but worked their way up to tending the rooftop greenhouses. They spend their days growing organic lettuces, baby carrots, tomatoes, peppers. Although the work can be difficult—many hours bent over, shuffling along rows of seedlings on your knees—he likes the act of cultivation. As he works, he sometimes imagines the honeyed sweetness of his family's barley, the taste of village buckwheat. Rows of wheatgrass under plastic tarps on the top of a ten-story building seem an odd simulacrum of what it means to be a farmer, but that is how things are now.

Yutok gets dressed, drinks a glass of water, grabs his MetroCard and keys, and leaves the apartment. He steps out of his building onto Newkirk Avenue, heading for the Q train. The street cleaners passed through only minutes ago. The asphalt is alive with steam. It is already hot.

# THE GROUND BENEATH OUR FEET

The 7 train jostles and jolts like a Coney Island roller coaster. Suspended above the Brooklyn-Queens Expressway, tenements and strip malls, billboards tagged with graffiti, prewar rooflines with their turrets and gargoyles, I enter a world in which city blocks are countries unto themselves. Queens is a geography of perpetual transition. When people from Mustang who could not read English first arrived in this urban landscape and needed to navigate their way home, they told one another to follow the signs marked with a *thapje*, a frying pan: the letter Q.

I take my first trip to Jackson Heights in spring 2001, months before the 9/11 attacks that would shift American and global lexicons around words like "immigrant" and "Asian." I am on my way to the Himalayan Yak, the first restaurant of its kind in this polyglot neighborhood, for a meeting of the New York Mustang *kyidug*. This word combines happiness (*kyi*) with suffering (*dug*) and describes a community social service organization. The meeting is being convened by the District Development Committee chairman of Mustang to discuss the idea for a motorable road through the district. The meeting will be about politics, pride of place, and questions of development—half a world away.

The subway doors yawn open. Roosevelt Avenue disorients. I spend fifteen minutes scanning storefronts. A Sikh dentist offers teeth cleaning specials. An Ayurvedic pharmacy doubles as a video rental store. I hear Tagalog spoken at an intersection. Across the street is a Colombian *carnicería*. When I reach the Himalayan Yak, I pause, self-conscious. Am I dressed modestly enough? Hip enough? Should I be wearing a *chuba*?

The head of the *kyidug* and the chairman greet me at the door. A middle-aged man from Tshug is taking attendance. I sign my name on line 39. "Sienna" becomes *Si-ye-na* in hesitant Devanagari. By the time the program starts, more than fifty people will fill the room.

The event begins with the screening of a short video, produced in 1993, the year after Lo was opened to foreign tourists. Masked dancers twirl against the backdrop of the royal palace in Monthang and a piercing blue sky. The narrator speaks of hidden kingdoms, Buddhist treasures, exotic rituals.

"Is that Tibet?" one woman asks.

An image of King Jigme Dorje Palbar Bista in full ritual regalia flashes across the screen. "Is that some important lama?" asks another.

An ex-nun from Monthang raises her voice. "It is the *cham* at Tiji. That is Lo Gyalpo," she says, referring to the king. "Can you not recognize your own place? Your own people?"

The other woman is quick to respond. "How would I know what Monthang looks like? I've never been north of Kag!"

As the event proceeds, the chairman discusses plans for a "green road" that will stretch someday between Monthang and Beni Bazaar before joining the paved ribbon of highway leading to Pokhara. His diasporic constituents are surrounded with more roads than they can count, and yet they are ambivalent about the seemingly fantastical project in Mustang.

I am struck by the fact that I recognize the landscapes from which this group of Mustang New Yorkers hail with a different sense of detail and immediacy than some of them do, at least with respect to one another's hamlets, even as they can navigate Queens far better than can I. The scope of human experience depends so much on the boundaries of mobility, boundaries defined by political-economic circumstance and by social norms. You can get to Manhattan but not to Monthang.

The chairman speaks about the bridges he's had built and his goal to provide each Village Development Committee with two landlines by the end of that year—no small feat in the middle of a civil war. He makes a plea, in Jackson Heights, for people to donate toward the cost of a bulldozer—a *single* bulldozer—to help build the road in Mustang.

"The people of Mustang and other laborers have been digging this road by hand," says the chairman. He's written a proposal for Nepali Rs. 150,000 that was secured from the district budget, but they need an additional Rs. 200,000. His audience remains polite, if skeptical. Although his maternal lineage links to Lo and he speaks Logé, this chairman is Thakali—and a powerful Thakali at that. Those from Lo and Baragaon can be wary of Thakali control of trade and resources along the Kali Gandaki corridor. As I stand in line at the buffet, I ask a friend from Dzar what he thinks of the bulldozer idea. "Even in New York, it is Nepali politics. People question the hearts of leaders. We are always wondering if money will go to development or to their own pockets."

Conversations over *momo* and chow mein revolve around questions about how this road would be built, across high mountain passes, through the deepest gorge in the world. People discuss what they see as its benefits and drawbacks. It might allow easier access to health care, particularly in moments of emergency, and might be important when disasters, such as earthquakes, strike. It might decrease the costs of transporting Mustang's goods to lowland markets and bringing up commodities for local and tourist consumption. It might disrupt tourism, because foreigners like to walk, but they don't want to trek on a road. It might open up new tourist markets for Indian and Hindu Nepali pilgrims who want to experience the Muktinath *darshan* but not the walk. It could make Mustang a more important site of cross-border trade with China. It could make Loba more vulnerable to Chinese influence. It could encourage theft of objects that define Mustang's cultural and religious heritage. It could make people rich. It could make people feel poor.

Revisiting this meeting nearly two decades later leaves me with slow-motion whiplash. The road has been completed with state and donor resources. A journey between Monthang and Kathmandu that once took weeks can now be traveled in less than two days, notwithstanding landslides and punctured tires. There are bulldozers aplenty. Landlines are obsolete in a country that now has more cell phones than people. You can send instant messages from the Kora La, the pass that marks the Mustang border between Nepal and Tibet—never mind that your phone will switch over to China Central Time as you approach the concrete pillars that mark national boundaries. Each of the possible outcomes discussed with the chairman on that spring day in 2001 has come to pass, as have other impacts of the road that the collective imagination—both in New York and in Nepal—did not fully anticipate.

Roads are infrastructures of governance and mediums of time-space compression. A place that once felt vast, where journeys were measured in hours of walking or riding, seems smaller. Travel is calculated in liters of petrol, the click of odometers, the price of a ticket. An environment that once held a certain kind of quiet—save the lilt of horse bells and the sounds of water and wind—is now a cacophony of horns, car stereos, and the incessant rumble of construction equipment. While it is more convenient to cook on gas cylinders than firewood or dung, and while it certainly requires less effort to catch a ride than to walk, many Loba did not fully consider what this entrance into the fossil fuel economy would mean for rapeseed and barley, for horses and miniature donkeys, for water and waste. And people could not have known that the substance that marbles riverbeds in iridescent green-gold threads, that paints some rock faces in silvery white, is uranium, waiting to be mined.

The chairman, for his part, now owns a restaurant in northern California. A Congress Party man, he and his family were Maoist targets during the civil war. They left Nepal in the mid-2000s, seeking political asylum in America. Now that he is a U.S. citizen, the chairman returns to Mustang occasionally and remains invested, from a distance, in development endeavors: wind and micro-hydro, cash crops. The chairman's wife, who used to run the best hotel in Jomsom, has less interest in returning to Nepal, where she was deeply shaken by political violence and where, as she described when we saw each other in 2014, "Everything is finished, broken." In California, she has become a yoga aficionado, joining in *asana* competitions when she is not cooking lentils and curried vegetables in Wine Country.

There is an apartment building in Brooklyn known as *bahra bahra*, which means "twelve twelve" in Nepali. It indicates the street address. In 2001, a handful of people from Baragaon lived there. Some traveled from this residence to the Himalayan Yak for the meeting about the road. Now the entire building is peopled with Mustang households. Whole villages are contained within this tenement *dzong* of brick and stone. We remake geographies of dislocation into geographies of home.

## BORDER CONSCIOUSNESS

In September 2016, after the annual *tshongra*, a brief window of time when the international boundary between Nepal and China opens for commodity exchange, Kunzom, Yangjin, and I decide to visit the border. We set off in the early morning, by jeep, with a plan to pick up the abbot of Namgyal monastery on our way north. As we drive out of the walled city, I take in all manner of soil, sediment, and stone: a chalky mountain of borax, iron-colored gulches. Tibet rises in the distance, the plateau undulating like a fleet of camels. The notion of a border makes little sense here, for we are already somewhere else, but geopolitics instructs otherwise. This location has been the site of tension between two nation-states for decades, just as it has been a place of lucrative and sometimes contentious trade for centuries. Here, the "Tibet Question" is much more than hyperbole. Rather, it is a location where literal struggles for power and control have occurred.

Our jeep driver weaves through the cluster of single-story homes that make up the hamlet of Namgyal. He brings the vehicle to a stop at the foot of a massive monastery. "Be quick," he says.

We can't escape tea with the abbot or a tour of his institution, which is being renovated with funds from the Indian embassy. They seem to have spared no expense. Meanwhile, emissaries from China have, in recent years, invested in a new computer lab and other material improvements to the Nepali government high school in nearby Tshoshar—the one high school in Lo—and they have installed a 50-megawatt solar field in Monthang, out near where the horses once raced during Yartung, the midsummer harvest festival. Out near the sky burial site.

We stand on the roof of what will be the new monastic living quarters. The abbot tells stories about the marks Guru Rinpoche left on this landscape. These religious parables are colored with secular jokes. This Buddhist monk does not take himself too seriously. As he speaks of sacred geography, I think about the political machinations that scar this place: Chinese and Indian influences on Nepali sovereignty and culturally Tibetan ground.

As we descend from the top of the monastery down through the second and first floors, the abbot tells us that the hardwood pillars have come not from forests in southern Mustang but from Malaysia. "Jungle to desert," he laughs, his eyes bright with wonder.

We load up and head north again, along the seam of land that divides the eastern and western segments of Lo. Much of this wide valley has been taken over by boulders. In 1986, an up-valley glacial lake outburst flood sent tons of moraine tumbling down into this series of settlements, leaving stones the size of dinosaur eggs in its wake. People died. Animals perished. Fields were damaged beyond recognition. People remember this moment of dev-astation, but they struggle to find words to describe the sound.

As we drive, the abbot shares tales of his years of monastic education in India, his trips to Singapore and Taiwan to do rituals. "Buddhist countries, yes, but no good for people from the snow mountains. It was so hot. All I wanted was to be naked and plunge my body into some cold river," he says, breaking for laughter, "but nobody wants to see a naked monk!"

I take in the abbot, visage and countenance. He wears unlaced women's sneakers, size 7 hand-me-downs, scuffed at the toes. His polarized Ray-Bans shield eyes that sparkle. A fraying garnet pashmina is looped over his left shoulder and around his waist, protecting the belt of his kidneys, prone as they are to coldness. On his wrist, prayer beads; across his back and chest, a Patagonia down jacket. His baseball cap is the color of a corn kernel,

covering his shaved head. The only outward sign of trauma is the unevenness of his cheekbone when he smiles. Then, you can see the place where
skin parted and reformed as scar. He smiles often. His limp only reveals
itself when he walks quickly. It can almost be mistaken for a skip.

We travel up, up toward the vast and spare space that separates Nepal
from China. I think about what bodies remember, about what the body of
the land remembers.

At the customs post, we are greeted by guards. Although the post will,
in future years, be expanded in anticipation of new north-south transport
links across the Himalaya, right now it is a modest cluster of brick and
cement buildings. The wall that surrounds these structures comes up to the
chests of the guards and is fringed with shards of caramel-colored glass—
the fractured remains of repurposed beer bottles, sunk into cement that was
once wet.

The men look bored. One decides, on the pretense of "security," to join
us on our jaunt up to the Kora La. He climbs into the back of our jeep. He
is chatty, but each word is swallowed by his dust-soaked scarf. He speaks of
long winter days in late September and of the impossibility of this place. He
speaks of China's strength and his own state's weakness as if he were describing the opponents in a World Cup match. All odds and inevitability.

We climb and climb, the jeep's tires moving across switchbacks. Many
years ago, I approached another segment of the international boundary on
horseback during an excursion to the king's summer pastures. Then, as now,
we came across yak grazing on stubbly sedges. Then, as now, we saw the
shadowy outlines of yak hair tents on the horizon—the homes of the nomads
who live here. Then, as now, I was aware of how politics has reshaped the
lives of animals and people—specifically the closing of the border to trans-
humance after 1960. The practice of humans herding animals across land
was, for centuries, a core tenet of Tibetan and high Himalayan life. This way
of life was predicated on mobility, a more ecologically circumscribed but
no less important *khora* between summer and winter pasture. All of this
was threatened when, as many Loba put it, "China ate Tibet."

We crest our climb and approach the international boundary marker. An
elemental whir enlivens the world outside the tinted windows of the jeep.
Snow powders the western hills. Sun gallops in long strides across the eastern horizon. Straight ahead of us, stretching north, is the strip of earth that
stands for a road. It is all ruts and washboard bumps, ribboning across these
plains. Clouds move so fast that even a rainbow cannot keep up. The world
ripples in shadow and light. A gust mounts its assault and then subsides.

The only points of stillness are found in tussocks of grass and clusters of wildflowers, at once tough and delicate, awaiting the sandpapery tongues of yak.

We stop to take selfies at a hollowed-out *chöten* where, half a century earlier, an unarmed group of local men were fired on by soldiers of the People's Liberation Army, who killed one local and wounded several others. This moment of sovereign intrusion—Chinese soldiers on Nepali soil— flashed across American and British papers and then, like a bulb, burnt out. It remained an international embarrassment, an "incident," but one poorly remembered and often improperly retold.

"See the solar panel?" The abbot points in a northeasterly direction. "See that metal fence? Up on that hill? They are watching. Everybody wave to the Chinese!" The red-robed monastic leaps out of the car, although it is still moving slowly up the road. The driver brakes, curses, and then refuses to go farther.

"No problem. We walk!" This religious man, who carries joy, takes the hand of the Nepali customs agent and leads him off toward the concrete border marker. Kunzom and I follow them. Yangjin, conscious of the roughness that can come to hands and face from wind and sun, spends time bundling up: mittens on her fingers, a hood pulled over her head.

I scan the ridge. Tears stream from my eyes, not from sadness but from the meeting of air and flesh. Everything seems blurred around the edges, but I can make out the thread of wire fencing that runs across the horizon. It is much easier to spot the CCTV camera that, powered by photovoltaic cells, has no doubt tracked our movements. What do the people behind these cameras see?

Before the winter of 1999–2000, there was no fencing up here. But in January of the new millennium, a much younger monk than the one with whom we are traveling today, the seventeenth Gyalwang Karmapa, escaped from Tsurphu, his central Tibetan monastery, traveled west to this border, and crossed into exile. This was a devastating moment for the political apparatchiks in Beijing, since the Karmapa had been hailed both by His Holiness the Dalai Lama and by Chinese leadership as an authentic *tulku*, or reincarnate lama. Loba recall, with both pride and fear, their small but crucial role in helping to lead a spiritual master to a land of intellectual and religious freedom in India. (Now the Karmapa is married and splits his time between Himachal Pradesh and New Jersey.) The Nepali army and police— themselves in the midst of engaging Maoists in a civil war—were not pleased with this incident, given what it revealed about the lack of state vigilance and how it recalled geopolitical tensions during the Tibetan resistance era. In subsequent years, Loba said that Chinese and Tibetan agents began searching them for pictures of His Holiness during *tshongra*.

Soft power works on sovereignty at the border too. Starting in 2010, for several years, Chinese trucks bearing food aid—rice, barley, sugar, tea— came across the border and deposited these unnecessary and unrequested "gifts" in villages throughout Lo, as with other northern border regions of Nepal. People were not sure what to make of this. Unlike regions west of Mustang where food shortages and outright famine do occur, Mustang is not a food-deficit area. And yet many villages in Lo received burlap sacks filled with offerings of Chinese governmental largesse, stamped with the words "Tibet Development Aid." People wavered on whether or not they should eat this stuff or even feed it to their animals. Some used the grain to make alcohol. Others were wary of pesticides. Many wondered aloud about the karmic consequences of accepting Chinese aid. Interestingly, the same logic did not seem to apply to Tshoshar's high school computer lab or Mon- thang's solar panel field. When talking about these issues with a friend, he put the situation plainly: "The Chinese don't have to conquer us with their army, the way that they did to Tibet. They have already conquered us eco- nomically, with their money and their things."

Today, many in Mustang want the border to become a major commer- cial outpost as well as a new tourist route to Mt. Kailash and Lake Manosa- rovar in western Tibet. This stretch of land is certainly easier physical terrain to navigate than Humla's Limi Valley and the steep climb to Purang—the standard route from Nepal to these sacred pilgrimage sites. However, I find it difficult to imagine that the Chinese will allow such passage. The possi- bility of uranium mining, most likely to serve Chinese military markets, combined with the dynamics of depopulation and climate change leave me skeptical about a future hitched to tourism. But I could be wrong.

Farther down the road, much farther than we dare to walk, although we would still be on Nepali land, I see the faintest outlines of a gate. This silvery- blue apparition seems like a door to another world but also like an archway suspended in sky. It floats like the apple in Magritte's *Son of Man*. In 1964, when this painting was completed, Tibetan men fighting the Chinese here in Lo were boiling the soles of their shoes for soup, hanging their hopes on American assistance, and waiting for metal birds to drop bullets from the sky.

We walk on toward the border for some time and then retrace our steps. Above us, a lammergeier lilts and swoons, rapacious yet calm.

PROFIT AND LOSS

Twenty years ago, virtually no buildings stood outside Monthang's wall. This labyrinthine settlement was a sealed cell with one official entrance: a *chöten*-lined gate through which only the king could pass mounted. Today, it is as if two cities live on this land, one inside the confines of a more archaic order and another seeping out from the wall, a semi-permeable membrane through which property and influence flow, as if by osmosis. The circumambulation path that rings the wall has become a thoroughfare, paved with cobblestones and lined with cement culverts. Guest houses, schools, private homes, curio shops, and restaurants rim the town. You can order a cappuccino at the Kagbeni Lodge, even though this might require the restaurant owner to fire up the generator. Monthang's electrical supply is fickle. It comes in and out with the wind.

In the past, miniature donkeys, horses, and cows were herded out the gates of Monthang each morning and brought home by twilight. Now there is nary a donkey to be found, and although the other animals still roam Monthang's hillsides, the rhythm of animal sentience has all but been replaced by creatures that feed on diesel and petrol. Tractors make the rounds each week, collecting the town's discarded beer bottles and soda cans, plastic bags and cardboard boxes, only to dump, bury, or burn them in waste pits on the edges of town.

Yangzom flips omelets with the flick of a wrist. On this summer day in 2014, she's been in the kitchen since dawn, alongside the Tamang man she's hired to help run her guest house. Their establishment is neither the newest nor the fanciest hotel in Monthang, but it was the first to be cast in concrete. Yangzom's kitchen bears little resemblance to the spaces in which she learned to cook. Instead of an earthen stove fed by dung and brambles, to which chimneys were only added in the 1990s, she cooks with gas. Instead of a simple pantry stocked with barley, wheat, and buckwheat, some white flour, loose lentils, and sugar brought up from the lowlands, she stocks cans of tuna and Cadbury's cocoa, peanut butter, Nutella, spaghetti. Instead of relying on a copper cistern that must be filled by hand, water is now piped from a large tank on the roof into faucets affixed to a stainless-steel sink.

Yangjin and KC sit beside the proprietress, tossing gossip like a hot potato, before turning to the questions at hand—queries about agriculture, food, and tourism.

"It doesn't pay to grow things anymore," says Yangzom. Yangjin and KC nod. We have heard this refrain often. "We have to pay Rs. 600 per day, sometimes more, to each lowland laborer—and this doesn't even include the cost of food and alcohol! We keep planting fields, but fewer. It is cheaper to bring things from Pokhara than to grow," Yangzom continues. "But our food still tastes better."

Yangjin asks for an example. "Are you still growing *tsuk*?" She refers to rapeseed that people harvest for oil and fodder.

"We were until last year, but then we did the numbers and we stopped." Yangzom reaches for the calculator that she uses to tally up tourist bills. She pounds on the "clear" button with her index finger, then begins the math.

"This is what it costs to grow and harvest enough *tsuk* to make one jerry can of oil, counting labor, pressing, all of that." Her fingers fly, then come to rest on the number 8,000. "And this is what it costs to buy the same amount of oil and bring it from Pokhara." She types in the number 7,000.

"We'll probably always grow a field of wheat, barley, and buckwheat. Same with peas. We like eating them too much," says Yangzom. "But the rest? There is no benefit. Just like keeping animals. Look how much my husband loves horses. He used to live for them!" Yangzom's spouse made his small fortune as a horse trader. "Now, he just keeps enough horses for *pony trek*," Yangzom continues, referring to the practice of putting oversized foreigners on under-sized equines and leading them along trails for a hefty hourly fee. "The cost of fodder is high. Finding people to watch the animals is difficult."

This conversation prompts calculations. The first formula, located in the past, goes like this: Domestic animals graze on surrounding hillsides. Some of their dung fertilizes the grasslands. Other dung is collected, dried, and stored in homes for cooking fires. Hearth ash is used to "flush" human waste down dry toilets with the help of a little water ladled by hand. This mix creates rich organic fertilizer, which is then used on fields, which are themselves irrigated in strictly monitored rotations. After harvest, when summer and early autumn give way to colder, shorter days, domestic animals graze on agricultural stubble, gleaning sustenance and depositing natural fertilizer on the fields in what you might call a neat ecological loop. This is not to romanticize the work involved in keeping this system going. Women and children are responsible for collecting dung and firewood, for fetching water from streams and village taps, and, often, for shepherding animals. This labor can get in the way of other things, including school. Dung and wood smoke damage lungs. Pulling up brambles for kindling can hasten soil erosion.

Now consider this differential equation, located in the present: Far fewer domestic animals graze on hillsides. Far fewer people—mostly poor locals and lowland laborers—collect and process dung to fuel those hearths that have not switched to gas, itself bought in cash and brought up in vehicles that run on fossil fuels. Those dung-fueled hearths that remain in Lo no longer produce sufficient ash to operate dry toilets, and sawdust from the hotel construction boom cannot make up for this loss in organic matter. Meanwhile, everyone knows that tourists want to shit while sitting on porcelain bowls and flush the waste away with copious amounts of water. Hotel proprietors have installed indoor plumbing and septic tanks. They supply toilet paper. After a few years, the septic tanks must be pumped out. And, while the demands for irrigation water have diminished—what with all the fallow fields—a certain life force has also begun to dwindle, itself a product of elemental imbalance: of water and wind, of earth and fire, but also of consciousness.

## VALUING HERITAGE

We leave the warmth of a kitchen in Tsarang and walk toward the village's monastery. It is late September 2016. The harvest is winding down, but most people are still out in their fields. Dogs are fierce here, untethered. We carry stones in our palms and talk loudly as we round corners.

Tsarang is the second largest settlement in Lo. The village sits on a plain between two river valleys: the Kali Gandaki to the east and a glacial tributary to the northwest. The village's borders are marked by elaborate *chöten* and the presence of two massive structures: the palace and the monastery.

The palace, a whitewashed five-story edifice, dates to the fifteenth century. Its libraries once housed gilded statues and Buddhist texts, including a copy of the *kangyur*, the 108 volumes recording the words of the Buddha, written in gold leaf. Now, although the physical structure has been repainted and reinforced, the lucrative trade in religious antiquities combined with disuse have left the palace a shell of its former self.

The monastery is painted vermillion. A wall snakes around it, striped in earthen pigments: white for Avalokitesvara, charcoal for Manjushree, and red for Vajrapani. This triad, Rigsum Gompo, are *dharma* protectors. The monastery's founding is associated with the visit to Lo in 1427 of Sakya Norchen Kunga Sangpo, one of the most esteemed religious teachers of that era.

At the monastery gates, we are greeted by the low, lazy growl of a mastiff and the clamor of monklets leaving the prayer hall. They search for their sandals, hungry for tea and *tsampa* after morning recitations. The *umdze*, or chant master, and another senior monk, a *geshe* in charge of monastic education, are inside. Sunlight bisects the dark interior. Great beams of dust-soaked luminescence shine from the second-story windows like lasers. The *umdze* is directing traffic.

"Careful with that one," he says, as two novices maneuver through the hall with what looks like—indeed what once was—a tree trunk. "Set it to the side!" he barks.

Rows of low cushions and tables have been pushed toward the outer walls. The area in front of the main shrine has been taken over by a growing stack of PVC pipes, each of which contains *thangka*, scroll paintings. These are centuries-old works of silk and hand-stitched brocade of deities rendered in cinnabar and lapis lazuli.

At the height of its prominence, the Tsarang monastery was said to have housed more than a thousand monks. While some traveled from nearby culturally Tibetan regions to receive their monastic education, most were from Mustang families. Today, the monastery's novices number about fifty, the majority of whom hail from regions other than Mustang.

Two monklets pry open the duct taped ends of one of the PVC pipes. They extract and unroll a gorgeous piece of art in devastating condition. They place the *thangka* on a tarpaulin spread across the wide-planked wooden floor.

"Look at this one," the *geshe* comments. "It is Kagyud. But instead of a Kagyud lama with his hundred-thousand *bodhisattva*, it is a Kagyud lama with his hundred-thousand shits!" The *umdze* erupts in laughter. "We like to talk about being *rimé*," he says, speaking of non-sectarian Tibetan Buddhism, "but we still like to crap on each other. . . . This time the birds and mice have done it for us!" He snaps a picture of this painting with his rose gold iPhone.

Kunzom has an equally sharp tongue. She respects these senior monastics for their liturgical knowledge, but she has little tolerance for inept monastic management. "You call yourself a Buddhist?! How have you let things get like this?"

"Ah, I see we have the wrathful form of *khandro* Kunzom here with us today," the *umdze* answers with a smirk.

"Seriously, what made you decide to open all of these paintings today? Did these young ones have nothing else to do, no studying?" She gestures toward the novices, who keep their mouths shut and their heads down. "And are you making a list of these things or just counting the moth holes?"

"If we make a list of all we have, it is just an invitation to thieves." This is an argument many here have made before, a narrative with a long social history, one tied to the opening up of Lo to foreign tourism in the early 1990s but also the illicit sale of the region's artistic treasures to museums and private collectors in Europe, North America, and elsewhere.

"That is crazy thinking," Kunzom responds. She has worked with leading scholars of Tibetan art on projects aimed at documenting the material heritage of Lo. "If you have a proper *inventory*," she says, using the English word, "you would be able to stop thieves and learn more about your own history. Or are you too busy with WeChat and your trips to Singapore?"

The *umdze*'s face flashes with anger. "And you would do what? Make an exhibition of these things in some foreign country? Put them under glass?"

"Either way, many of these things are going to end up somewhere else. Why not know where? Why not have some control over how?" Kunzom responds.

The value of Mustang's material heritage and its stewardship are polarizing topics. Some egregious robberies have occurred—from monasteries, from the consecrated centers of *chöten*, from cave complexes—in the past and the present. At the same time, millions of dollars and two decades of foreign and local labor have been invested in restoring Lo's most impressive architectural and artistic religious monuments. This work, while well intentioned, has been controversial. It has provided valuable training in *thangka* painting and art restoration for some but has left others wondering who "owns" places like Monthang. Simultaneously, people from Lo and Baragaon have invested their own resources in creating new temples, monuments, and community centers, not only in Mustang but also in Pokhara and Kathmandu. Fundraising efforts and real estate searches are afoot for such a place in Queens.

Still, questions of form and function remain. Statues and *thangka* have been stolen and sold, as have *sung*, consecrated relics placed inside statues as well as *chöten*, to sanctify them. Meanwhile, new statues are commissioned in Nepal and brought to New York to grace household shrines. Some are consecrated, but others stand hollow—for lack of time and energy, for lack of resources, if not for lack of faith.

THE SHAPES OF WATER (A *HUNDREDS* REDUX)

Hardly any snow fell in Lo during the winters of 2014 and 2016, but rain soaked through September, damaging crops. Flat roofs are made for shoveling, not for deluge. In winter 2015, Lobsang posts a picture of horses cresting a mountain pass, gaskin-high in the remains of a blizzard. Winter 2019 was a wolf: it ravaged yak, sheep, goats, horses. I have watched the face of Nilgiri for twenty-five years, intermittently. The mountain has molted from white to black. This is a different kind of calving than icebergs, signaling the birth of a new *abnormal*, here at the Third Pole.

Kathmandu newspapers call residents of Dhe and Samdzong "climate refugees." Glacial streams cease to flow, desiccating groundwater reservoirs. Algae overtakes a drinking source. Villagers become subjects of relocation. Dhe's move proceeds from the grassroots. A new village sprouts at lower elevation where apples grow, thanks to solar pumps that harvest the Kali Gandaki's flow. Samdzong's resettlement is contentious. Lo royalty gifts land, but *ra-lug* prefer higher pastures. Water rights remain unresolved. And without water, no life.

Sometimes there is too much water. In 2011, a suspension bridge was stretched across the Panda Khola. Before this, reaching Lubrak when the river swelled was tricky. People called the river "crazy." Rain has always riled up this aquatic creature. Now, the creature of monsoon is less predictable. Downpour doesn't necessarily forecast flash flood. River ravaged the hem of this village in summer 2017, ripping out fields and drowning the seventy-year-old *chöten* that marked Lubrak's twelfth-century founding. What water gives, water can also take away.

October 2012. Sandy. Nawang sends a picture of Loba praying, taken inside a Brooklyn home. No electricity means no tea, but *mani* happens anyway. Nawang's uncle: "New York is our place now. We must honor *yul lha* here, in times of disaster." Village gods can travel. Elemental imbalance begets practice: a reckoning, a form of insurance. I wonder about other kinds of insurance and the crumbling infrastructures on which Mustang New Yorkers build their future.


POPLAR AND JUNIPER

Some decades ago, if you had visited the hamlets of Tshoshar and Tshonup, you would have encountered a virtually treeless landscape of cliffs, caves, and sparse fields. In fact, Tshoshar comprised a series of half-cave, half-built structures. Small verandas extended out from grottos, their inner walls lacquered patent leather black from years of dung smoke and butter lamps. In Tshoshar today, some villagers still live in these hybrid cave-homes, but many have moved out into settlements, some of which were re-formed after the glacial flood of the mid-1980s.

For all the ways that Mustang has abandoned cliff dwelling, caves remain a fundamental feature. Here and in nearby settlements, teams of anthropologists, archaeologists, and mountain climbers have found the human remains of Himalayan ancestors, illuminated manuscripts, treasure palaces of religious art, death masks wrought from precious metals, Silk Road beads, Buddhist figurines that predate what was thought to be the official arrival of the *dharma* in this place, and compelling evidence for the Tibetan plateau's pre-Buddhist past, as described in a 2017 *NOVA* documentary, provocatively titled "Secrets of the Sky Tombs."

Yet while caves remain a constant across Mustang, trees have transformed this place.

When I first visited Tshoshar in the mid-1990s, ACAP's tree planting efforts were nascent. Locals were skeptical about the benefits of these skinny little saplings planted near streams. Few people grasped the long view: a world where dappled shade might interrupt the intensity of sun, where domestic animals could be fed on culled branches, where roots would guard against erosion, and where these swiftly growing, spine-straight columns could be turned into income. Although ACAP's reputation in Mustang remains mixed, this eco-development is one that many people view as a success.

Yangjin was a child when this tree planting began. While visiting her home in Tshoshar in the summer of 2012, I pull out my computer and show her a photograph that my stepfather took of the area in 1996. She gasps. "My god! It looks like a desert. There is nothing. No green." Now, more than twenty years later, stalks of barley pulse to the same rhythm as waving switches of Himalayan poplar (*Populus ciliata*), or what in Nepali are known as *bhote pipal*. In high summer, the land undulates like an emerald sea. Come autumn, the sea turns gold.

Gold is an apt analogy, for these trees have become a form of currency. One small poplar beam brings in roughly the same profit as a sheep. The sale of ten poplar trunks can cover a term of boarding school tuition. Investing in a plantation could, over time, pay for a jeep. Poplar presents a much easier prospect for profit and use than the pine that grows in southern Mustang and in neighboring districts to the south. Hotel construction has further enhanced the value of these quick-growing deciduous trees, even as trees themselves are being overtaken in some construction projects by cement.

*Populus ciliata* might be an exotic species in Nepal and across the Tibetan Plateau, but it has come to feel native. And this is precisely the point of their planting, on a much grander scale, across Tibet. I recall a conversation with Namdul, the late King of Lo's Lord Chamberlain. His mother immigrated to Lo from Shigatse in the 1950s, along with the woman who would become the queen. Given the timing, Namdul's mother was never able to return to Tibet. But he accompanied the Lo royal family on a sojourn there in 2002. In speaking of this trip, he recalls how the queen could not recognize anything. "She said that everything she knew had been remade with roads and trees."

Stands of poplar line the tiled streets of Lhasa and the banks of the Yarlung Tsangpo. Cadres of agricultural workers, mostly immigrants from other parts of China, propagate, plant, irrigate. That poplars grow quickly and with a high germination rate, that they take well to sandy, loamy soil, and that they need both moisture and sun to flourish have aided in rewriting the story of the ground in Mustang and across China's Tibet. In addition to roads, schools, and medical clinics, these trees are often cited as an index of development. They embody a civilizing impulse.

But there are other trees in Mustang and in Tibet. These trees have been used to meet material needs, but their history bespeaks Earth's consecrated nature, its sacredness. These are junipers.

Gnarled with ruddy, reddish bark, sometimes dwarfed in stature, *Juniperus recurva* is a Himalayan native from northern Pakistan to Yunnan Province, China. The tree thrives at high altitude. It depends on wind for pollination between male and female specimens. *Shukpa*, as juniper is called, is one of the raw materials used to make Tibetan incense.

Tibetan textual histories, particularly of places like Reting, tell us that these trees are divine. Located in a valley north of Lhasa, Reting not only shelters a sacred juniper grove but also is the seat of the Kadam lineage of Tibetan Buddhism, later enfolded within the Gelug school, from which the Dalai and Panchen Lamas emerge. Consecutive incarnations of the Reting Rinpoche played very important roles in the searches for successive Dalai Lamas, and this figure of the head of Reting Monastery has been included in many high-profile controversies in modern Tibetan history. Tibetologist Ulrike Roesler writes that the roots of Reting's 21,000 junipers are intertwined; specific trees stand for individual Buddhist masters; layers of juniper bark represent the seven *gyalwa*, or "victorious ones" who will teach humanity in the age of degeneration; other Reting junipers represent precious substances—crystal, gold, copper, turquoise—and mark the four directions; some trees reveal the face of Yama, Lord of Death; other trees are known to have sprouted from hair of the Tibetan king, Songtsen Gampo, which was cut and scattered at Reting.

Smoke from juniper incense or even the earthy blue-green fronds themselves have long been used for *sang*, fumigation offerings. From pre-Buddhist times to the present, juniper stills the fluctuations of the mind. The tree associates with springs, abodes of *lu*, the serpent spirits that, like the junipers themselves, crave clean water and sheltered places. And, like *lu*, they do not appreciate disturbance.

As Roesler recounts in her history of Reting, local monks say that one of the junipers tried to protect the monastery when Mao Zedong's Red Guards fired at the buildings. In another contemporary story, when Chinese soldiers began cutting one tree, a *lu* merged from under the tree and scared off the soldiers. The soldiers tried to kill the *lu* and, in the process, split the trunk. An ecologist would tell you that this split occurred well before the time when Red Guards came to Tibet, probably from a lightning strike. Still, the arboreal scar is a way to remember the human capacity to injure and to blame.

Ancient juniper forests are found in Mustang, particularly on stretches between Samar and Ghami. Most people describe it as a tree in decline—a decline they attribute to the presence of the Tibetan resistance soldiers in the region during the 1960s and 1970s. Of course, it is convenient to assign the responsibility for a species' decimation to a desperate group of people who are no longer present. It is less convenient to accept responsibility for deforestation yourself.

ACAP staff and some local farmers are trying to revive Mustang's juniper forests. This is an act of conservation and an act of faith. An ACAP officer with whom I spoke in 2016 said, "We must collect seeds and keep them in the apple orchards as seedlings. Soil needs to be a mix of 75 percent clay, 25 percent sand. Each little tree needs a metal fence to protect it, and we need people to water them in summer. It will take some commitment, but it is possible to reforest." I appreciate his optimism with respect to restoration ecology, but I keep wondering about life beneath the surface, about the worlds of soil and bacteria, of slope and aspect, of pH and micronutrients, of serpent spirits and the ways people scar land. In 2018, bulldozers severed junipers limb by limb as they built the road. People collected the remains of these trees and vowed to use them. It felt like tidying up after a massacre.

In a story called "She Unnames Them," published in 1985 in *The New Yorker*, the writer Ursula K. Le Guin speaks of "unnaming" animals and plants, by which she means stripping them of language we have foisted upon them for our use and benefit. A yak, after all, does not need the word "yak" to know itself, Le Guin reminds her readers. This is a radically imaginative act that decenters the human. She ends this piece by speaking of trees: "My words now must be as slow, as new, as single, as tentative as the steps I took going down the path away from the house, between the dark-branched, tall dancers motionless against the winter shining." As I read her description of these sentient beings, my mind conjures junipers.

## TENTS AS A CAUTIONARY TALE

Nawang calls me from New York. His voice cracks. "My mother is cold. She is sleeping on the ground," he says. After many hours of trying, he had finally been able to reach someone in the village with a phone and to speak with his mother. "Everyone is scared. Some are afraid to leave their houses. Others won't go back inside."

The days following Nepal's devastating 7.8 magnitude earthquake on April 25, 2015, pass in a blur of sleeplessness and Facebook scrolling. I ache to be there. Yet I also realize that I will be more help from a distance, raising awareness and funds for affected communities. Images tumble in of familiar landmarks now leveled and hundreds of thousands of Nepalis racked by grief and shock. I know these pictures are partial representations of reality, but they still disturb. The internet becomes a strange safety net, catching those of us tied to Nepal as we fall into new forms of connection.

Minutes after I speak with Nawang, a Facebook post reveals that an old friend, someone who had spent many years in Kathmandu and now lives in the U.S., has tents to send to Nepal. I reach out, asking if twenty tents can be sent to Ghiling. This friend knows Nawang, and when I tell her that it is an effort to help his community, she agrees. I mention that physicians from my small New England town are heading to Nepal soon and that they are willing to take the tents. These physicians have spoken of airline baggage waivers—promissory notes against further suffering.

For most of Nepal's roughly 30 million people, living with uncertainty is old hat, given the legacies of political instability and civil war, the dynamics of out-migration, the economics of social difference, and the nature of nature from the plains to the high mountains. However, the spring of 2015 tore into lives and landscapes, exacerbating fault lines of inequality and prompting new forms of national solidarity. Official numbers put the death toll around 9,000, with more than 700,000 homes destroyed or damaged and about 2.5 million people internally displaced. The immediate news from

Mustang is that although there were no deaths, there was destruction. The two most impacted villages in Mustang were Ghiling, where Nawang is from, and Namgyal, a hamlet north of Monthang. Between them, about a hundred structures were damaged or destroyed.

Two days after talking to my friend, twenty six-person tents arrive at my office. They are called, somewhat ironically, the Eureka model. If they hadn't been donated, I would call them an impulse buy. A colleague helps me carry them up from the delivery truck. I clear a corner of my office, stacking the sleek, mineral gray duffels against the wall. Each one weighs twenty-five pounds. Two can fit into a suitcase. Four will max out the international baggage allotment on passenger airlines. Meanwhile, the physicians' baggage waivers fail to materialize. Suddenly, the weight of these gifts feels enormous. The cluster of pristine shelters in my office makes me regret my decision. I think about Madeleine L'Engle's tesseract from *A Wrinkle in Time*. I wish that I could use my mind to bend matter and beam these polyester folds across the world.

When I call Nawang to tell him that the tents have arrived but that the baggage waivers have fallen through, he is devastated. Like so many people living far-away-so-close to this catastrophe, Nawang is desperate to get these shelters to his village. He considers using funds he has been raising in New York for Ghiling's reconstruction to pay airline fees. However, the logic of this choice falls away quickly. Even if the tents get to Kathmandu, they still have to reach Ghiling. There might be a road to Mustang, but sending these temporary shelters to the village requires additional time, money, and goodwill. I am angry at myself for falling into a habit of mind that so often characterizes humanitarian aid and development failure—energy and resources expended without giving rise to their intended effects.

Nawang and I try to determine what to do with these material gifts that have quickly become existential burdens. As solace and as strategy, I turn to Elaine Scarry's *Thinking in an Emergency*. A colleague who works in Haiti, and who lived through a similar experience after the 2010 earthquake, recommends it. I devour this slim volume. Scarry instructs, "The habits of everyday life often fail to serve in an emergency. But in the absence of our ordinary habits, a special repertoire of alternative habits may suddenly come forward."

Meanwhile, these tents take on a social life of their own. Four travel from New Hampshire to Kathmandu with the medical relief team, who agree to pay the extra baggage costs. Four are sent to a friend in Wyoming who is heading to Nepal. Two go with a Nepali Dartmouth student, going home to help.

The pile grows smaller. Still, I cannot shake the irony that I am now shuttling a petroleum product in the form of shelter from place to place, using fossil fuel to do so, in the hopes of providing emergency relief in the wake of a natural disaster that some interpret as Earth's enraged response to all we are doing to her.

That leaves ten.

Nawang convinces a friend in New York to take them to Kathmandu. This time, baggage waivers are secured. But the friend is in New York, and the tents are in Hanover. I call our local coach service, which runs between the Connecticut River Valley and Grand Central Station. They will not carry the tents. "I'm sorry, ma'am," says the coach representative, "but we cannot accept unaccompanied baggage." In our not-so-new world order, I cannot send tents alone to New York in the barrel of a bus.

So, Nawang comes from New York to collect this cargo. We shove as many as we can into travel-worn duffels that have made the trek between the U.S. and Nepal many times. To put these virgin shelters into such seasoned containers is, at some level, to prepare them for the journey ahead: across oceans, into the stream of Kathmandu traffic on the backs of motorcycles, along the potholed Prithvi Narayan Highway to Pokhara, up toward Beni Bazaar in a battered bus, past waterfalls and the imminent threat of landslides, around switchbacks of cornmeal-colored powdery earth, alongside juniper forests, and, finally, home.

Some weeks later, I receive a picture from Nawang's younger brother, who helped to send the tents north from Kathmandu. The soft luminescence of a solar bulb, salvaged from a home and strung up inside this 10-by-10-foot shelter, reveals a dozen schoolchildren laying cheek by jowl, playing games and watching videos on mobile phones, sheltered from the dust and noise of deconstruction and adult discussions about rebuilding. The tents serve a purpose, albeit one that is no longer directly connected to their initial impetus: a son's desire to staunch a mother's vulnerability, a body sleeping on disturbed ground.

The earthquakes' aftermath unfurls over weeks and months. Nawang makes T-shirts with the slogan "I Am Helping to Rebuild Nepal" and sells them at fundraising events in Queens and Brooklyn. Along with others from the New York *kyidug*, he helps to raise nearly $100,000 in relief, some of which goes to Ghiling.

When Nawang arrives in Ghiling some months later, he learns that many other tents made it to his village: bulky olive-colored army shelters, used as communal kitchens and rendered slick with grease and smoke; white festival tents, their felicitous brocade belying the seriousness of their purpose; trekking equipment bought for outrageous sums; simple lean-tos of blue tarpaulin, distributed by Buddhist relief organizations and representatives of Nepali political parties.

As much as I view the tents critically—a cautionary tale against rapid action decoupled from careful thinking—they are also reminders that the possibility for charity is only ever as good as the nimbleness of implementation; that commodity chains come to live in the people and machines that carry things; that "relief" is a synonym for the Nepali phrase *milaune manche*, meaning "those who get things done."

The skies crackle and roar with monsoon that summer of 2015. Clouds bloat and groan like bellows. There is an eerie symmetry to it all: avalanche as downpour, thunderstorm as quake. This sense of precarity worsens in the coming months, as a political crisis over Nepal's newly promulgated constitution leads to a five-month blockade of the Nepal-India border. The blockade, in turn, causes the skyrocketing of commodities prices—essential medicines and cement, cooking gas and petrol, onions, biscuits, and soap—and sets everyone on edge.

In Lo, members of the Tshoshar Youth Club trek to Gyakar Tsho, a glacial lake tucked into the folds of Mustang's trans-Himalayan ridges. The massive flood in the mid-1980s is on everyone's mind. I watch a video of young men traversing moraine, depositing *chinlab*, blessed substances, at the edge of the lake, at the glacier's skirt. They do this to honor and appease local deities, "to keep the glacier happy," a friend explains. "To keep it in place." Sacred geography ground-truths environmental precarity.

To feel the instability of the ground beneath our feet is not metaphoric. In a geophysical and karmic sense, we are *all* living in a state of temporary protected status. Still, some remain much more vulnerable than others.

Earthquakes remind us that the borders between built space and ecologies are permeable. To know Himalayan history is to cultivate an engagement with this animate earth. To reckon damage and destruction is to realize how cosmological and physical structures—from sacred mountains to household shrines—undergird social life, even in and through diaspora. Still, recovery is messy. It takes a long time. It is a process that demands *upaya* (skillful means) and methods of action that emerge from wisdom and compassion.

At least that is the ideal. But to practice *upaya* is no small thing. As I think of our imperfect efforts, lines from Leonard Cohen's song "Anthem" fill my head:

> Ring the bells that still can ring
> Forget your perfect offering
> There is a crack in everything
> That's how the light gets in.

To crack open is not to succumb but to sense our way through, however we can.

### STONES AND SILENCE

The three o'clock jeep from Monthang swings through Ghiling. From the second floor of the Kunga Guest House, where we are having tea, I watch the vehicle careen into town. This is the last jeep of the day heading south, on the last day of my Upper Mustang permit in 2016. We need to catch this ride.

We shout. We whistle. The owner of the guest house frantically dials what he thinks is the driver's number. But none of these efforts slow the vehicle: a tin can on wheels, hurtling through space to the hip-hop rhythms of Drake.

Two minutes later, the jeep has passed up and over the ridge leading from Ghiling toward Syangbochen. We are left in its wake. A cow's muffled mastication. A woman's labored breathing, under the load of buckwheat on her back.

Kunzom spends the next half hour pacing along one of the neat walls that mark agricultural territory, a barrier made of round stones. She curses and shouts into her phone. "I don't care if you thought we weren't here. We had reserved seats. Paid you for them this morning! That good-for-nothing driver didn't even slow down!" Kunzom's head comes to my shoulders. She wears a size five shoe. I could carry her up a mountain if I had to, but there is nothing diminutive about her. People say she is just like her older brother; however, to be sharp-tongued and persuasive is not a compliment when you're a woman.

Yangjin and KC huddle into each other, scrolling through photos on their phones. Unlike previous field seasons, KC will stay in Ghiling, helping her mother and aunts through the harvest. Her city hands have calloused, her skin has darkened under mountain sun. Yangjin is returning with Kunzom and me to Kathmandu.

I sit, watching light grow golden across the Annapurna massif. There are worse places to be. We could wait for another vehicle, or we could walk. The plan has been to reach Kag by evening. But that possibility requires moving through the landscape at a steady four-wheel-drive clip.

"Let's go," Kunzom announces. "They're sending up another jeep from Tsele, but we should start walking. It will take a couple of hours." She does not need to say that any distance we can cover now will mean less driving in the dark down that zipper of road carved out of a cliff.

I recall an incident that occurred while this stretch of road was being built. Massive boulders tumbled down atop a bulldozer, crushing it and killing the two workers in its cab. A third worker narrowly escaped. People attributed this tragedy to inexperience and second-rate engineering, but they also saw this accident as the manifestation of *sabdak* and *tsen* wrath—local deities whose habitats were disturbed by the construction and who were taking revenge.

We gather backpacks, secure hats with scarves, hug KC goodbye, and set off. I am happy to be walking. The slowed pace allows for memories: of mule trains and deep breaths, of wind and time. I am young and old here, by turns. Kunzom and I first walked this road together twenty years ago, when Yangjin and KC were pre-pubescent village girls with very different prospects, when the notion of a motor road remained an abstraction, when the King of Lo still branded sheep and bathed horses in the high pastures at the start of summer. Twenty years before that, people made the trip from Monthang to Kathmandu once a year for winter trading, if at all. And twenty years before that, venturing south inspired people to instruct those left behind in the distribution of property, the care of children. Who knew what awaited in the lowlands?

Echoes of the heart are not nostalgia.

We walk up a chalky hillside, past the *chöten* that marks Ghiling's edge. Kunzom calls us to a shortcut, and we scramble up a ridge toward a small pass. A young boy catches up with us. His navy blue trousers hang above his ankles, though his loafers seem to fit. He is a *rongba* adoptee of a local family who run a lodge in Syangbochen, and he attends the Ghiling school, class five. Sometimes he hitches a ride to or from school in a local jeep or on the back of a motorcycle. More often than not, he walks. With the short-cut, it is an hour each way. The nylon cords of his book satchel cut into his shoulders, but that doesn't slow his pace. I struggle to keep up with him. Kunzom and Yangjin walk more slowly up the mountain.

The boy and I sit together at the top of the ridge. I offer him a sliver of dark chocolate. In the distance, snowcapped peaks rim a fuchsia sky.

The boy runs down the other side of the mountain, toward home. By the time we arrive at the lodge, he has shed his uniform for a Boston Red Sox hoodie and is slurping instant noodles. A few minutes later, we hear a horn. Our jeep has arrived. We grab our things. Kunzom attempts to pay the woman of the house for our tea and is refused.

Thirteen people in a jeep is an unbearable, if standard, practice. Four people in a jeep feels luxurious. We head south, our young driver navigating the switchbacks toward Bhena to the soundtrack of a Tibetan love song. Dusk brings a sense of stillness, even as we move. The outlines of junipers and musk roses texture the long shadows of evening.

"Stop!" Kunzom commands. "Stop the car." We all jump in our seats.

"What's wrong?" I ask.

"Look over there, under that rock. Get out of the car slowly." Kunzom's voice is commanding, even at a whisper.

"What is it?"

"Snow leopard." Kunzom points to a dappled boulder, the size of a small car, positioned about fifty feet from the road. "Just underneath."

It takes a moment for my eyes to adjust to the low light. Then I see the creature. The cat's ears flick: twin pyramids on the horizon of its face. A spotted tail wraps around a muscled body. We wonder at the animal. The animal tracks us. It lounges, regal and perfectly camouflaged.

Twenty years ago, snow leopard numbers had sunk low across the Himalaya. Like wolves, they killed livestock. Like musk deer and black bear, they fetched a handsome price when dead. Now, after two decades of strict conservation policy combined with out-migration and decreasing numbers of domestic animals, the population is surging.

In 2016, in the village of Marang, it was said that a snow leopard mother and her two cubs killed more than one hundred goats in one murderous evening. Eyewitness claimed that at least half of the goats had died by stampede, suffocated under the weight of their brothers' fear. Other villagers believed that even three snow leopards could not have done so much damage. They spoke of *hri*, vampires.

"Are you not scared, *didi*?" the driver asks Kunzom as we observe the animal, and the animal considers us.

"No, *bhai*," she answers. "Not scared." We stand, sheltered by stones and silence, watching this inscrutable being as last light bleeds from the sky.

In Tibetan, wrathfulness also bespeaks protection.

We climb back into the jeep and make our way to Tshug in the dark.

# PART VI

# LOSS AND TRANSFORMATION

Bring a heart that barters; that is not afraid to split.

—TSERING WANGMO DHOMPA, "HOME, A TRANSITIVE"

IN THE *KHORA* OF MIGRATION, AS WITH THE *KHORA* OF SENTIENT
existence, an end signals a beginning. To what extent are the ends of kinship bound up with the ends of life? How are enduring rituals refashioned

in the wake of new mobilities? And how is this refashioning of collective action also a rebirth of identity and belonging?

People from Mustang create and recreate community through movement. But what does this mean for elders—people who move more slowly or who shy away from travel? Ways of being in the world that might seem distinctly American are reclaimed and recast to serve new needs, in Nepal and New York. Patterns of culture from one side of the world infiltrate the other. Change and continuity, like loneliness and communion, live as two halves of the same reality. Whether in a Mustang village, Kathmandu, or New York, families and larger social networks reach out to one another. Sometimes the language of a grandfather is no longer the language of a grandson, but to pour tea or hold the crook of an elbow is to practice a grammar of care. Many languages are necessary. Sometimes none feels sufficient. Like tea, these transformations are bitter and sweet.

Like "Blood and Bone," the first story in this book, "Three Seasons in the Fire Monkey Year" is a tale of three women in three locations. The women are all seventy-two years old in 2016. One lives in Kathmandu, another in Jackson Heights, and the third in the village of Ghiling. These narratives illustrate what it means to age; they also present questions about what it means to "age in place" and demonstrate how older individuals are cared for by younger generations and, increasingly, caring for one another.

The final ethnographic chapter, "Between Presence and Absence," marks the passing of time, of certain relational forms, and of people. The scene of a village funeral meets an unexpected death in New York. Folded within these losses are examples of how those from Mustang do not turn away from suffering, including that which can come at the end of life. Rather, people embody practices that are Himalayan, Buddhist, and American as they make sense of loss and honor one another through different forms of death— literal and cultural experiences of great transformation. Sometimes the care such moments require is accomplished virtually: messages sent as data and pixels to draw one's kindred close. Other times, care is practiced in the flesh: in the circle of a dance, in the performance of ceremony.

# THREE SEASONS IN THE FIRE
# MONKEY YEAR

In the early days of the Fire Monkey year, a damp fog blankets Boudha, on the easterly edge of the Kathmandu Valley. Given her cataracts, Sonam does not notice. She bears this milky quality of vision without remark. Like the ache in her knees, this is simply a body experiencing age. She is a grandmother, after all.

This morning, like each morning when it is not raining, Sonam walks out the metal gate of the house her son purchased with money he earned driving a taxi in New York; past the dogs sleeping beside the garbage pile, curled around one another for warmth, their mange a reminder that she is fortunate to have two legs, a conscious mind, humanness; past the shuttered butcher shops with their lazy flies that dot bloodstained concrete and, even so, make her hungry for meat; past the kiosks selling prayer beads, *kathag*, and incense with its hint of sandalwood sweetness; past the Tamang women who scoop butter into brass lamps and twirl cotton whisks between their teeth, dawn light glinting off the golden rings in their noses; until she comes face-to-face with the *stupa*.

Sonam's palms touch and move to her head-mouth-heart, prayer beads gathered in the gap between her fingers. She blows warm breath on cool orbs of hardwood and the little metal tassels on this rosary. Sonam's gesture—to touch her folded hands to head-mouth-heart—is an embodied act that signals body-speech-mind, *kon chog sum*, the three jewels of *buddha*, *dharma*, *sangha*. There is so much wrapped up in this plain act, announcing her place in the family of beings.

Sonam enters the clockwise flow of morning circumambulation. Placing her prayer beads in her right hand, she walks and prays. She feels the fog through her aprons, in her joints. The slate pathway and red brick gutters encircling the *stupa*'s girth have been swept clean. Pigeons gawk and coo, a great gray swarm of feathers. Custodians of this sacred place scoop corn kernels from plastic buckets and scatter them across the plaza in offering to these birds. It sounds like cloudburst. Construction workers, intent on restoring the *stupa* to its pre-earthquake self, don hard hats the color of mandarins and climb bamboo scaffolding toward the cairn's spire.

As Sonam moves past the first Sakya monastery, she notices two old men, backs bent toward each other, spinning prayer wheels. She knows these men's stories, just as other people who circle the *stupa* know hers.

Sonam has long since given up on counting the number of times she walks around the *stupa*. Her name means "merit" anyway. Instead, she walks until her breath grows quick, until sunlight cracks through the early spring haze. Milarepa, the Buddhist poet-saint, spoke of drinking from the mountain stream as a metaphor for the *dharma*. Here, elder mountain people drink from the stream of circumambulation. It sustains them.

With Losar now passed, Sonam rests exactly six twelve-year cycles deep in the turning of this Wheel of Life. In Western years, this makes her seventy-two, but it is easier to speak of the Wood Monkey. It is easier for her to remember that Tuesday is a day of obstacles and that any medicine she takes on Thursdays will have a more potent effect. Astrological assurances anchor her, even as they tell her that she cannot resist temptations, that she may die suddenly far from home. She runs her tongue across her gold-plated tooth—this indulgence also a desire to carry wealth on her person. In this, she is like her late husband, a nomad from eastern Tibet, turned Tibetan resistance fighter. He battled the Chinese when they swept in a lifetime ago with their stiff manners, their skinny legs and sharp tongues, their promises of liberation.

She remembers his death in the Fire Dragon year. After the Tibetan resistance was forced to abandon their bases in Mustang, the unlikely couple passed one Losar together with their infant son, a chubby child who tumbled through her womb door into the village of Ghara. She knows sin—quick-tongued and prone to gossip, she'll admit it—but her husband killed a man. He made it through the fighting years but died an early death after a fall from his horse. It is he who she prays for as she walks around the *stupa*, knowing also that, whoever her husband was, he has long since passed into another life.

Sonam finds Karchung waiting for her under the billboard for the Kunzom Guest House. This is their regular meeting spot, though neither of them can read the sign. They are so used to this routine that even a simple greeting—*thangbo ü dé?*—seems like too many words. They have more important things to talk about. These old women clutch each other's hands and head toward Pema's tea shop—nothing more than corrugated tin in one of the last open spaces behind the *stupa*. This place makes the best sweet tea, and, if you ask for it, the adolescent girls who fry eggs and churn chickpeas will make flatbread with wheat flour brought down from Mustang.

The old women settle into dingy plastic chairs, once white.

"Did the son call?" asks Karchung.

"Called last night. Line crackled like thunder. He said the Nepali lawyer is not hopeful," Sonam answers. "Son said it cost three *lakh* just to get him out of jail until the judge makes a decision." Sonam calculates in rupees the cost of her grandson's bail, set by a family court in King's County, Brooklyn.

"All that money just to let a boy return to his family? Sounds like a bribe to me." Karchung reaches for the tin of snuff she keeps in her fanny pack along with her rosary and the cash her daughter-in-law doles out for tea and butter lamps each week. Her friend begins to cry. She needs something stronger than sugar to get her through this conversation.

"I fed him from my own mouth. Maybe he has my bitterness," Sonam whispers.

"*Kon chok sum*! We all fed them from our own mouths. You took care of that grandson. What was it? Four years? Five? While his father worked in that Chinese restaurant, paying off his visa. No, that child has made his own obstacles. Look how hard his father works! And without a mother!" Karchung voices the thoughts that Sonam cannot.

"Medicine that heals is not always sweet. Caring words are not always pleasant," Karchung offers a proverb. Sonam thinks about how Karchung learned, through circles of village gossip that went around the world, that her son had taken up with a Tibetan nanny with a green card, not long after he arrived in New York, even though he has a wife and two children in Boudha.

"Frank words make listening easier," Sonam answers, also with a proverb. She swallows a sip of tea. The two old women sit in silence for a time.

In truth, neither of these women knows much about the daily lives of their children and grandchildren, all of whom live in New York. But Sonam does know that her only son, Gyatso, has a good heart. He does his best to care for his only son, her grandson, Dawa. There is simplicity to Gyatso. He lacks malice. Dawa was newly off his mother's nipples when she became pregnant again and then lost the child when it was the size of a turtle in her womb. Then she went crazy. There was no other word for it.

Gyatso cared for his wife, but she could not climb the mountain of her grief, so he put their son in Sonam's care for a time. It was only supposed to be for the winter, as he headed off for the sweater trade, and his wife was left to tend the house, the horse, and their three cows in Mustang. They found his wife's body at a bend in the river near Jomsom.

"If your son were less of a man, he would be chasing women and wasting his money on drink," Karchung offers. Sonam wishes Karchung would be quiet now, but she is just getting started.

"Gyatso made a home for that boy. Gave him opportunity. Papers. School. And what does he do? Wastes his brain on those black cigarettes. Fights. Steals. Acts like those good-for-nothings with their sunglasses and hair like roosters!" Karchung spits on the ground, gestures with her chin toward a group of young men, all K-pop hairdos and swagger, lounging on a bench beside the tea shop. "At least in America young people can earn good money if they don't want to study. But what has that grandchild done?"

Dawa was born in the Earth Rabbit year. He was a kind and cautious child. Sensitive. Sonam instructed him in the small joy of saving insects. Although emptying and refilling the water offering bowls was usually a woman's job, she let him help. His tiny hands poured with elegance. But there was *nga rinpoche* in him, a propensity toward pride, a need for comfort. This, too, she indulged. He seemed to crave smooth days, without shouting neighbors, without thunderstorms.

Dawa had been so small when his mother drowned herself that Sonam believes he has no memory of her. Maybe she is wrong.

SUMMER: JACKSON HEIGHTS

Rigsang had grown accustomed to the fleshy warmth of summer in Pokhara. It had taken her a few years of living in the lowlands, but after she turned sixty, she was released from the embarrassment of her skin and came to enjoy stripping down to her undershirt and cotton pants under the banana tree, airing out the tangle of amulets around her neck. She, a woman raised in the high, dry air of Mustang, had adapted to heat and humidity. In fact, she had come to crave it.

But Jackson Heights in July undoes her. One of the first English words she learns after coming to New York is "air-conditioning." Even so, this fake coolness complicates matters. She can never quite figure out if she is cold or hot in New York. Machine-made shifts in the wind play with her sense of the elements, in the world and in her body. She feels unsettled when the flush of cool air inside the Delhi Heights Restaurant envelops her. Her grandchildren take her here on weekends to get her out of their small apartment. The tweens and their *ibi* do not have much to talk about, but the flavors they encounter, in this Indian fast food restaurant on the corner of Diversity Plaza, are familiar to all of them. Amidst the whir of AC units and the multilingual din, they take comfort in *samosa*, greasy and crisp.

The sharp edges of fried dough challenge Rigsang's dentures, but they would be truly impossible to eat without those fake teeth her son had bought her. Still, she enjoys these snacks. They remind her of the Water Sheep year when Angyal, her late husband, had taken her on pilgrimage to India: Dharamsala, Tsho Pema, and Bodh Gaya, where they received the *Kalachakra* empowerment from His Holiness the Dalai Lama.

Angyal died three years ago. His sickness, too, had taken her to India. The bodily shifts from fat and chili peppers to gastric ulcer to malignancy is so well known in their circles as to be predicted, but, still, nobody dares to breathe the word "cancer." She remembers medicine that seemed like poison, trickling into Angyal's veins. She remembers holding hands with this man she grew to love, who first saw her as a feckless, timid bride. In their old age, he did not doubt her strength; he leaned on her. "I will not live long. I wish to go home." They had left Delhi and returned to Pokhara, where she stood vigil to ensure that his desire for a good death was met.

Here in Queens, Rigsang and her grandchildren—Mingma and Tenzin, aged eleven and thirteen—eat their greasy snacks together in the too-cool fast food spot. When they finish, Mingma takes her *ibi*'s arm and leads her outside, into the wall of heat that is New York summer. Sunlight filters through the train tracks along Roosevelt Avenue. *What sort of people build tunnels to move underground and block the sun with all this iron?* Rigsang wonders. She feels dizzy. Her daughter-in-law insists that her dizziness is just high blood pressure and that she should stop drinking so much Tibetan tea. But Rigsang knows these vertiginous flushes are more about wind and heart than butter and salt. Melancholy settles in like sweat at the nape of her neck, between her thighs. It is a bodily longing.

Rigsang recalls the moment when she decided to leave Nepal and come to this strange, discomfiting city. "What are you going to do all day?" Rigsang's eldest son, Norbu, posed this question on a clear morning in the Pokhara autumn, when it was also a hazy evening in New York. This was not a new conversation. Norbu's pixilated face pulsed on the screen of the iPhone he had bought and sent to her.

"Your family is here now," he continued. Of course, "here" meant New York. Norbu was an American citizen. His wife and children settled in Queens on the heels of his naturalization. Rigsang's two daughters lived in Kathmandu, but she had no desire to live with either of them. Nor did she get along well with Norbu's wife. She was beautiful. Her desire for material comfort bothered Rigsang, in part because she recognized the same impulses in herself. But she lingered on the thought of being closer to her grandchildren. Mingma and Tenzin were in diapers when they left Nepal.

"Okay, I will come," Rigsang relented. "But I will not sell the house in Pokhara." That was more than two years ago now.

This noblewoman has not lived in Mustang for decades. Even so, back in Nepal, Rigsang did not lack for company the way she does in Queens. Even in Pokhara, she belonged. She enjoyed the comfort of her house, not far from Phewa Lake, with its view of the Peace Pagoda from her roof. She looked forward to winter trips to Kathmandu, when she and her sister-cousins would gossip, drink tea, and circumambulate Swayambhu to bookend the days. She even enjoyed the occasional late-summer excursion to Mustang, when the air was inviting and the buckwheat greens were sweet.

But Angyal's death made her lose her bearings. Grief becomes a drunkenness. It makes you unsteady on your feet. Norbu arranged for her plane ticket, found a distant relative to rent the house in Pokhara, and traveled from New York to Nepal to collect his mother. She followed, almost too obediently.

Sometimes Rigsang wishes that she could leave this body behind. She is seventy-two, like the numbered street on which the family's apartment in Jackson Heights is located. A Wood Monkey woman, Rigsang is quick-witted and prone to flaunting her wealth. In the village of her youth, her family had the most beautiful headdresses, pearls like drops of nectar, turquoise the color of a glacial lake, *dzi* that she learns from her son can be sold for $20,000 in New York, the same price he once raised for his visa. Now, those jewels live in a metal box under the bed in the corner of a bedroom she shares with her granddaughter. Rigsang has no desire to wear them anymore.

Upon arrival in New York, Rigsang hopes for independence. She memorizes the shape of the numbers 7 and 2 and has Tenzin draw her a map of the neighborhood. It is an attempt to orient. But, although Rigsang speaks three languages, English is not one of them. The thought of leaving the confines of Jackson Heights, where she can at least find a Nepali or Tibetan on most corners, frightens her. Instead of expanding her world, this move to New York contracts it.

Rigsang then begins threatening to return to Nepal. "At least I could die among people I know."

Until she hears about the Sherpa *gönpa* on 75th Street.

Going to the *gönpa* is her daughter-in-law's idea, although Rigsang does not like to admit it. "I hear it is clean. They serve tea and feed you lunch. A monk comes once a week to give teachings," she says. "It is better than sitting here staring out the window all day long."

"You should try going," Mingma adds. "You could meet people." Mingma does not feel comfortable speaking Logé, but she knows the word for "effort" and the one that means "companion," and she strings them together best she can, trying to please her *ibi*.

"It is clean here," Rigsang retorts, her chest heavy. "All the people I need to meet, I have met. Half of them are dead, and the other half run around like headless chickens all day, until they collapse in front of the TV."

Still, soon enough, Mingma will be laughing with her grandmother, calling the program Rigsang now attends three days a week "*ibi* daycare."

The Sherpa *gönpa* stands in an old church. Even though Rigsang feels a bit uncomfortable at first walking the few blocks on her own, not knowing whom she might meet, she gets used to it. The wood floors feel warm in winter, and the yellow walls remind her of her Pokhara home.

Rigsang now looks forward to these days. Even though she and the other elders—sometimes as few as twenty, sometimes twice as many—do not always speak the same languages, do not wear their aprons in the same way, there grows a kindred sense among them. Come June, they will be bundled like schoolchildren into buses and driven to a place called Upstate to visit a large Sakya monastery. They will picnic and circumambulate the main temple. They will sit for hours on the grass, drinking tea and airing out their tired feet, taking naps or playing with grandchildren—theirs or those of others.

It ceases to matter that Rigsang's father had been a Nyingma *ngakpa*, even though the weekly *dharma* teachings are given by a Kagyud monk. Her ears grow accustomed to the sound of the Baragaon women she befriends, the tone of their speech so much sharper than Logé, with its smooth, trailing endings. Now, as she walks to the *gönpa* together with two women from other parts of Mustang, the boundaries of their villages re-form into new territories of belonging.

Rigsang cannot remember exactly when she had learned that the money that funds the weekday gatherings, which allow her thermoses of tea, Zumba and yoga classes, and soft meals of black *dal* and lightly salted cauliflower, come not only from the monthly dues her son pays but also from death rituals taking place back in Nepal. At first, the idea bothers her. But she comes to settle on the thought, not unlike the spinning of her prayer wheel, that this is a different kind of *khora*. A turning of the possibilities for life.

## FALL: GHILING

"Did you hear the cranes?" Angmo asks her neighbor, PaDoka.

"No. But I felt them in my back and kidneys," PaDoka answers.

The change of seasons here is a physical reckoning, for all creatures. Horses sense the cold in their hocks as they carry burlap sacks of grain between fields and homes. Mastiffs strain against their tethers, wanting shelter inside. Sheep and goats huddle together as they move toward market, their horns marked in red, indicating impending slaughter. Demoiselle cranes fly south across the Himalaya, their necks and legs stretched long as arrows, fixed on the target of India's temperate wetlands and the future possibility of rest.

These two elder women sit beside a cast iron stove, Chinese lettering embossed on its potbellied side. The hearth is framed by wooden strips set into a rammed earth floor. A chimney pipe bisects the room. PaDoka can easily remember the days before this stovepipe, when the hearth was a three-pronged burner forged by the local blacksmith and smoke filled the room, escaping only through a small hole in the ceiling. Then, smoke stung her eyes incessantly. *Sometimes the Chinese make useful things*, she thinks as she stokes the fire awake.

It is mid-morning, on a day between buckwheat harvest and the work of threshing and winnowing. Angmo's back bends, mimicking the gentle curve of a sickle, except there is nothing gentle about the work of subsistence. It exhausts the young people. It wrings out this old woman.

Had this been a harvest day, they would have already spent several hours bringing in the bounty they'd grown. Had this been a threshing and winnowing day, they would have already settled into a rhythm of pounding sheaves with wooden paddles and shaking neat black grains from their chaff. They would have felt this exertion between the shoulder blades.

Although buckwheat is still threshed by hand, villagers now use a machine for wheat and barley. It costs a thousand rupees an hour because the diesel is brought up in trucks from Beni. Still, the machine is cheaper and more reliable than hiring lowland labor.

"Snow on the ridge when I went to pee in the night," Angmo announces.

"Drink tea." PaDoka picks up her aluminum kettle, the one used for salt butter tea, and insists that Angmo sip from a porcelain cup. Another Chinese thing. These two elderly women are friends. They are also kin. The village is a tangle of blood and bone, alliance and descent.

PaDoka fills Angmo's cup, takes a long sip from her own cup and refills it. She smooths the kettle with a rag and sets it on the burner. The rag and her hands are both black, but the kettle shines.

The two women feel no obligation to talk. Words come slowly, between sips.

"Kunga Tashi got hit by that younger wife again last night," Angmo gossips. "I don't know why he ever thought it was a good idea to bring her into the household. He couldn't handle the elder one."

"You would think the *genba* would put a stop to it," says PaDoka, speaking of the village headman. "But he is weak. Those people just fight until they get too tired and need to sleep." People say the young wife has witch in her, but she is a hard worker.

The drama of village life unfolds like this. Someone raises the specter of jealousy and sparks a row. Old scars split open at night, like grain sacks thrown to the ground, and are then sewn up again by morning. Everyone needs one another, especially now.

True, the community school thrives, but women like Angmo and PaDoka find little they can relate to in the children's talk of "maths" or the Nepali national anthem. True, there are some young adults around—those nursing the wounds of failed attempts to go abroad, those farming and caring for aging parents. Yet it seems that the only people who really *live* here are at least fifty. At seventy-two and sixty-seven, PaDoka and Angmo remain backbones of this place. Like their age-mates, they guard patterns of subsistence. They know the harvest songs. They remember *yul lha* in their prayers.

Were these women from wealthier families, their children might tell them to give up agriculture. Young people say, "Why plant fields when rice from Pokhara is cheap? When the Chinese send you sugar and tea?" The economics may be accurate, but to sew and reap are not solely rational acts.

For some who remain in the village, the concession to their children has been to plant fewer fields. The gentle terraces of fertile land beyond the *chöten* at the village edge are fallow. But this is not really a concession. Even with cheap rice, there are fewer mouths to feed. *People don't have enough children*, PaDoka thinks. Even though she heard the scream of a newborn just last week. Even though squeals of delight—games played with sheep knuckles and rubber balls—can still be heard from the village daycare.

"When will the monks come?" Angmo asks.

"Next month. On the fifteenth day," PaDoka answers. This occasion— chanting and offerings made in her home at the end of the village—will be done to acknowledge her dead husband. Born in the year of the Iron Dragon. Died in the year of the Wood Sheep. Seventy-six is a respectable age in most places, especially in the mountains. He had not been ill, but he had been tired. One evening, he did his prayers and said goodnight. In the morning, he did not wake. This was his *karma*: to die cleanly, without pain.

In actuality, the one-year anniversary ritual should be taking place now, but it is bad luck to mark death while new grain is being brought in, so Pa-Doka offers incense on their roof to purify and pacify. The village lamas will wait for one more cycle of the moon before they properly honor her dead.

"Has he sent money?" Angmo asks.

"None has come to my hands," answers PaDoka.

She thought she was barren after many years with no children, but eventually she birthed a son. That son was raised in the village, but he lives in New York. He calls sometimes. He has never returned.

There are rumors that her son has a gambling problem. The last time they spoke, he promised money for rituals. The money did not come. What to do? More reliable relatives in Kathmandu send cash. The *genba* performs his duties. Offerings are accounted for. Rituals are completed. PaDoka marvels at the money it costs to send the dead on their way: a stack of thousand-rupee bills as thick as her wrist. She remembers when a five-hundred-rupee note felt like a fortune.

Just then, *karang karung*.

"The cranes," PaDoka says.

Unlike the birds, she has no desire to leave this place.

# BETWEEN PRESENCE
# AND ABSENCE

We know before leaving Kag that we will arrive in Dzar to a funeral. News of the grandmother's death travels quickly, between villages and across the world.

The *chöten* marking the entrance to the village has been ritually closed to contain the spiritual pollution associated with death, so we enter the settlement from the side, passing patchworks of planted and fallow fields, by turns verdant and tawny. We arrive at Tsultrim and Rinzin's home before the funeral procession has begun. Tsultrim is scrolling through images on Facebook of his granddaughter's first day of kindergarten, in Brooklyn.

"Rinzin is with the other women, preparing to cry," he says, as greeting. Unsentimental, Tsultrim sips a cup of Himalayan chrysanthemum tea, his antidote to hypertension. He was once a thin man, but now he jokes that his belly is like that of a baby, six months in the womb.

Soon, the wail of trumpets and the pulse of *damaru* pierce the kitchen's calm. "The procession is coming," says Kunzom.

From the roof of Tsultrim's home, I see a human train of grief stretching out along the row of *mani* stones and prayer wheels that line the village entrance. Monks and householder priests, dressed in shades of red, wait on the far side of the *chöten*, ritual instruments in hand. Village women are cloaked in white, wearing turquoise headdresses that run along their neat parts, hair glossy with apricot oil. I recognize the shape of one figure as Rinzin.

By the time we make it downstairs, the funeral procession is passing Tsultrim's home. The corpse, a small triangle of human form that has been washed and wrapped in cotton, is held aloft on a palanquin carried by four village men. We join the mourners. The melancholy resonance of horns, cymbals, and drums are familiar, but I am not prepared for the laments.

Women shuffle along in their rainbow-striped aprons, their voices caught between song and wail. I see Rinzin closely now, tears running down her plump cheeks; Kelsang, a woman about my age who came to Dzar as a bride from Lubrak; and Janchuk, once the manager of a Loba-owned hotel in Kathmandu, now returned to the village. We lock eyes. Now is not a time to talk.

For all the ways that Tsultrim seems cynical and unmoved by grief, I watch his face as we walk. The winds of emotion shift. Perhaps this is the result of seeing his beloved mourn. I cannot know for certain.

I cry. Not because I knew this woman. Not because I understand the subtleties of this funerary rite or the complexities of this grandmother's story. But because the dirges offered up as part of the ritual process for one person resonate with the loss of a way of life—if not the life force of the village itself.

There are no people under forty in this procession. Most are decades older.

The villagers gather behind the old fortress. Men prepare to walk the body up the mountain where it will be kept until the cremation. Ritual is precision. They will set fire to the body after buckwheat harvest, lest smoke from the pyre offend deities of place and interrupt the reaping. Rinzin and other women huddle together at the edge of the village, their faces smudged and wet. They sing once more as the body ascends.

But ritual is also about paying attention to intention.

Later that afternoon, we talk about the woman whose funeral it was. *Ibi* Sangye was eighty-seven. She is remembered as recalcitrant, argumentative. These character flaws do not excuse the neglect she experienced in her infirmity, according to Tsultrim and Kunzom. Her immediate family no longer lives in the village, and those who bore responsibility for her care did not take care of her. She spent some seasons working the fields of others for her keep. She lived off alms at the Muktinath nunnery for the last five years of her life.

"Village people can be so *hypocrite*," says Kunzom. "I really don't like this. People wail one minute and then gossip the next. This is not how you should take care. People think it is okay as long as you do the ritual. This is like a TV serial, not real sorrow."

Tsultrim nods. "Just by doing the right things at the right times we are not necessarily treating people well."

I notice Rinzin's silence. She putters around the kitchen, smoothing a rag, removing a dish. Eventually, she speaks. "It is true that *ibi* was not looked after as she should have been. It is true that people are forgetting how to care for the old ones. But we are all getting old. There are fewer of us to take care of each other. Sometimes we speak with two mouths. Sometimes there is sin. Even so, we need to sing. We need to cry."

The next morning, we encounter an ancient-looking woman—a living version of the *ibi* now deceased. She has tipped over while weeding her buckwheat field. The weight of her *doko*, slung on her back and balanced by a sisal rope across her forehead, is too much for her. She lies like an upturned turtle, arms and legs moving slowly. I climb over the wire fence separating field from path and help her up. Kunzom, who of course knows the family to whom this grandmother belongs, asks why she is out working in the fields alone.

"Who else is there to do the work?" comes the whispered response. It is truth, unadorned. The woman rights the strap of her *doko*, grips the sawed-off trekking pole that serves as her cane, and heads home.

## VIRTUAL NETWORKS, ACTUAL CARE

My phone tells me that I have 952 unread messages. This is not a reflection of my popularity. It is WeChat.

First developed in China, where it was released in 2011 as Weixin (which means "micro-message"), WeChat has nearly a billion monthly users—the vast majority of whom are Chinese. It rivals both Facebook Messenger and WhatsApp in terms of reach and scope. I use WeChat to communicate with friends in Mustang, Kathmandu, and New York as well as those in Tibetan areas of China. Although the app handles all manner of feeds and functions—pictures and videos, walkie-talkie and GPS capabilities, an endless array of emojis—mostly I send voice messages.

When the app launches, my phone screen displays a human figure silhouetted against the moon. My hand holds the gravitational pull of virtual connection and the human relationships beyond the screen. I cradle the phone close to my mouth. I have to resist the urge to shout as if I were bridging a physical divide, the way phone calls from Nepal used to sound.

When I visit Dolma in Queens, we scroll through WeChat together. It is a sort of time-space travel. She shows me the shrine room that belongs to her relatives in Lhasa. We listen to a group of women singing in Logé, arms swaying with silken grace, feet shuffling in the dirt. We watch videos of lamas giving *dharma* teachings. She shares with me the latest voice memo from a mutual friend in Kathmandu.

As Dolma and I huddle together in her Woodside living room, I consider how this app forms a network of care. Although WeChat groups can serve to perpetuate gossip, sometimes causing personal embarrassment or increasing intergenerational tension, these virtual links can undergird actual social safety nets. People donate funds to help with medical crises or reward promise in a young person through collective educational sponsorships. These "technologies of the self," as social theorist Michel Foucault might call them, channel the voices of loved ones and distant community members alike in ways that are particularly useful if you don't read or write. The app informs people about weekly in-person *mani* gatherings, but WeChat can also hold virtual space for prayer.

One of the WeChat groups to which I belong is named for a specific monastery in Lo. According to the moderator, members can come from Mustang or other Tibetan communities, wherein "Tibetan" means *tsampa* eaters from India, Nepal, or China, those who have interest in Buddhist history and practice. People self-identify using powerful *dharmic* avatars: King Gesar, Atisha. Tibetan, English, Nepali, Hindi, and Chinese languages are represented in message threads. There is a post-national, pan-Tibetan feel to the group's flood of sight and sound. Someone shares pictures of a Sakya monastic school in south India; another member posts a video of people burning crates of Chinese alcohol in a central Tibetan village, worldly vice going up in smoke. And yet the virtual group also retains very real links to Mustang. Some members choose WeChat IDs that indicate localized Loba identity. A New York taxi driver who was once a monk in Mungod identifies by his natal village, Marang. Someone else posts a fragment of a religious text found in one of Mustang's caves, itself a screenshot from a *NOVA* documentary.

Group moderators make explicit a set of ethical norms. Members are reminded that this is a space for right speech, not for lewd jokes. A specific form of civil society is at work here. Each day of the week has a different theme, and auspicious days are devoted to cyber ritual practice. A flood of Guru Rinpoche GIFs comes through on the tenth day in the lunar month, for example. Saturdays are good to upload videos or audio recordings of songs. People post announcements about religious figures coming to Kathmandu, Sarnath, or New York to give teachings. Images of Buddhist masters in *thugdam*, death meditation, go viral. People post flickering butter lamp GIFs, strings of *namaste* emojis, prayer beads wrapped through animated fingers, steaming cups of butter tea offered up in virtual *phorwa*. Like most of the time we spend on social media, lingering in the simulated community of such groups seems to be a form of what Nepalis call "time pass," but it can also be a form of everyday religious practice within the unrelenting busy-ness of New York.

Despite the air of piousness, occasional posts are laugh-out-loud funny. An obese Chinese man dressed up as a potbellied "Laughing Buddha" figure sits on a stage, lit with disco lights, behind his *doppelgänger*, carved in stone. A village toddler tries to eat his dinner, only to keep falling asleep in his food. An Indian television anchor speaks in earnest Hindi about the danger of radiation posed by laptops and mobile phones—a message being sent, of course, over mobile phones.

Sometimes I hear familiar voices. Close my eyes, and the app becomes an enchantment. I am transported to a hearthside ritual or the sounds of offerings in a Mustang monastery. This magic cannot conjure the feel of foreheads touching. It cannot, as yet, reproduce a waft of incense. But it can foster a sense of connection.

On a scroll through posts, an image catches my eye. In the picture, several middle-aged men from Lo stand together in a hospital corridor. One is dressed in a hospital gown. The preceding posts express gratitude for the funds that the sick individual received through the group. Unsurprisingly, the particular illness from which this person is suffering is not named, but the messages indicate that this man will remain in the hospital for some time.

I swipe right. The next image reveals the same man in the gown, now seated cross-legged in his hospital bed. He is reading a *peja*, its bright orange covering spilling across white sheets. The man is backlit. He rests in a field of fluorescent light. I think about the fact that someone was present to take this picture and that others are waiting across boroughs and continents, hands cupped around their phones, to receive this message.

These, too, are vital signs.

IN PASSING

Outside it is summer, but spring lingers on the shoe rack. Leather boots rub up against flip-flops. Pairs separate. Sneakers and sandals fold at odd angles. If you were to cross into this Brooklyn apartment, there would be no dirt to speak of, but the threshold is all dust and chaos—lives lived in passing.

A photocopied list of American idioms sits on the coffee table. It is an artifact of an adult literacy class in which one of the members of this household is enrolled. The paper is tea stained, as is the table on which it rests. These idioms bespeak the murky nature of assimilation. Each phrase is pregnant with tacit knowledge, presumed continuities of culture and history that are more like keys to locked doors than a means of communication. To read this list here, in this place where seven members of an extended family cohabitate in a two-bedroom apartment, where they try to look after one another but also keep secrets and lose the ability to speak with one another, is to acknowledge one form of the ends of kindship. Sometimes families crack apart, even if they sleep under the same roof.

From this living room in New York, voices from Nepal fill my head.

As she brings in her buckwheat harvest, a seventy-three-year-old mother confides, "I hope to see my son before I die." I tell her that I hope so too. We do not talk about the fact that her son is banned from the village for a violent crime of which he is accused and that he left a village wife for a woman in New York, whom he was later arrested for beating.

An old man from the hamlet of Phuwa, now living in Kathmandu, tells me, "The houses of our forefathers are being abandoned. The roof leaks when it rains. I have *tension* over this. I dream of the village, but then I wake up in Kathmandu. What to do?"

"It is really challenging to do this thing called *save culture*," the Kag *khenpo* professes, "especially if the whole family is away, in a new place. When we lose our roots, there is a loss of identity and language. This creates *mental torture*. All the focus on money does not help." As a culture broker who navigates between foreign organizations intent on preserving Mustang's religious heritage and the daily needs of a monastery now filled with little monklets from elsewhere, the abbot lives these points of tension.

I think about these words as I snap a picture of the literacy class idiom list on my phone. It is a fieldwork instinct.

Some months later, I spend time with this photo, re-reading each idiom. The list becomes an act of back-translation. To find a story in each saying is a way of writing the family silences to which I have become attuned.

Someone is tucked into a shiny leather couch, shiny like a black-eyed pea. *Safe as a pea in a pod.* But don't peas get shucked? Isn't there a certain violent displacement within this possibility of refuge? The man on the couch has worked from three in the morning until three in the afternoon, as what they call a "stock boy." Never mind that he has not been a boy for half a century. In this household, he is uncle and son, brother and father, depending on who is asking. He rests in the midday quiet between shifts. He is beyond tired. What would happen to this family if he did not wake?

Cold rice congeals around traces of chili and a chicken bone. The scum of butter tea made in a blender coats a mug, the kind you buy at the dollar store. A woman stares at the sink and sighs. Outside, the gloaming descends in a humid haze. She hears grandfather snoring in the storage closet they've turned into his room. Everyone else is at work or who-knows-where. She sucks in her breath and resists a wave of nausea. They said at the clinic that she would feel the baby move. She has told only her boyfriend, who is not from Mustang, not Nepali, not American. *Let the cat out of the bag.* Why confine an animal like that in the first place? When will it be too late to speak what people already know?

He stole the headphones months ago now, from a Best Buy up in Flushing. It was not his first attempt. But this success emboldened him. He loved the world those headphones afforded. They numbed the smallness of the apartment. They granted this Loba kid who had joined a Sherpa gang a certain deafness—to family, to his own disorientation. After the next robbery, when the police pin him to the sidewalk, he thinks of those headphones. *Caught red handed.* He has been in America long enough to know he is lucky they didn't shoot him. What of this can he manage alone? How will his parents be notified? After he has done his time, will the headphones still be there, under his pillow?

She had been tall when she arrived at JFK, but she was only eleven. Given the difference between Tibetan and American reckonings of age, they put her into eighth grade, even though she had only completed class six at a mediocre Kathmandu boarding school. Her guidance counselor said that she would soon find classes *a piece of cake.* But there is no sweetness in failure. To recall the sugary film on her tongue from the confectionary at her niece's birthday party brings up bile, not pleasure. She lays on the mattress she shares with her cousin-sister, staring up at the water-stained ceiling, wondering how she will tell her mother—the one who thinks six years of education is enough for a girl—that she must repeat this year of school. Nothing sweet or easy about it.

Her shoulders splinter in pain after a fourteen-hour shift at the nail salon. She dreams that she's been threshing barley. Each form of labor carries a

similar ache, sharp and pronounced like her father might have described
a Brahmin's nose. But threshing never made her temples throb as if her
head might explode. Nails do that. She tells her boss, a Korean woman
who lacks empathy, that she is *under the weather.* She is granted one day
off. She sleeps through that day. Her dreams are of roiling monsoon
clouds over Kathmandu, a spring snowfall that dusts the plains above
Tsarang, a rainbow that dissolves into streams of technicolor acrylic
polish. Mustang sunsets are lipstick red. Rivers run gumball blue.

Her framed certificates of academic accomplishment are placed behind
glass in a cupboard that doubles as the family shrine. She feels embarrassed that these marks of her success sit beside pictures of lamas, near
the water offering bowls and butter lamps. But where else would they be
placed? When the acceptance letter arrives—to study at a famous
university, far away from New York—she does not bother to hide the piece
of paper. Everyone in this household is too tired or too distracted to pay
attention. Still, she is *between a rock and a hard place.* She is this family's
rock, but she can feel herself begin to harden. She finds little comfort in
ambition. Instead, it sits in her belly like sediment, accruing to stone.

Grandfather couldn't care less about being in *Nu-yok,* but he finds himself
here, nonetheless. The land in the village was sold years ago, and now
nobody remains in the house in Kathmandu they'd worked so hard to
build. Cancer took the *nama* who was left in Nepal to care for him. Then
he was alone. His son called him to this foreign country. What could he
say, *no?* After all, this is where the money for living comes from. But this
place does not suit him. *Not my cup of tea.* The air and water do not agree
with him, nor does this house. He lives boxed in with his relatives, the
young ones he cannot understand and the middle-aged ones who feel
more duty than love. His *phorwa,* gilded with silver filigree, sits beside his
bed, near his prayer beads. The tea bowl still smells of butter and wood
smoke, after all these years.

## RELEASE OF CONSCIOUSNESS

Wangchuk and I are in my mother's kitchen, chatting about the ocean—
which he has just seen for the first time while visiting my childhood home
in California—when my mother's friend Lourdes rushes in through the

front door. It is 2003, and it is this *amchi* from Monthang's first trip to the United States.

"Where is your mom?" Lourdes asks in lieu of a greeting. Dark circles form shadowy half-moons under her eyes. Her thick hair is pulled back. She wears no lipstick, which is unusual. Lourdes seems short of breath, confused. She smiles weakly at Wangchuk. My mom hears her friend and comes out to join us. Lourdes bursts into tears.

"Dad just died. I don't know what to do," she says to my mother. "I feel like I should do *something* but I don't know. . . . Do you have some sage?" she asks. As someone who grew up around Chumash Native Californian communities, I recognize Lourdes's request for this sacred plant as a way of ritualizing death—even by relying on practices that do not come from her own culture.

My mom holds her friend, tells her to take a deep breath. "We will figure it out. It will be okay," she says.

"He is at home, around the corner." Then the words pour out. "My brother is there, but he is not very useful. He just thinks we should call the ambulance. But I feel that we need to *do something*. Otherwise, they will just come and take him away. That can't be it, can it? He was resting, and then he was just gone. I knew it was coming, but I guess I didn't know it was coming. I have no idea what to do."

Lourdes's mother was a Nicaraguan Roman Catholic. Her father was a Russian Jew. This and other exigencies of family life seemed to have left her at a loss when faced with this rite of passage. "The girls are at school," she says, speaking of her daughters, both younger than ten. "He didn't seem to be in pain, just sleeping. But then he wasn't breathing or moving."

Wangchuk can see that this American woman is upset, but he cannot understand her words. I explain. "This is a friend of my mother. She lives nearby. Her father is in the house. He just died. She thought he was sleeping but then he had no breath. She is upset because she doesn't know what to do."

As both an *amchi* and a *ngakpa*, Wangchuk is well versed in death. "Doesn't she have her own religion?" he asks.

"Yes, but also, no. She is confused. Her mother and her father had different religions. She is not sure what her father would have wanted. Her brother is there, but he just thinks they should call the hospital to take the body away."

My mom introduces Lourdes to Wangchuk, telling her that he is a Tibetan doctor and a Buddhist priest, visiting from Nepal.

"Is there something *he* can do?" Lourdes asks.

"She is wondering," I translate, "If there is something you can do for her father." In this tender moment, I am acutely aware of the crisscrossed possibilities for misunderstanding and cultural appropriation. I feel oddly protective of Wangchuk, far away from home and thrown into a circumstance that he knows how to handle but that is still, in other ways, outside his comprehension. I am also acutely aware of my role as interpreter.

"We do *phowa*," he says, referencing a release of consciousness ritual. "We recite the *Bardo Thödol*." This is *The Tibetan Book of the Dead*, a text that is a guide through the *bardo*. Normally, death rituals are done every week for seven weeks—forty-nine days of practice to light the path through the in-between realm, away from one life and toward its next manifestation. This carefully delineated process helps to curate grief, channeling support for the dead and invoking resolution within the living. It is a ritual process of affection, a profound expression of care.

"I cannot do all," Wangchuk says, "but I can do something that will be of benefit. We should go now. It needs to be done immediately."

I explain Wangchuk's offer to Lourdes, as he goes to retrieve the ritual texts he has brought with him, along with his *dorje* and *drilbu*, from his duffel bag. I don't even pause to consider that he has traveled with these Buddhist ritual implements. Of course he did. He always does.

This, too, is emergency preparedness.

Lourdes leads us around the corner to her house. Her brother opens the door. He does not look pleased to see an entourage, particularly one that includes a foreign-looking person.

"This is a friend of Sienna's," explains Lourdes. "He is a Buddhist priest from Nepal, he's offered to do some prayers for Dad." Although I have no idea about the nature of their sibling relationship, I sense the effort it takes for Lourdes to keep calm. Her brother is guarded.

"Lourdes, what are you thinking? We're not Buddhist—no offense," he says, directing this last comment toward Wangchuk.

"Please," Lourdes asks. "I can't imagine having him taken away, just like that. *Please*." I whisper an interpretation of this exchange to Wangchuk. The siblings talk quietly for a moment before her brother acquiesces.

We are led to the back bedroom, where Lourdes's father has left this life. The room is cool. The man looks as if he could be napping. His thin cheeks are marked with stubble. He has a full head of hair, mostly gray. His eyes are closed. As I take in this visage, I consider the dissolution of different cycles of living in Tibetan worldviews—the external signs like a thinning body, how the five senses slip away, and the end stages, when the internal winds dissolve into the drop of life at the heart.

"I will sit here," says Wangchuk. He speaks in low tones. "Tell the daughter and son that they should sit and remain calm. You can sit too, if you want." I translate.

Over the next hour or so, we sit, listening as Wangchuk's voice fills the room with what is both prayer and practical instruction—words to guide, to dispel fear, to conjure compassion, to make peace with the certainty of death. As I listen to my friend, gentle and clear as he performs this work, I am overcome with awe for the ways he can abide with a stranger at this most intimate time. Still, I notice how relatively unprepared, how uncomfortable, so many of us remain when faced with the end of life.

Wangchuk reads his text, then wraps it up again in its saffron-colored sleeve. He rises, places a small bit of *chinlab* inside the mouth of the deceased, and drapes a *kathag* over his head. We follow Wangchuk out of the room. Not knowing how to acknowledge this effort, Lourdes bows and offers a *namaste*. We take our leave.

By early evening, Wangchuk looks exhausted. Jet lag notwithstanding, he seems emotionally spent. I settle him into a guest bed and bring him tea. When I come to get him for dinner, the ritual practitioner is fast asleep. I let him rest.

CEREMONY

The first time I saw the Dö Gyab ritual, I was twenty-two. It was winter. Snow fell, blanketing the village—an auspicious sign during this ritual cycle. I fell asleep on more than one occasion in the corner of the village *gönpa* to the mesmerizing sound of recitation and ritual drums and cymbals that went on late into the night. At that point, I understood very little of the Tibetan spoken here, and I was a novice when it came to the arc of ritual practice. Instead, I relied on two other more senior anthropologists who were also present and on conversations I could have in Nepali with the villagers I knew, to get a sense of what was going on.

During breaks, we were served cups of tea and, as day turned toward evening, grain alcohol. I watched as *ngakpa* formed butter statues to honor the tutelary deities of this Bön hamlet. During cycles of *cham*, householder priests cast and recast themselves as protectors, as tricksters and wanderers, as a god with the head of a deer or a wrathful creature crowned with a garland of human skulls. I watched them create an effigy that serves to concentrate and then dispel nefarious forces. The *ngakpa* attacked this image with arrows and daggers before they cast it out of the village.

Two decades after I observed that first Dö Gyab, I find myself back in this village for this same ritual moment. It is late September 2016. I have arrived alone, but I do not feel alone. This is familiar territory. After a lunchtime visit with Karma, we head to the monastery for the *cham*.

"It was a long time ago, when you last saw the Dö Gyab," Karma says as we walk down the path from her house toward the village temple, which sits like the head of a flower in the middle of this cluster of homes, unfurling like petals in all directions.

"Twenty years. We're both more wrinkled now," I say. "And we aren't freezing!" I add, recalling the layers of long underwear and woolen aprons I wore to keep warm those many years ago.

"Yes, we had to change the timing, otherwise nobody would be here," Karma answers. The Dö Gyab used to be practiced in winter. However, given the exodus of people from Mustang, and the increasing draw of Pokhara and Kathmandu as places to spend the cold months, villagers reinvented their ritual calendar. Now, the Dö Gyab occurs in autumn, when it is pleasant to visit the village and before people head south for trading, pilgrimage, and rest. Despite a slightly different format, *ngakpa* still enact a living history with their voices and bodies, calling in supplication and offering, dispelling obstacles, enticing good fortune.

Karma and I arrive at the monastery to find the aging row of *ngakpa*, including the reincarnation of the village's founding lama, setting up their low tables and ritual implements along the walls of the inner courtyard. The senior-most *ngakpa* greets me warmly, clasps my hands.

"We're all getting old," he says, "but we still know how to call the gods," he gestures to the *ngachen*, which he is stringing from the ceiling. I tell him that he is looking well, to which he responds, "We've stopped drinking. Can you believe it?" He holds up his mug of tea and gestures to the row where his four fellow tantrists will sit to perform.

Another senior tantrist adds, "We have to take care of ourselves. Otherwise, who will do this work? But," he continues, with a grin, "we are teaching some younger generations the masked dances." I delight in his delight.

Karma takes her place in the monastery kitchen, working with other women to prepare refreshments. I step over the raised threshold into the *gönpa*. I prostrate three times, feeling the coolness of the wood floor beneath my feet, hands, and forehead. The *gönpa* looks kempt. The masks to be used in the dances make a neat row under the windows.

I settle in alongside the wall adjacent to the row of ritual officiants. Over the next half hour, the room fills up: with children from the village school; with Nepali visitors and a few foreign tourists; with people from elsewhere in Mustang; and with every local resident currently in the village. The space brims with chatter, until the *cham* begins.

Cymbals guide the rhythm. Slowly. *One. Two. Three. Four.* Then *five-six-seven* in quick succession. Brass clashes and sizzles, the *ngachen* bass in the background. Masked dancers, dressed in flowing brocade robes, raise their feet at angles that remind me of a prancing horse. They pivot, twist, and stomp to a tempo that turns this dirt floor into a divine domain. The only thing that gives away the dancers as merely human is their footwear. Sneakers and scuffed loafers peer out from underneath gowns.

As I watch the masked dances and take in the completeness, if also the transitory nature, of this consecrated moment, I think about the words that open Leslie Marmon Silko's novel *Ceremony*:

and in the belly of this story
the rituals and the ceremony
are still growing

The dynamics of dispossession and structural violence about which Silko writes, in her book about Native American experience, departs from Mustang's history in many ways. And yet something of both the pain and the reclamations that center Silko's work seems to be mirrored here, now.

I think, also, of anthropologist Keith Basso and his insights from many years among the Western Apache. "Knowledge of places is closely linked to knowledge of the self," he writes, "to grasping one's position in the larger scheme of things, including one's own community, and to securing a confident sense of who one is as a person."

At a time when so many people have left, when place-based practice and the knowledge that comes from living on and through one's own land are jeopardized, when language splinters, dissipates, and shifts like storm clouds, when the future is uncertain, this feeling of a village's fullness, endowed with ritual life and the wide-eyed curiosity of children, with the patience of grandparents and the hard work of householders, moves me deeply.

When I ask people what Mustang will be like in twenty years, the answer I often get is the phrase *ki rongba ki tongba*. This code-switching response combines Nepali and Tibetan to assert that Mustang will either be inhabited by lowland Nepalis (*rongba*) or it will be empty (*tongba*). Often, this feels like an apt assessment—complexity distilled into a slogan, like a bumper sticker. But not today.

Karma knows that I must return to Jomsom this evening. During a break in the *cham*, I signal to her from across the courtyard, and she rises to walk me down to the edge of the village. It has been too short a visit.

"This was like a dream," she says, as we embrace.

Later in her book, Silko writes, "It was a restless, dry wind that felt as if it blew out of dusty thin years of the past; it smelled of emptiness and loss." In recent years, I have often felt this sort of wind in Mustang. However, this evening, the swiftly moving air sweeping up the Kali Gandaki gorge feels alive. Like the ceremony I have just witnessed, it is a wind unburdened—shaped by the past but also wholly present.

I walk back to Jomsom at dusk, my body flush against the face of this wind.

THANKSGIVING

In November 2014, Ken, Aida, and I gather in Brooklyn to celebrate Thanksgiving with people from Ghiling. Like the Fourth of July, this quintessentially American holiday has been refashioned into a moment of community celebration for people from Mustang because many of them have the day off. Ritual calendars have adapted to meet work schedules and public holidays.

My family and I spend the earlier part of the day in the nineteenth-floor apartment of a friend of a friend, watching the Macy's Thanksgiving Day Parade from a terrace overlooking Columbus Circle and Central Park South. From that vantage, we stare down at bulbous blow-up versions of cartoon characters and listen to the thunderous cacophony of marching bands and megaphones. Central Park's overstory glows red and gold against a low sun, inching toward winter solstice.

After the parade, we take the subway to Brooklyn and enter a different world. Nawang meets us at the station and escorts us to a three-bedroom townhouse in Ditmas Park where the Ghiling Thanksgiving party is being held. As we walk inside, we are met by a different register of eclectic sound: the soft clatter of dice and shells, the words *para para para*, and the muffled spat of *sho* as a dice game is played; great gasps of steam from pressure cookers; a mix of Logé, Nepali, and English. People take notice of us for a moment and then go back to their playing and socializing.

Three or four circles of people, some all-male, others mixed gender, arrange themselves on the living room floor. They play games, animated as they sip Coke or tea, beer or whiskey, in front of the wooden cabinet that houses a TV, family photos, and the household shrine. All the furniture has been pushed up against the walls to accommodate these circles of play. The coffee table has been repurposed into a space to stack drinks and bulk containers of biscuits, deposited near the door.

Ken talks with some of the men. Aida and I go off to explore the kitchen. Three women vie for places at the stove, stirring vats of *dal* and frying up potatoes. The air is thick with turmeric and caraway, ginger, cumin, and chili.

One of Nawang's uncles greets me. "This may not be Mustang," he says, "but we still cook as if it is." He points to the ceiling, directing my attention to an intricate lattice of wooden rods that form faux rafters on which strips of meat have been hung to dry. In the corner, the carcass of a newly butchered goat lays limp. Several women squat on the floor, kneading glutinous lumps of flour and water into dough for dumplings.

"Have tea. Have Coke," they offer. We perch on stools and help to make the *momo*. Aida is somewhat disoriented but also welcomed into the bustle of preparation, that is, until she is pulled away by a group of young women who offer to do her nails—an offer in which she delights.

Nawang's uncle pummels goat meat into submission. The *momo*-making team and I continue our kneading and rolling. While we work, I learn that more than sixty people—roughly seventeen full households—from this one village are now in New York. When I ask about how they feel the Ghiling community is doing at this point, here in America, all agree that life is good. People are making their way. This house is owned, not rented, by a Ghiling family. The women beside me speak of their work in nail salons and as nannies with nonchalance. It is work, and work must be done. At the moment, they are happy to be with one another, embodying the labor of community, bantering about the vicissitudes of urban village life.

Later that evening, I sit on the couch beside Ken and Aida, chatting with one of the first people to have arrived from Mustang to New York. His round face pleats into smile lines as he speaks frankly of the past. "When I first came here, in 1998, there were few of us, all men, most married. We worked construction. It was not secure and sometimes dangerous. Now, the situation is much better." He describes how most of the men over thirty from this village still do construction, but many of them have worked their way out of the occasional economy and are now employed by larger companies. Many have health insurance. Some are unionized.

"In the summer, we dangle our bodies over the air of Manhattan, like Spiderman," he says. "In winter, we work indoors, painting, wiring, finishing. At the beginning, it was difficult to know whom to trust. We had to go to Chinatown to one of the labor agencies. Now we don't need agencies. The village is its own agency! We depend on those we know. And if we ever needed to go through an agency, now there is a Nepali one in Queens, so we don't have to deal with the Chinese."

I remark on the size of the house, three bedrooms with a finished basement. "It is a beautiful home."

"I wish that I had tried to buy a house sooner," he replies, "but at first we thought we would be here for four or five years, earn some money, then go home. This is how it was in the 1980s when some of us went to Japan or Korea. But America is different. After five years or so, we began to understand the *system* and see the benefits. So, we stayed. This was also such a bad time in Nepal. What was there to go back to? Now we bring our families, and it really becomes *comfortable*." The man and I speak, mostly in Nepali, about the similarities and differences between Mustang and Tibet and about what it meant to be a Himalayan New Yorker.

"And the village? How does it feel to be away for so long?"

"I miss the village for the peace of mind you can have there and also the different kind of work. Taking care of animals and fields is difficult, but it brings a special satisfaction," the man reveals. "But the *system* works so much better here. You can count on things. In Nepal, just to pay an electric bill you have to go to an office and stand in line, and, even then, you still might have to pay a bribe. We can be lazy in Nepal, but we cannot be lazy here."

The man pauses, stretches, and moves his empty plate to the floor. "Here, the challenge is no *time*. We do not get to see people. This sort of party doesn't happen very often. Losar, weddings, those big moments are also different. Too much *pressure* to show what wealth you have. *Buy car. Buy house.* Like that. Most of the time it is the same routine every day. No change. In the village, there is routine, but it is not the same. You notice things. Cows and horses give birth. We pay attention to the weather and to people's heartminds. If something important happens, we can stop to *take care*. Here, it is more difficult to stop. Work goes on, *dung-dung dung-dung*, like the beating of a two-sided drum."

I listen, taking in the poetry of his descriptions—the rhythmic monotony of the rat race as if it were a *damaru*, the image of a calf or foal slick and wobbly with new life. Each of these ways of seeing Mustang and New York reveals distinct articulations of a sort of stability that cannot be replicated from one locale to another. In each, there is the possibility for success and failure; in each, the possibility of being held if you fall.

The man leans over toward an elder gentleman in the corner and introduces us. At seventy-eight, he is the most senior person here. After seven years of work, he became quite ill with *tsa drip*. Temporarily paralyzed, he spent the better part of a year in a Queens hospital, being cared for not only by the *system* but also by his fellow villagers. Now, he explains, "I have no need to work. My family is here. They look after me. All I have to do now is pray."

We are joined by a man about my age. He is from Kag, not Ghiling, but he married into the village as a Brooklyn *makpa*. We talk about his journey.

"I went to school in Pokhara and Kathmandu. At that time, I had no concept of going abroad. I liked Nepal," he confesses. "I went home after passing the SLC and I lived in the village for two years. One day, a *sadhu* was passing through on the way to Muktinath," he says. "We gave him alms, and he insisted on reading my palm. This was long ago, maybe 1997, and just at the time when the first people were coming to New York. I had no ambition to leave. But the *sadhu* said, 'Soon you will go to a foreign land.' I was happy in the village. I had been working with a foreign scholar on a research project. Everyone was surprised by how much I liked it. But then, my mother began to tell me I should go. She reminded me what the *sadhu* said."

"What do you think of what the *sadhu* said?" I ask.

"I think maybe he just knew this *trend* of the youths was coming. But maybe he could really see the future. I don't know. I gave him a bag of rice before he went up the mountain."

As the evening wears on, the room grows steamy with bodies. Among the men and women playing cards, bets are dealt. The kitty spills out of a plastic bowl. In one of the back bedrooms, young men get drunk and play guitars. Another bedroom is turned into a makeshift nursery for the infants and toddlers among us. We stay until the children are sleeping, until the gambling circles grow smaller and more serious.

Two days later, we meet Nawang for brunch. He looks exhausted.

"Are you okay, *bhai*?" I ask. "Did you stay out too late drinking and playing cards?"

"Actually, no *didi*. I have some bad news." He looks at Aida, who is just eleven at this time, and says, in Nepali so she cannot understand, "Someone died. Is it okay to talk about it?" Ken and I nod yes. Although we can be protective, we do not feel the need to shelter our child from death.

Nawang shares what happened. One of the men at the party, someone in his mid-fifties and by all accounts in good health, was found dead in his bed in the early morning hours after our Thanksgiving celebration. He had not been in New York very long. "He just got his first paycheck in the days before he died," says Nawang.

We learn that the man had been talking, that Thanksgiving evening, about his gratitude for life. "I don't know, but it was almost as if he was predicting what would happen," Nawang confides.

I sit with the human propensity to reconcile the unexpected with efforts to remember, to claim, to attribute. Nawang relays the fact that this man stopped drinking alcohol several years ago but that he consumed a lot of Red Bull that last evening of his life. "Maybe it did something to his heart." Given the cardiac dangers of so-called "energy" drinks, this does not seem unreasonable.

"What did you do?" I ask.

"I had to talk with many people. Police. Morgue. Medical examiner. At first, they wanted to do an autopsy, to find an answer. But after I talked with the family and explained what 'autopsy' means—that the body is disturbed—they decided not to do this. Instead, we went by our own custom."

Nawang helped the aggrieved family manage official bureaucracy around the experience of death in New York as well as ritual arrangements back in Nepal. "Yesterday, we came together and collected money for the funeral, about four thousand dollars, and also money to pay off his remaining visa debt," he says. "We got what we needed. Four lamas will come for the cremation. It will be on Monday, the right day for him." Astrological calculations were done in Nepal, but we all live under the same stars.

As Nawang describes the mechanics of managing a funeral across time, space, and culture, I think back to a moment, four years prior to this one, when I sat in the incense-drenched room of his uncle's house in Brooklyn as we marked the passing of Nawang's own father back in Nepal. His outpouring of grief then seems the inverse of his composure now—his sense of obligation, his gentle response to the needs of others. In each instance, people hold one another. In each instance, duty meets devotion in ways that reinscribe care and belonging. Ways of being present, even in absence, are maintained.

This, too, is Thanksgiving.

# CONCLUSION

I do not think that I ever, in fact, returned home.

—MARY OLIVER, *UPSTREAM*

And so it is myself I want to turn in that direction
not as towards a place, but it was a tilting
within myself.

—MARIE HOWE, "ANNUNCIATION"

IN SEPTEMBER 2018, TWO LOBA MEN DIED. ONE PASSED AWAY IN Kathmandu. The other ended his life in New York. The men were brothers. They died within one twenty-four-hour period.

The elder brother succumbed to cardiac arrest. People spoke of how, when the body was discovered, the man's hands were folded under his cheek. He looked to be at peace. Although estranged from his wife, this man lived within a circle of community. People spoke of his jovial nature, his generosity, the cups of tea they had enjoyed together in the hours and days before his passing.

The younger brother's death was determined to be a suicide. The man's body washed up in the East River. Although some people suggested foul play, given the unexpected nature of this event and the fact that this brother was financially successful, many also said that they were unable to know his heart-mind.

The uncanny nature of these deaths produced a collective sense of disease in people from Mustang living on both sides of the world. *Death happens, but why two brothers? Why in the same day?*

In each case, the men died alone. The exact times of their deaths were impossible to determine, hampering astrological calculations for funerary rites. Navigating the logistics of death in Kathmandu was straightforward. Setting into motion the retrieval of the New York resident's body from the city morgue proved challenging, for reasons that had to do with bureaucracy—with claiming this person as Nepali, let alone as Loba. There

227

was dissonance between official papers and the lived experience of identity. This Himalayan New Yorker remained at once visible and invisible, even in death. Nevertheless, the work of seeing these brothers through the *bardo* proceeded apace, in New York, in Kathmandu, and in the village of these brothers' births.

◆  ◆  ◆

I arrive in Kathmandu the day after the fourth week of death rituals, mark weeks five and six in Lo, and leave Nepal hours after the forty-ninth day rituals are completed for these brothers. In Mustang as in Kathmandu, people are wrapped up in the service of honoring these mortal ends of kinship. Female relatives spend hours cooking, cleaning, serving tea, and facilitating the mostly male labor involved with other aspects of death: ritual practice, the disbursal of property, the payment of debts.

Another way to say this is that while men manage relations to land and lineage, women manage the web of social relationships on which care and belonging rest. Grief, coupled with remembering the dead, are collectively embodied acts. Each demand time, resources, attention. At the forty-ninth day rituals for these brothers in Kathmandu, people remark on just how much money it now costs to die ("as much as a wedding") and how the cultural requirements of being present to honor death preclude the possibility of other kinds of labor ("We need one person per household just for showing up to funerals").

People in Mustang and Kathmandu thought about these facts in relation to their kin in America. When death happens, money circulates, itself a way of recognizing blood and bone, tying up the loose ends of kinship. But in New York, time to collectively practice the culture of mourning are confounded not only by inflexible work or school schedules and the annoyances of mass transit but also by more internal changes linked to acculturation, generational divides, and the senses of alienation and isolation that can accompany late capitalist lives. A common saying, popular among Loba and itself the title of a film made by Lhaksam, an exile Tibetan artist, rings in my ears: *Nu Yok ma ré. Mi yog ré.* It is not New York. It is slavery.

Still, everyone along the path that is the *khora* of migration bears a certain spiritual responsibility to honor these brothers' deaths and to live out their consequences, in presence and in absence.

◆  ◆  ◆

Nearly two years after the King of Lo's passing, I walk on the roof of the palace in Monthang with the man people still refer to as Gyalchung. With this title, he is the "little king" or crown prince, though he has taken up his father's mantle. We look north, toward the Nepal-China boundary. I ask about the future of cross-border trade and tourism, having witnessed on this trip the significant infrastructural development that has occurred since I last drove the road up to the border in autumn 2016. Locals now call this rural highway a "third gear road." It is wide enough for lorries in places. With this widening has come increasing numbers of domestic Nepali tourists and Indian pilgrims as well as new risks and hazards, at once human and environmental: accidents, landslides. In this, Gyalchung seems deferential to the political will of others, in Mustang and Kathmandu.

We speak about plans to build an airport on territory that belongs to the village of Tsarang, near a new Nepal Army garrison erected and populated in the past two years. I question the necessity—let alone the wisdom—of this proposal. He maintains an agnostic cool with regards to the airport's possible future and its potential impact on Loba land and people. It is, after all, a campaign promise of his nephew, now the mayor of one of Lo's newly drawn rural municipalities.

We speak about the People's Republic across the border: its strength, its looming pressure. There is candor in our conversation about the caravans of Chinese-plated SUVs, with their tinted windows and souped-up shocks, that whir across the international border and roll into Monthang on a regular basis, stirring up dust and political suspicions with impunity. The Loba rumored to be Chinese informants live as open secrets in their own village. There is no need to name them, but we acknowledge their presence.

We walk along the roofline, past a shrine of Tibetan antelope and wild yak horns and piles of beautifully carved pillars and crossbeams that have been rescued from several palace rooms that were severely damaged in the 2015 earthquakes. These spaces have inched toward repair, but the palace's future remains uncertain.

From this vantage, we peer down onto the roofs of other households. On one, an aging *ngakpa* is performing a ritual that must be done before members of this family head to India for winter trade. Another house stands out. It is the home in which I once lived, with Dolma and her family. It is not empty, but neither is it well maintained. Weeds sprout from the roof. The garland of firewood that crowns the structure is uneven and dusty.

Out beyond the edges of the wall stands Gyalchung's own boutique hotel, a gorgeous building fashioned in Tibetan style but one that is noticeably separated from the town itself. This distance feels at once physical and emotional. I remark that one of the many new hotels being erected in Monthang stands taller than the wall. Even in its half-formed state, the guest house looms, cement and iron crowding not only the parapets but also an ancient poplar in which a serpent spirit dwells.

"What do you think about people building so close to the wall and taller than the wall?" I ask.

Gyalchung shrugs. "I don't have any right to say this can't happen."

I am reminded that *monthang* means "plain of aspiration." This is a place where many conflicting forms of aspiration are playing out and where the socioeconomic divides between those with means and those without is widening. While one person from Mustang can leverage enough capital to build this hotel, can afford to purchase the latest Land Rover or buy a home in Kathmandu or Jersey City, others live very different lives.

A few days earlier, I met an elderly woman on the trail between Monthang and Tshoshar. She was from Samdzong, one of two villages in Lo being relocated for lack of water. She left her home in the old village at first light and had already crossed a mountain pass by the time we encountered each other. The woman shuffled along, ill and alone, with only the equivalent of a few dollars tucked into the folds of her cummerbund. She would use this money for medicine—either from a government health assistant or a local *amchi*. She claimed only two dozen goats, the clutch of turquoise and coral at her neck, and a dilapidated house in a village with no water as her valuables. Socioeconomic stratification has existed in Mustang for centuries. But such stark disparities are, in many ways, new.

So, too, are shifts in Mustang's built landscape. The understandable local desire for different forms of creature-comfort have twined with projections about what tourists want and the real-time impacts of a shifting climate to create a perfect storm of aesthetic transformation. You can see such changes in Monthang but perhaps nowhere as starkly as Kag.

Not long ago, a singular structure dominated the view of this village: a monastery, whose carmine walls were buttressed by the remains of a fortress in an otherwise uniform landscape of rammed earth and mud brick structures surrounded by agricultural fields. Today, the town is an architectural menagerie. Telephone wires and the steel poles that prop them up rest beside rows of prayer wheels and *mani* stones, themselves bookended between *chöten*, just down the road from the jeep stand. New hotels built of cement and painted the color of toothpaste and cotton candy tower over an old wooden bridge. A bodega sells cell phone recharge cards and Khukri

Rum, powdered milk and Panther condoms. And yet, when you enter the inner passages of the village, you are framed by Mustang's social history. Low lintels grace the imperfect angle of home.

When I comment on these architectural shifts to an aging noblewoman of Kag, herself the owner of one of the most important houses in the village, her tongue is swift. She has no patience for nostalgia. "Tourists are crazy! They think we should only keep the old places. But do they not live in cement houses? Do they not have *attached bath*?"

Another friend is a bit more ecumenical. "We have seen a hundred years of change in ten or fifteen years," he says.

◆ ◆ ◆

I am walking around the cluster of sacred sites that make up the Muktinath temple complex. The consecration ceremonies for a renovated monastery and a newly installed giant stone Buddha statue have just been completed. The statue itself cost nearly half a million *dollars* and was donated by one of Mustang–New York's wealthiest individuals, who has returned from Queens for these ritual festivities. People from across Lo and Baragaon have come to Muktinath for this event. It is a rare conjoining of Mustang's many worlds.

On the circumambulation path, I meet a woman from Monthang and her teenage son. We exchange pleasantries and comment on the auspiciousness of the day. The broad valley shimmers in the afternoon light. As we part, I am reminded that this woman's husband has been in New York for nearly all of their son's life. This man has failed to make papers, but he has not failed his family. His wife owns a lodge in Monthang. Their children attended good schools. And, unlike some partners, this physically estranged couple speak every day. But presence-in-absence doesn't quell longing.

In seeing this mother and son, I recall a conversation I had a few months prior with another person from Monthang who has lived in New York for eighteen years without returning to Nepal. As we sat in his living room in Elmhurst, he spoke about seeing his younger sister face-to-face when she arrived in the States a few years ago. "We have talked over the years, but it was still like meeting someone I didn't know," he said. "I'm not sure what I was expecting, but it was like somewhere in my heart I thought she would still be seven, not a grown woman." Such temporal incongruities are the split ends of kinship.

Not long after that conversation, I found myself in another Queens apartment, this one occupied by Dolma, her husband, and their two unmarried daughters. We spoke about the price of rent and the cost of living in New York as well as the house they own in Kathmandu—including the headaches associated with renting it. It was purchased as what might be called a retirement investment. This middle-aged couple are steadfast in their desire not to die in the U.S. but uncertain of the home's usefulness in the long run.

Dolma served lunch. Over a meal of curried potatoes and buckwheat bread, she shared her ideal version of growing old. "My hope is that we spend three months a year in New York, three months in Kathmandu, three months in Monthang, and three months to travel or go on pilgrimage," she said. "We will do *khora* around the world, to see people and be in places we love." This is, indeed, a lovely vision. But it is one complicated by so many practicalities, small and large.

As we ate, Dolma's daughter chided her mother for the fact that she has refused to sit for the U.S. citizenship test. This opportunity is hers for the taking, since she has a green card and has resided in New York for more than five years. The rest of the family are citizens. But Dolma's shame about her lack of English has stopped her. And, even with a U.S. passport, returning to the place of Dolma's birth in central Tibet, where her sister and mother live, was impossible for other reasons, although it remained Dolma's primary motivation for considering taking the test.

In all these cases, external factors shape the mechanics of mobility. Sometimes, *khora* lives in the mind while the body is still, when movement is constrained. Sometimes to be present is also to sense the negative space of absence.

Returning to the day of celebration at Muktinath, I am reminded of another sort of dream, another way of being that illuminates paths not taken. During the consecration rituals, the son of Muktinath's hereditary lama— the person whose responsibility it is to steward this sacred abode—takes his place beside his father. High-altitude sun, clear mountain views, and Tibetan Buddhist pageantry lend this moment a sense of grandeur. The young man wears the robes of a *ngakpa*, like his father. Beside him is not only his father but also a Nyingma master from Tibet. They chant in unison.

I stand in the crowd beside the young man's mother. This woman has experienced more than her share of suffering, but her smile is genuine, empty of bitterness. She has spent most of her adult years in Kathmandu. The stresses of her social role at this high-stakes event, combined with the rarefied atmosphere at nearly 13,000 feet, to which her body is no longer accustomed, leaves her dizzy and depleted. Still, she seems happy. Five years ago, her son was keen on a life in New York. He aspired to be a disc jockey and wanted nothing to do with Buddhist philosophy, let alone inheriting the family responsibility for this place: its nunnery, its temples and shrines. But a series of events—good mentorship, a father who could have forced his will on his son but did not, and a quiet form of divine intervention—led this young man toward another path, one of study and practice, of envisioning a future for this place on his own terms.

"I left my phone in the kitchen. Can you take a picture?" his mother asks, glowing with pride. I click a few images of father and son, of change and continuity, against the backdrop of natural splendor.

◆  ◆  ◆

I spend some time in the home of Karma and Yungdung after the Muktinath festivities. Karma and I delight in each other's company. We sip tea by day and modest cups of homemade *arak* after sunset. "We are drinking again," she admits, "but only a few sips to clear the path for sleep."

Yungdung watches a Nepali game show on the television in the next room. Karma and I laugh at twenty-year-old jokes and speak seriously about the challenges she and Yungdung face in a village whose own existence is threatened not only by out-migration but also by environmental change. The *chöten* that signified the founding of this village was swept away by a flood in 2017. It has been rebuilt on a shale and scree ledge above the main settlement. Yet newly constructed retaining walls and fields were this year's monsoon casualties. The river threatens houses at the base of the village. Still, people persist, embracing—as one must in this community that clings to a cliff—a certain confidence in verticality and a healthy fear of water.

The morning of my departure, Karma places an offering scarf around my bowed shoulders, then takes my hands in hers. Our foreheads touch.

"The world is small," she says. "It keeps turning, just like *khora*."

We live in and through this turning.

# GLOSSARY

**ABBREVIATIONS**

L    Logé
N    Nepali
Skt    Sanskrit
T    Tibetan
W    Wylie transliteration (the system used most widely to transliterate Tibetan words into the Roman alphabet, to preserve accurate spellings)

**agi / apa (T, L), a gi / a pa (W)**  father
**ále (L)**  money
**ama (N, T), a ma (W)**  mother
**amchi (T), em chi (W)**  physician, practitioner of Tibetan medicine
**ani (T), a ni (W)**  nun, aunt
**ani-ashang (T), a ni–a zhang (W)**  cross-cousin [marriage]
**arak (T), a rag (W)**  distilled grain alcohol

**bahini (N)**  little sister
**bardo (T), bar do (W)**  intermediate state
**bhote (N)**  culturally Tibetan person (derogatory and slang)
**bhote pipal (N)**  Himalayan poplar, *Populus ciliata*
**bu (T, W)**  bug, insect
**bukampa (N)**  earthquake

**cham (T), 'chams (W)**  masked dances
**chang (T, W)**  beer, usually from barley
**changsa (L)**  wedding ceremony
**chikya (L), phyi skya (W)**  foreigner
**chinlab (T), byin rlabs (W)**  blessing
**chori (N)**  daughter
**chöten (T) / stupa (Skt, N), chos rten (W)**  reliquary mound, shrine
**chuba (N)**  Tibetan-style dress

**churpi (N), chu ra (W)**  dried cheese

**crore (N)**  ten million, one hundred *lakh*

**dai (N)**  elder brother

**dal bhat (N)**  rice and lentils, Nepali national dish

**dalit (N)**  "untouchable" castes

**damaru (T, N, Skt), da ma ru (W)**  two-headed drum

**darchog (T), dar mchog (W)**  vertical prayer flags

**dewachen (T), bde ba chen (W)**  "heaven," great bliss, *mahasukha*

**dharma (Skt, N)**  [Buddhist] religion, duty

**doko (N)**  woven conical basket

**dorje (T) / vajra (Skt, N), rdo rje (W)**  ritual thunderbolt scepter

**dralog (T), sgrwa slogs (W)**  ex-monk

**dresil (T), 'bras sil (W)**  ceremonial rice pudding

**drilbu (T) / ghanta (Skt, N), dril bu (W)**  ritual bell

**drokpa (T), 'brogs pa (W)**  nomad, pastoralist

**drumbu (T), grum bu (W)**  rheumatic disorders

**dukhor (T), dus khor (W)**  rotating credit system

**dzema (T), mdzes ma (W)**  beautiful girl, woman

**dzi (T), gzi (W)**  black-and-white agate, highly valued

**dzinbu (L), 'dzin bu (W)**  wild chives

**genba (T), 'gan pa (W)**  headman

**geshe (T), dge bshes (W)**  Tibetan Buddhist doctorate

**gönpa (T), dgon pa (W)**  monastery, hermitage, temple

**gonyé (L)**  caraway seed

**gyakpa (T), rgyags pa (W)**  fat, chubby, "healthy"

**hajakpa (L)**  unspeakably bad (slang, profanity)

**hrewo / hremo (L)**  nobleman / noblewoman

**hri (L), sri (W)**  vampire

**hromo / hrowo (L)**  paternal aunt / uncle

**ibi (L)**  grandmother

**janajati (N)**  ethnic group, principally associated with minority ethnicities in Nepal

**jasta (N)**  tin

**jhankri (N)**  shaman

**jindak (T), sbyin bdag (W)**  sponsor, patron

**ka kha ga (T, N)**  first three letters of Tibetan and Nepali alphabets

**kaliyug (Skt, N) / dü nyemba (L, T), dus nyams pa (W)**  a "degenerate age"

**kathag (T), kha btags (W)**  offering scarf

**kawa (T), ka ba (W)**  central vertical pillar

**khandro (T) / dakini (Skt), mkha' 'gro (W)**  "sky dancer," female deity

**khaubadi (N)**  looters posing as Maobadi, from the verb "to eat"

**khenpo (T), mkhan po (W)**  abbot

**khorwa (T) / samsara (Skt), 'khor ba (W)**  cyclic existence

**khurma (L), khur ma (W)**  load, things carried

**khuwa (T), khu ba (W)**  semen

**kora (L), skor ba (W)**  circumambulation

**kyekar (T), skye dkar (W)**  birth horoscope

**kyemen (T), skye dman (W)**  woman, wife

**kyidug (T), skyi sdug (W)**  social service organization


**la (T), bla / la (W)**  life force

**lakh (N)**  one hundred thousand

**lam (T, W)**  road, path, way

**lama (T), bla ma (W), guru (Skt, N)**  religious practitioner

**lé (T) / karma (Skt, N), las (W)**  laws of cause and effect

**lhapa (T), lha pa (W)**  medium, oracle

**lokta (N)**  two *Daphne* species, used for paper

**lonak (T), lo nag (W)**  "black" year of obstacles

**Losar (T), lo gsar (W)**  Tibetan lunar new year

**lu (T), klu (W)**  serpent spirit, *naga*


**makpa (T), mag pa (W)**  matrilocal groom

**mani (T, N), ma ni (W)**  prayer (stone or wheel), jewel

**mantra (Skt, N)**  prayer

**Maobadi (N)**  Nepali Maoists

**martsa (L), dmar tshwa (W)**  dried chili powder mix

**mitini (N)**  ritual / fictive "sister," close friend

**mo (T, W)**  divination

**momo (T, N), mog mog (W)**  steamed dumplings


**nagarikta (N)**  Nepali citizenship document

**nama (T), mna' ma (W)**  bride, daughter-in-law

**ngachen (T), rnga chen (W)**  large ritual drum

**ngakpa (T), ngags pa (W)**  tantrist, married priest

ngotsa (T), ngo tswa (W)  shame, embarrassment

nöpa (T), gnod pa (W)  harm, injury

nyelu / nyemo (L)  illegitimate son / daughter

nyetsang (T), gnas tsang (W)  lineage-based trading partners

nyingjé (T), snying rje (W)  compassion

nyung ne (T), snyung nye (W)  Buddhist fasting, purification practice


peja (T), dpe cha (W)  unbound religious text

phalba (T), phal ba (W)  commoner

phorong-morong (L)  household (not joint)

phorwa (T), phor ba (W)  wooden drinking cup

phowa (T), 'pho ba (W)  ritual practice at death

pipal (N)  sacred fig tree, *Ficus religiosa*

puja (N)  religious ritual


rajya (N)  nation, nation-state

rikhor (L)  petty trade (usually in winter)

rimé (T), ris med (W)  non-sectarian Tibetan Buddhism

rinpoche (T), rin po che (W)  esteemed religious teacher

rolang (T), ro langs (W)  zombie

rongba (L), rong ba (W)  lowland Nepali (derogatory and slang)

ropani (N)  measurement of land (approximately 500 square meters
   or 1/8 acre)

rü (T), rus (W)  bone, (patri)lineage


sabdak (T), sab bdag (W)  earth-owner spirit

sadhu (N)  Hindu renunciant

sagul (T), sa 'gul (W)  earthquake; also a gloss for the creature on whose back
   Earth sits

sang (T), bsang (W)  fumigation rituals

sasum (T), sag sum (W)  polyandry

sathi (N)  friend

sayom (T), sa yom (W)  earthquake

sem né (T), sems nad (W)  illness of the heart-mind

sha paglep (T), sha pag leb (W)  meat-stuffed bread

shukpa (T), shugs pa (W)  juniper

sogtsa (T) / nadi (Skt), srog rtsa (W)  central life channel

srinmo (T), srin mo (W)  demoness

**thangka (T), thang ka (W)**  Tibetan scroll painting

**tharchang (L), thar chang (W)**  retirement ceremony

**thugdam (T), thugs dam (W)**  death meditation practice

**tongba (T), stong pa (W)**  empty, neglected, desolate

**torma (T), tor ma (W)**  ritual offering cake

**tsadrip (T), rtsa sgribs (W)**  illness of spiritual pollution, often similar to a stroke

**tsampa (T), tsam pa (W)**  roasted barley flour

**tsen (T), btsan (W)**  nefarious spirit, demon

**tsham (T), tshams (W)**  religious meditation retreat

**tshé (T), tshe (W)**  life, life span

**tshong gyug (L), tshong rgyug (W)**  trade returns, bringing home trade

**tshongra (L), tshong ra (W)**  trade bazaar

**tsi (T), rtsi (W)**  astrological calculations

**tsuk (L)**  rapeseed

**tulku (T), sprul sku (W)**  reincarnated religious figure


**ulu bulu (L)**  secret sexual relations

**umdze (T), dbu mzad (W)**  chant master

**upaya (Skt)**  skillful means


**yartsa gunbu (T), dbyar rtswa dgun 'bu (W)**  caterpillar fungus, *Ophiocordyceps sinensis*

**yerma (T), gyer ma (W)**  Sichuan pepper

**yidam (T), yi dam (W)**  tutelary deity

**yul lha (T), yul lha (W)**  local, regional deity

# ESSAY ON SOURCES
# AND METHODS

I first journeyed to Mustang in 1993, as a nineteen-year-old undergraduate student on a study abroad program in Nepal. This initial excursion led to a post-graduation Fulbright Fellowship that, in turn, facilitated three years of living and working in Nepal (1995–98), including more time in Mustang. During my Fulbright Fellowship, I did research with *amchi* and other healers throughout the district, studying ethnoveterinary care and the role of horses in Mustang's culture and economy. This included spending time in "upper Mustang," which had only recently been opened to foreigners. The region's full name is Lo Tö Tsho Dun, the Seven Principalities of the Kingdom of Lo. Below Lo, in the unrestricted yet still culturally Tibetan region of the district, is Baragaon, a name that means "twelve villages" in Nepali but that comprises nineteen settlements. Lo and Baragaon have distinct, if interconnected, histories. People throughout this region speak variants of Tibetan. In these early years, however, I communicated primarily in Nepali, using what Tibetan language skill I possessed at the time around the edges of conversations and for specific concepts. These years generated the material and the inspiration for my first book, *Horses Like Lightning: A Story of Passage through the Himalayas.*

An initial impetus for the project that led to that book was meeting anthropologist Charles Ramble on a crisp fall day in Kathmandu in 1993. He had come to lecture to my study abroad group about his research on religion and social history in Mustang. We struck up a conversation about horses. Many years later, Charles's scholarship as well as the example he set for long-term, multi-dimensional engagements with people from Mustang, particularly with his collaborator Nyima Drandul, informs how I work with people from Mustang as well. Charles is an exemplar when it comes to language, not only in how he narrates history and culture in his scholarship but, equally, in how he has modeled fluency in varieties of Tibetan, including those spoken in Mustang. My formal instruction in Tibetan only began during graduate school, but it benefited from two years of living in Lhasa during my PhD study. This, combined with continuous work with people from Mustang, has led me to a reasonable fluency with variants of Tibetan spoken in Mustang, but I remain in awe of Charles's abilities and grateful for his scholarship.

Much earlier work on Mustang by Giuseppe Tucci, Michel Peissel, David Snellgrove, Christoph von Fürer-Haimendorf, and David Jackson have helped me to understand this region in the larger contexts of the greater Nepal Himalaya and Tibet, as have more recent archaeological, historical, architectural, and ethnographic work by Mark Aldenderfer, Ramesh Dhungel, William Fisher, and Michael Vinding. Social science research conducted through the Centre for Nepal and Asian Studies at Tribhuvan University, led by Professor Ram Bahadur Chhetri during the 1980s, has further instructed me in dynamics of change and continuity, particularly in Monthang. Christian Luczanits's expertise on the artistic heritage of Mustang and John Harrison's meticulous renderings of Mustang architecture—as well as his fieldwork companionship—have enhanced what I know about the region's past, present, and possible futures. The ethereal and yet exacting paintings by Robert Powell and Bidhata KC, along with Kevin Bubriski's photographs of the region, have contributed to how I see this landscape's poetry. I first read Manjushree Thapa's *Mustang Bhot in Fragments* in 1996 while I was living with a family in Monthang, along with Pushpa Tulachan, a Thakali from lower Mustang and a PhD candidate in anthropology at USC at that time. Manjushree's reflections on her year in Lo and Pushpa's groundbreaking though unpublished dissertation have guided my understanding of so many Mustang dynamics: domestic politics, kinship networks, migration, trade, and the tensions between personal aspiration and family expectations.

More recent scholarship on social, infrastructural, and environmental change by Galen Murton and Fidel Devkota as well as our conversations contribute to how I see and write about the region. Likewise, my ideas have been shaped by scholarship that focuses on other Himalayan borderlands and on the concept of the "border" in Himalayan studies—work by Ken Bauer, Geoff Childs, James Fisher, Kabir Mansingh Heimsath, Martin Saxer, Sara Shneiderman, Wim van Spengen, Dan Smyer Yü, and Jean Michaud, among others. Joanne Watkins's book on Manang was particularly influential early in my thinking about migration and mobility in Himalayan communities and about the roles of women therein—themes that Prista Ratanapruck's more recent work on Manang also illuminates.

I cannot overstate the extent to which Geoff Childs's scholarship, friendship, and collaborative spirit have shaped my thinking about many issues at the heart of this book, from a focus on the life course in Himalayan places to how education and out-migration are intertwined. I've worked with Geoff on several projects, the data from which shape this book. The first, on which biological anthropologist Cynthia M. Beall was the principal investigator, focused on the links between high altitude biology, kinship networks, and household situations and women's reproductive lives. This project, funded by the National Science Foundation (NSF; BCS-1153911), involved intensive biocultural fieldwork in 2012 in Mustang and in northern Gorkha District, where Geoff has worked for decades. My collaboration with Cynthia on these themes continues. We spent the summer of 2019 together in Mustang, again funded by the NSF (BCS-1831530), delving more deeply into the relationship between culturally Tibetan people's adaptations to living at high altitude and women's health. Our work together laid the foundation for Part I of this book.

In subsequent years, Geoff and I have supported each other's interests in migration: sharing methodological approaches, reading each other's work, and publishing independently and together on questions of social and demographic change. Geoff's PhD student and collaborator Namgyal Choedup has been a key part of this work, and their co-authored book, *From a Trickle to a Torrent*, makes incisive ethnographic and demographic points about the ways that educational goals and practices, the phenomenon of "Tibetanness," and political, environmental, and economic change are shaping Nepal's high Himalayan communities. Our books are distinct in structure and focus, but they are kindred spirits.

The devastating 2015 earthquakes brought Geoff and me together again for a project spearheaded by linguist Kristine Hildebrandt and funded through an NSF RAPID award (1547377). In this effort, we worked with young community researchers from Mustang, Manang, and Gorkha to document how people in these places narrated experiences of natural disaster. It has been a fruitful collaboration across disciplines and languages, resulting in an open access archive of these interviews and multiple publications. The Mustang team was comprised of Nawang Tsering, Yangjin, KC, and a young *amchi*, Tsewang Gyurme. Research from this project informs Part V of this book.

That project's focus on the relationships between language, culture, and social transformation is echoed in other applied, interdisciplinary efforts in which I have been engaged. These collaborations—rooted in New York and seeded by Nawang Tsering—involve partnerships with the Endangered Language Alliance (ELA), anthropologist and linguist Mark Turin, and filmmaker Kesang Tseten. This work has included *Voices of the Himalaya*, a project that uses the medium of open-access video storytelling and documentary film to talk about language, migration, and social change among Himalayan New Yorkers. We are now working on a project, funded by the Peter Wall Foundation (Mark Turin, PI), focused on representing linguistic diversity and supporting language revitalization across the city through digital language mapping tools, in which Himalayan and Tibetan communities will feature prominently. A map of New York at the front of this book shows Mustang variants of Tibetan alongside other related languages and dialects, as they plot onto distinct neighborhoods in the boroughs of Brooklyn and Queens. This is a representation created by cartographer Molly Roy and built from ELA's groundbreaking Languages of New York City analog map, which serves as the foundation for our digital mapping work.

But how did I get from Nepal to New York and back again?

I first visited a friend from Mustang in New York in January 1998, an event I recount in Part III of this book. At the start of the new millennium, while a graduate student at Cornell, I began making trips from Ithaca to the city and other parts of New England to visit people from Mustang. My nascent efforts at thinking through these experiences included two early articles (2002, 2004). Although I conducted most of my dissertation research in China's Tibet Autonomous Region, I made regular trips to Mustang during this time (2002–4). Both before dissertation research (1999–2002) and after, while writing my PhD in Ithaca (2005–6), I kept meeting friends from Mustang, now in New York, and was able to invite others from Mustang to Cornell.

Between becoming a mother and starting a tenure-track job at Dartmouth, I did not return to Mustang until 2008, this time with my daughter, Aida, in tow. Over the past decade, I've spent a total of nine months back in Mustang, with additional time in Kathmandu and Pokhara. Trips to New York have been interspersed between Nepal-based fieldwork. Nawang Tsering and I first embarked on formal research together in New York in 2011, focusing on the theme of everyday religion and belonging. Our work together has continued in the intervening years, including through some of the projects described above. After more than two decades of connection to

Mustang, I began to conceive of this book in earnest in 2016. Since that time, the book itself has become an object of inquiry and a subject of conversation: I shared early drafts with many of the people described herein. Their responses, in turn, shaped my writing and revising process.

Scholarship on mobility, diaspora, transnationalism, and globalization informs my understanding of the *khora* of migration between Nepal and New York. Each of these keywords, if you will, corresponds to vast literatures. I have read widely, but I still feel as if I've only cracked the surface. While the etymology of "diaspora" points to population dispersal, many social theorists have worked to problematize ideas that would have diaspora emerging from singular origin stories or assert that it feeds only on nostalgia for return. Rogers Brubaker, Avtar Brah, Kim Butler, James Clifford, and Stuart Hall have helped me to wrestle with the ways that diaspora, as a concept and as a sociopolitical experience, does not give way to easy answers about home or identity. As Laura Ogden has written, "Moving beyond the 'homeland orientation' has enabled scholars of diasporas to understand diasporic identity and subjectivity as always political and relational . . . and often constituted by modernity's spatial-racial ordering" (2018, 66). Thinking about this work in relation to the cyclic nature of *khora* as well as the multifarious ways that origin and return are configured and reconfigured for those from Mustang has been instructive.

The work of Nina Glick Schiller and Peggy Levitt, among others, have shaped my thinking about the category of transnationalism as it relates to identity and belonging. Sara Ahmed's work on narratives of migration and estrangement has helped me to think about the possibilities for isolation and forms of cultural discontinuity that migration can produce. Vinay Gidwani and K. Sivaramakrishnan prompt me to think, specifically, about the circularity—the roots and routes—of migration. Of all that I've read on globalization, Anna Tsing's *Friction* sticks with me the most, not only because of her masterful ability to move between ethnographic and theoretical registers but also in the ways that she elucidates how the movement of ideas, people, and things in late capitalism give rise to so many forms of conflict and possibility, sometimes simultaneously. Robert Smith's ethnography, *Mexican New York*, Dan Reichman's *The Broken Village*, and Seth Holmes's *Fresh Fruit, Broken Bodies* all draw from Latin American contexts, but they have served as intellectual touchstones as I've moved between Nepal and New York.

Lisa Åkesson's work on Cape Verdean transnational families, Caitlin Fouratt's engagement with Nicaraguan transnational communities, June

Hee Kwon's work on the entanglements of love and money in Korean Chinese transnational migration, and Dinah Hannaford's analysis of the ways that marriage, migration, and remittances are connected through transnational Senegalese lives have allowed me to think comparatively about the power of remittances. Levitt's scholarship on forms of what she calls "social remittances" has furthered my thinking about two social institutions central to Mustang's *khora* of migration, namely *dukhor* and *kyidug.* Nepal's Centre for the Study of Labour and Mobility has produced seminal publications about Nepali migrations, many of them spearheaded by Bandita Sijapati. These are essential reading for anyone who wants to understand migration in and through Nepal. Work on the topic by David Seddon, Jagannath Adhikari, and Ganesh Gurung also stand out. *Facing Globalization in the Himalayas*, edited by Gerard Toffin and Joanna Pfaff-Czarnecka, and *Global Nepalis*, edited by David Gellner and Sondra Hausner, have been useful sources for thinking about these worldly dynamics through a Nepali lens. Other recent Nepal-centric scholarship (Adhikari and Hobley 2015; Gurung 2015; Maharjan 2015; Mulmi and Shneiderman 2017; Sato 2016; J. R. Sharma 2018; S. Sharma et al. 2014; Shneiderman 2015a, 2015b; Speck 2017; Yamanaka 2000) has led me to points of consonance and dissonance between their interlocutors' experiences and those from Mustang. Dannah Dennis's wonderful short story "Fifty-Three Kilos" resonates and was a delight to find while writing this book.

Equal to this body of work, literature has guided me. Tsering Wangmo Dhompa's poetry and her memoir, *Coming Home to Tibet*, have helped me to feel my way through what I cannot know. Teju Cole's capacity to tack between genres while writing about Nigeria, America, and places between have inspired me from the sentence level up. Others, too, among them: Viet Thanh Nguyen, Nadeem Aslam, Tenzin Dickie, Jenny Erpenbeck, Ocean Vuong, Pico Iyer, Chimamanda Ngozi Adichie, Jhumpa Lahiri, Jamaica Kincaid, Mohsin Hamid, Zadie Smith, Michael Ondaatje, and Richard Blanco.

Speaking of writing, one need only look to Zora Neale Hurston's oeuvre or Elenore Smith Bowen's *Return to Laughter* to know that the relationship between fiction and ethnography runs deep. Reading Ruth Behar's *The Vulnerable Observer* during my first year in graduate school was like a bolt of lightning: visceral, charged, transformative. It and her other work, which I have followed over the years, have shown me that being an anthropologist does not require living as a closeted creative writer. In a very different way, Kirin Narayan's work has done the same.

Her mastery of intersections between narrative and vernacular, theory and method and her treatment of women's experiences have had a profound influence on me. Paul Stoller's writings across multiple genres, including about the life of West African immigrants to New York, have given me confidence to be a storyteller and to write friendship into text. Kristen Ghodsee's interweaving of ethnography and short fiction in *Lost in Transition* gave me courage.

The work of many poet-anthropologists, especially Renato Rosaldo and Adrie Kusserow, have imprinted on me. Robert Desjarlais's phenomenological anthropology and sensory ethnography of Nepal have helped me to find my voice within this text, especially in writing about death. Ann Armbrecht has helped me to meditate on the meanings of home and how this links to place. João Biehl's *Vita* and *Will to Live* as well as his theorization of subjectivity and what he calls "an anthropology of becoming" have helped me think about life histories, mutuality, positionality, and the relationship between image and text. Carole McGranahan is a lively and caring interlocutor about so many things, from the writing life to ethnographic theory to Tibetan histories. I thank her, specifically, for helping me to navigate the murky waters of asylum and exile and for the comprehensive volume, *Writing Anthropology*, that she has hewn—an endeavor in which she has included me. Kathleen (Katie) Stewart's work slips under my skin. It makes me attentive to detail and how theory emerges, as she might say, on the side of the road. I take up the invitation, proffered in her collaboration with philosopher Lauren Berlant, *The Hundreds*, to hone and sculpt ethnographic work into clutches of meaning.

## PART I

I spent my early years of fieldwork mostly with older men, local veterinarians and *amchi*, in a place where Tibetan medicine was still a nearly exclusively male domain. Yet many of my most memorable experiences involved friendships with women and opportunities to learn about their lives. This included confronting—well before I became a wife and mother myself—the fact that pregnancy and birth could be precarious. What I would later come to understand within the frameworks of critical medical anthropology and global health, I first encountered in talks with Mustang women about their pregnancies: the live births and the losses as well as the distinct possibility that women who were in their forties or older, when I first met them in my twenties, had lived through the death of at least one child.

It was not until I spent time in Lhasa that I began to learn more about the circumstances under which many culturally Tibetan women conceive, gestate, labor, give birth, and—if they make it this far—care for newborns and young children. My dissertation involved working on a National Institutes of Health and Gates Foundation–funded project that ultimately resulted in the first randomized controlled trial of a Tibetan medical formula versus a biomedical pharmaceutical for the prevention of postpartum hemorrhage—a problem that kills more women worldwide than nearly any other complication of labor and delivery. During this time, I had the privilege of working with the Women's Division of Mentsikhang, the Tibetan medical hospital founded in Lhasa in 1916 that survives to this day. A second project in which I was involved in Lhasa focused more on rural women's pregnancy and birth experiences and the training of Tibetan midwives. This led to the creation of a non-governmental organization, OneHEART (now One Heart Worldwide), and its development of a women's health training curriculum and public health intervention, supported by the TAR government as well as by this American NGO.

These combined experiences form the basis for a body of scholarship on pregnancy, labor, and delivery in Tibetan contexts, written collaboratively with mentors and colleagues Vincanne Adams, Sue Ellen Miller, and Arlene Samen, among others. I reflected on what I learned about pregnancy and birth through these years in the TAR in several other articles, including one that took a constructively critical look at the oft-cited assumption that there was no such thing as a "traditional" Tibetan midwife. Stacy Pigg's work on the development category "Traditional Birth Attendant" and Sarah Pinto's ethnography on birth, loss, and dynamics of development in northern India have been key reference points in my own work on these topics. Likewise with the research of Andrea Wiley, Kim Gutschow, and Jennifer Aengst on Ladakhi women's experiences of the biopolitics of pregnancy and birth; Susan Heydon's study of the biomedicalization of birth in Sherpa communities; Geoff Childs's analysis of fertility, family planning, and demographic change in *Tibetan Transitions* as well as his careful treatment of child death in *Tibetan Diary*; Santi Rozario and Geoffrey Samuel's ethnography on ideas of birth pollution in Tibetan and Indian societies as well as Geoffrey's discussion, specifically in *Civilized Shamans*, of classes of autochthonous beings that can be recruited for protection or harm, including in relation to pregnancy, childbirth, and early childhood; Mona Schrempf's historical and ethnographic study of family planning and the politics of reproduction in Amdo; and Katia Buffetrille's engagement with the work of the Tibetan poet and women's rights activist Jamyang Kyi. This regionally focused scholarship rests on a broad foundation of work by anthropologists of pregnancy and childbirth, including but not limited to Robbie Davis-Floyd, Carolyn Sargent, Rayna Rapp, and Emily Martin.

I became pregnant during my second year of fieldwork in Lhasa. I passed the majority of my pregnancy (seven months) there, being cared for by Tibetan and biomedical doctors with whom I worked every day. This was not always easy, but it led me to a completely different understanding of the dynamics I was also studying as an anthropologist. I reflect on this experience in one of the hundred-word segments in "Finding the Womb Door."

This time working on women's reproductive experiences in Tibet set the stage for research on which I would collaborate with Cynthia M. Beall in Mustang, beginning in 2012 and continuing into the present. Like the work in Tibet, the focus of fieldwork was on eliciting reproductive histories and learning about the many factors that shape the reproductive lives of women. But unlike the work in Tibet, this project—centered on the connections between culturally Tibetan people's biological and genetic adaptation to living at high altitude and women's reproductive outcomes—pushed me to delve more deeply into the (sometimes uncomfortable) relationship between biology and culture, including what it means to do things like collect spit or urine samples while also interviewing women about sensitive topics such as miscarriage, contraception, and infertility. Margaret Lock's essential theoretical intervention—the concept of "local biologies"—has remained a guidepost through this work, helping me to conceptualize how the biophysical, genetic, environmental, cultural, and political realities of being Tibetan or from Mustang relate to pregnancy and birth. Together with other colleagues, Cynthia and I have published on this work, from articles that center on the EPAS1 genetic marker in Tibetan populations to work that explores what we learned through our reproductive history interviews and household demographic surveys about contraception, fertility decline, and out-migration.

Concurrent with this research, I have maintained connections with One Heart Worldwide, now located in Nepal. Experiences from our Tibet days shaped this organization's approach to creating a "network of safety" for women and neonates—a model that is now being translated to Nepali contexts. Since the organization relocated to Nepal, I've done a second wave of writing with Vincanne Adams and One Heart's founder, Arlene Samen, along with Nepali colleagues, focusing on what One Heart's approach can teach us about grounded global health work in an era that values metrics above all else.

A few other notes are warranted in relation to Part I. In "Blood and Bone," I allude to the presence of the Tibetan resistance, also known as Khampa soldiers, who were based in Mustang from 1960 to 1973, as they waged guerilla warfare against the Chinese People's Liberation Army. Although not directly related to pregnancy and birth, the presence of Khampa in Mustang certainly impacted local women (pregnancies, marriages, affairs, assaults) and left profound political marks on the region in other ways (for more on these topics, see Andrugtsang 1973; Cowan 2018; Knaus 2000; McGranahan 2010; Peissel 1967).

In the chapter "Finding the Womb Door," in which I conduct my own *Hundreds* experiment, following Berlant and Stewart, I refer to the Tibetan creation story, in which Tibetan people were formed from the union of a monkey and an ogress as well as to another primordial assertion to do with the "taming" of Tibet—represented by a demoness—by Buddhism. Janet Gyatso has written an influential piece on this topic.

I acknowledge Julia Cohen, Dartmouth '18, whose thesis on Filipina caretakers in New York City included the articulation of the term "negotiated intimacies" in relation to transnational women caregivers. While considering the roles that Mustang women take on as nannies for New York families, I learned from Tamara Mose Brown's *Raising Brooklyn*, which focuses on Caribbean caretakers; Nicole Constable's work on migrant mothers and the politics of female transnational labor; and Rhacel Parreñas's analysis of "long distance intimacy" between mothers and children within dynamics of migration and transnational caregiving. Jason Pribilsky's research on Ecuadorian male migrants to New York and their experiences in relation to marriage and parenting, alongside perspectives from women in Ecuador, helped me to think about the differences between initial and later waves of the *khora* of migration between Mustang and New York, particularly for men.

As for my use of the term "grandmother hypothesis," it is generally a way of explaining menopause in human life history, focusing on the adaptive value of extended kin and alloparenting. There are various criticisms and alternative hypotheses for this particular aspect of human evolution. I use the term only as a conceptual alliteration.

PART II

This part of the book focuses on education and migration. Geoff Childs and Namgyal Choedup's work on this topic in relation to Nubri remains a central source. Together with Melvyn Goldstein and Puchung Wangdui, Childs also explores the idea of "going for education" through a discussion of this dynamic in central Tibet.

One might ask why Phurba's age is different in Tibetan and Western years. Tibetan cultural practices link age to Losar, the lunar new year, and the astrological year of birth. A baby born just before Losar will be considered two years old in the new lunar year.

In the logics described by parents for sending their children from Lo and Baragaon away for school, I mention the Thakali. They are an ethnic group whose home territory corresponds with the Thak Khola region of lower Mustang. Consummate traders and culture brokers, Thakali are perceived by many Loba as being "clever"—a gloss for manipulative and strategic. Vinding's comprehensive ethnography, *The Thakali*, William Fisher's work on identity and ethnicity among the Thakali, and Turin's work on language and ethnicity among the Thakali all help to challenge and complicate such assertions. Childs's (2004a) insight about how cultural change often occurs in the name of cultural preservation is helpful in further unpacking these logics.

Although the circumstances under which children from Mustang have been sent to residential boarding schools are entirely different than forced relocation of Indigenous, First Nations, and Aboriginal children from the settler colonial societies of North America, Australia, and New Zealand, the net effects of these experiences can be similar in terms of language and culture transformation and trauma. In other instances, boarding school can produce effects (of social networks, social capital, and advancement) similar to what students experience by attending elite institutions in the U.S., U.K., or elsewhere. Kesang Tseten's film *We Homes Chaps*, about the Indian and Tibetan students at Dr. Graham's Homes in Kalimpong, is a moving portrait of these dynamics among early generations of Tibetan exile children.

I write extensively about the Tibetan medical institution described in "Going for Education," and Phurba's uncle and father, in my second book, *Healing Elements*. In the section "Reckonings" within this chapter, I describe how in the minds of many from Mustang, receiving a good secondary education has come to "require" winter schools or full-scale out-migration. However, there are counterexamples: two schools in neighboring Dolpa, Crystal Mountain School and Tapriza; Ladakh's highly innovative Students' Educational and Cultural Movement of Ladakh (SECMOL); and schools in Nubri mentioned by Childs and Choedup.

In speaking about the concepts "techniques of the body" and "technologies of the self" in relation to Mustang daycares, I am connecting to Marcel Mauss and Michel Foucault. Mauss articulated the former as actions that come to embody aspects of a culture, including in ways that produce or reproduce social norms, for instance around gender and class. For Foucault, technologies of the self are a form of biopolitics that focus on the ways people come to represent and embody social values by developing specific forms of (self-)discipline or expertise. In relation to Mustang daycares, both of these processes are occurring, with normative American values interwoven with local cultural frameworks.

With respect to the dissonance that older Mustang women often feel between their lack of educational opportunities and those of their children, especially their daughters, it is worth noting that women's literacy classes have taken off in Mustang, Kathmandu, and New York. One of the primary goals of these classes is to enable reading Tibetan scripture. In a 2014 piece on mother tongues and language competence, Turin addresses the ways that being able to introduce yourself in Tibetan as part of claims to identity in the Himalaya have become increasingly powerful—as is reflected in the experiences at the New York Mustang language and culture classes about which I write in the section "Sunday School."

Christian proselytizing and associated recruitment of Nepali children into Christian schools is a growing area of research and public scrutiny. Brot Coburn's (2017) exposé of one such organization in the *Nepali Times* focuses on a school in Nubri. Not unconnected from this issue (but also not the same) is the increasingly popular space that Korea occupies in Nepali national consciousness as well as in educational and employment opportunities within and outside Nepal. Heather Hindman and Robert Oppenheim have written about aspects of these trends.

PART III

One of the reasons that citizenship, belonging, and ethnicity can be so fraught in Nepal involves a document called the Muluki Ain. First promulgated in 1854, this national code divided the new nation-state's populations into regimented caste hierarchies in accordance with Hindu ideals (Höfer 1979). Although Nepal has been officially a multi-ethnic and multi-party constitutional democracy since 1990, and a secular federalist republic since 2008, caste and ethnic differences remain entrenched, driving socioeconomic inequality and political dynamics. According to the Muluki Ain, those from Mustang were not considered "enslavable alcohol drinkers" as was the case with some other ethnic groups (including the Tamang, one of Nepal's largest *janajati*, or minority ethnicities). However, people from Nepal's northern rim were still considered marginal citizens whose claims to national belonging were further complicated by their cultural, religious, and linguistic alignments with Tibet.

For many from these regions, including Mustang, identification with Tibet is a double-edged sword. Outside of Nepal, stereotypes about Tibetans are often positive, intertwining "model minority" Asian labels with associations of His Holiness the Dalai Lama, nonviolence, Buddhism, and compassion. As Don Lopez has articulated, the more troubling aspects of this dynamic can lead Tibetans to become "prisoners of Shangri-La": caught in a net of expectations that flattens complex identities into romanticized caricatures that can become internalized. One might hear echoes of W. E. B. Du Bois's double consciousness. Within Nepal, however, being associated with Tibet and Tibetanness can be a political liability, particularly as Nepal edges ever closer to China.

To complicate matters further, official state-issued documents that do everything from confer names on people to grant them land or citizenship rights and allow them to travel outside their country do not neatly align with lived experiences of identity and belonging. In fact, official documents might even obscure or erase a person's actual roots, even as they facilitate routes along the *khora* of migration. As I write about in "Paper and Being," the Panchayat period in Nepali history (1960–90) promoted a unified Hindu, monarchical nationalist agenda. Political parties were outlawed, and expression of ethnic *janajati* rights were suspect. This manifests in many ways, including the practice of giving Hindu names to high Himalayan Buddhist children. We might also consider what happened to many American immigrants at Ellis Island in relation to these experiences. Shneiderman's work on ethnicity and identity among the Thangmi/Thami in Nepal as well as Tina Shrestha's work on Nepalis "making paper" in the context of U.S. immigration draw attention to the fact that to speak of citizenship in Nepali requires the active verb "to make or craft" (N. *baanaune*).

When considering how to write about these complexities, I was inspired by details described in the Tshognam archives compiled by Charles Ramble and Nyima Drandul (2016a, 2016b). Specifically, I draw on details from HMA/LTshognam/Tib/23 and HMA/LTshognam/Tib/04 in crafting the story "Paper and Being." Later in the story, I refer to a Green Book. Called *deb jangu* in Tibetan, the full name for this document is *Receipt Book of*

*Voluntary Contributions to Public Funds of the Independent, Cherished [State] of the Tibetan People.* Contributions made to the Central Tibetan Administration, principally by exile Tibetans but also, for other reasons, by Himalayan people such as those from Mustang, are recorded in these books. First implemented in 1972, when the government in exile was still quite young, the Green Book functions as a physical symbol of belonging, pride, and solidarity. It confers no official legal status outside the government in exile, but it can be used as one way of "proving" Tibetan identity outside of the People's Republic of China.

The Mustang phenomenon of the sweater trade is described in Pushpa Tulachan's dissertation. Emily Amburgey, PhD student at University of British Columbia, and her research collaborator Yungdung Gurung are conducting new research on this phenomenon at present. Ramble has written about the history of trade in Mustang. Tina Harris's work situated in Darjeeling and Kalimpong complement what I have learned about Tibetan trade in Mustang. Don Messerschmidt (1978) describes what he calls "Dhikurs" and what I know as *dukhor:* rotating credit systems that help to facilitate the circulation of cash as a social and economic strategy, including to facilitate migration. This social institution has endured. However, as work by Galen Murton, Ken Bauer, and James Fisher show, the phenomenon of *netsang,* trading partners that once served important social roles in regional trade, is now declining with the rise to dominance of the cash economy.

In the section of the ethnographic chapter "Bringing Home the Trade" titled "Cost-Benefit Analysis," I refer to efforts at recruiting Mustang men into farm labor in California. I cannot think of this possibility without considering what I have learned from Seth Holmes on this topic. I thank my former colleague at Dartmouth, Lourdes Gutiérrez Nájera, for her perspectives on the ways that language—specifically not being able to speak Spanish as an Indigenous Mexican immigrant—can impact transnational migrant experience, including mental health and interactions with state authorities. These issues of labor migration, recognition, and *misrecognition* have become further complicated in the Trump era. In 2018, for instance, approximately one hundred Nepali men ended up in Immigration and Customs Enforcement detention centers in Oregon and Washington and were first misrecognized as "Mexican" or "Latin American" and not provided with translators who spoke Nepali.

Speaking of the nuances of language, Nicolas Tournadre's work on Tibetic languages and their classifications seeks to not only "locate" Logé and Baragaon variants of Tibetan but also describe the phenomenon of *ra ma lug,* the "neither goat nor sheep" code-switching conglomeration that many people in Nepal and New York speak. Turin's work on mother tongues and language competence points to the social effects of this semi-fluency.

The Himalayan Town Hall about which I write in the "Prayer Flags" section of this chapter was held in 2016 and organized by the office of Queens councilmember Daniel Dromm. It brought together city government, social service organizations, and several hundred individuals who self-identified as "Himalayan." The event included translation from Nepali and Tibetan into English. In this forum and in other contexts, varying numbers were put forward when it came to how many Himalayan and Tibetan people are in New York. Here, the number quoted was 50,000, although I have heard other estimates of between 20,000 to 30,000. For reasons outlined in Part III, precise numbers are impossible to determine.

If, after Aihwa Ong, we might speak of Himalayan people as "flexible citizens," then this needs to be tempered by considerations of statelessness, refusal of citizenship, contested identities, and experiences of exile, as Carole McGranahan and Fiona McConnell describe in relation to Tibet and Audra Simpson writes about in relation to Mohawk Indigenous experiences. We must consider the strategies for state recognition and border crossing that, in turn, link to approaches for maintaining cultural traditions and livelihoods, as Shneiderman documents in her work with Thangmi. We need to account for the ways that Nepalis who claim asylum in the U.S. craft their narratives, with urgency and ellipses, as Shrestha has written for Nepalis and as Bridget Haas has done in other contexts. And we must examine how people are shaped by the actuality and the specters of papers, documents that can make or break the prospects for individuals and families, now more than ever (see Gomberg-Muñoz 2017; Mulmi and Shneiderman 2017; Sadiq 2009).

PART IV

Kinship threads this book together, but it comes into focus most clearly in discussions of marriage, households, and extended family as they relate to the *khora* of migration—the topic of Part IV. The study of kinship has been a cornerstone of anthropology from its beginnings. Franz Boas, Claude Lévi-Strauss, Bronisław Malinowski, Ruth Benedict, Mary Douglas, Margaret Mead, and so many other disciplinary ancestors seeded their inquiries in forms of relatedness. Even so, a focus on kinship in some contemporary anthropological circles has been treated as parochial or passé—sometimes for very good reason (a propensity to "other" especially through the ways that kinship can demand classification). Yet as anthropologist Nancy Levine—someone who has spent much of her career thinking about marriage and kinship in Tibetan communities—recently reminded me, without kinship or with a misunderstanding of its importance, many anthropological fallacies can take root.

My thinking about kinship as it relates to marriage and the creation of households in Tibetan and Himalayan contexts has benefited from close readings of Levine's work, along with that of Melvyn Goldstein, Geoff Childs, Ben Jiao, Barbara Aziz, Sydney Schuler, Matthew Kapstein (chap. 6 of his reader *The Tibetans*), and Heidi Fjeld. In terms of comparative and overarching treatments of the topic, Janet Carsten's *Cultures of Relatedness* and *After Kinship* frame kinship as fundamentally negotiated and experiential. Susan McKinnon and Fenella Cannell's *Vital Relations*, and a special issue of *Social Analysis* edited by Kathryn Goldfarb and Caroline Schuster, which focuses on ideas of mutuality and difference in relation to kinship, were also helpful. Michael Peletz's review article—which puts kinship into context with Marxist, feminist, and historical approaches—allowed me to grasp some of the debates in this corner of the discipline. Daniel Miller's critique of the term "relationship" made me more conscious of slippages with this word in my own writing.

When it comes to thinking through kinship, transnational families, and the *khora* of migration, Loretta Baldassar and Laura Merla's edited volume, *Transnational Families, Migration and the Circulation of Care*, has been particularly on point. Their theorization of "care circulation" connects directly to *khora*, both in their foregrounding of cycles and circles and in how they challenge dyadic or unidirectional modes of caring across time and space. They define care circulation as "the reciprocal, multidirectional and asymmetrical exchange of care that fluctuates over the life course within transnational family networks subject to the political, economic, cultural and social contexts of both sending and receiving societies" (2014, 25). The original subtitle for my book included the word "care." Although I ended up changing the subtitle, modes of caring, questions about who cares for whom, and how this care relates to Buddhist conceptions of moral action over the life course remain important. In tandem with these interventions, Michael Herzfeld's (2015) article "The Village in the World and the World in the Village" resonated throughout my entire writing process, particularly in considering how marriage and intimate relations unfold across space. The concept of "ephemeral care" mentioned in the short story "Night Visitors" comes from David Citrin.

I titled the ethnographic chapter in this section "At the Threshold of This Life" after a Loba song that, along with other songs from Lo and my original poetry, formed the inspiration for a cantata by composer Andrea Clearfield (http://www.andreaclearfield.com/works/choral/tse-go-la/).

When describing myself dressed up in a *chuba* and heading off to a Loba wedding in Queens, in the first section of this chapter, I note points of similarity and difference with Tsering Bista's experience, as described in a photo essay and National Public Radio story, "Redefining the Bakhu."

Laura Ahearn's work on love, courtship, and modernity in Nepal has been useful in thinking through these practices alongside the *khora* of migration. The practice of cross-cousin marriage is noted in many ethnographies of the Himalaya, but I have learned about this dynamic most directly from conversations with David Holmberg and Kathryn March as well as from their scholarship.

Aidan Pine and Mark Turin have written an important piece about pleas to retain language in conditions of diaspora. Turin has written further on the ways that globalization can help to bolster endangered languages. This general theme has been central to work on which I have collaborated with Turin and colleagues at the ELA, mentioned above.

In the section titled "Sketches of Matrimony and Its Others," I refer to issues of non-binary gender and sexuality. Nepal has a mixed reputation regarding LGBTQ rights. Homosexuality was legalized in 2007, and the new 2015 constitution includes provisions such as the right to have preferred gender displayed on official documents such as passports and *nagarikta*, along with prohibitions against gender identity and sexual orientation-based discrimination. Yet most of the effects of such progressive legislation is only felt in urban areas. Gender-based violence, including related to gender identity and sexual orientation, is still common. In Mustang and among Mustang New Yorkers, the topic of sexual orientation and gender identity remains, for the most part, taboo.

Shneiderman's work on Chomo Khandru (2014) and Childs, Goldstein, and Wangdui's (2010) discussion of the gendered transitions occurring within larger dynamics of economic development in Tibet are helpful in understanding the roles of unmarried women in Tibetan societies, beyond just as nuns. Sydney Schuler's (1978) work on Baragaon women's lives describes bride capture in detail. When I mention "lower status" Loba, I am referring to caste difference in Mustang as it articulates with occupation (butcher, blacksmith, musician) and lineage.

As I describe the road in the section "Specters of Return," I am thinking broadly about dynamics of "development" (N. *bikas*). Stacy Pigg and Mary Des Chene have informed my thinking about this concept. Des Chene's 2014 letter to then–prime minister and former Maoist leader Baburam Bhattarai and Pigg's recent work of graphic ethnography, "The Penstocks," have been illuminating, in both content and form.

PART V

The dynamic relationship between people and land in the Himalaya and Tibet begins, for me, with an appreciation of sacred geography: namely, the idea that Earth is alive and agentive, both in its very formation and through the non-human beings that guard, possess, protect, and govern it. I have learned about these concepts from conversations with and the scholarship of Charles Ramble, Katia Buffetrille, Hildegard Diemberger, Toni Huber, Geoffrey Samuel, and Alex McKay.

The narrations of earthquake experience presented in "Gods and Demons" comes from Mustang-based data from "Narrating Disaster," the NSF-RAPID project mentioned above. See Geoff Childs and colleagues (2018) and Kristine Hildebrandt and colleagues (2018) for more on this project. Ben Campbell's work on the 2015 earthquakes includes a discussion of the term *sagul* to describe the creature on which the Earth sits. This is a Tamang language variant of what is also described in other Tibetic languages as *sangul*, wherein *sa* means "earth," and *gul* is a verb that means to shake or quake. It is interesting to me that this synonym for "earthquake" also comes to take agentive form—to be the name for a creature itself, on which the world rests. When referencing an earlier earthquake in Nepal, I am speaking of the major 1934 event. The *kaliyug* refers to the last of four stages that the world passes through within Sanskrit scriptures. In Tibetan, this era is glossed as *dü nyemba*, a "degenerate age." This age, associated with Kali, the wrathful form of the Hindu goddess Durga, is a time in which greed, loss of humility, and moral decline predominate. Referring to contemporary problems of both social and natural order—or reading natural disasters as products of degenerative human action—is a common theme in the Narrating Disaster corpus.

Frederick Weisman's documentary *In Jackson Heights* helped me to more fully appreciate the history of Queens, although the absence of Himalayan and Tibetan New Yorkers is notable. Kesang Tseten is working on a film that will address this gap.

When it comes to thinking about roads in the Himalaya, I have learned from Galen Murton, Kathryn Rankin, Austin Lord, Sam Cowan, and Martin Saxer as well as Phurwa Dhondup Gurung and Nyima Dorje Bhotia. I also point to several ongoing collaborative research projects involving researchers from Canada, the U.S., and Nepal. Some of this research focuses on "Infrastructures of Democracy: State-Building as Everyday Practice in Nepal's Agrarian Districts," and other research examines the relationship between post-conflict (Maoist civil war) and post-disaster (2015 earthquakes) reconstruction as sites of socioeconomic and legal transformations. Shneiderman and Rankin are principal investigators in both projects. The concept of time-space compression, which I mention in relation to roads, was first articulated by geographer David Harvey.

The official discovery of uranium in Mustang occurred in 2014 (see "Discovery of Uranium" 2014; Parashar 2014; "Uranium Found" 2016).

In speaking of Mustang's sacred geography in the chapter "The Ground beneath Our Feet," I mention Guru Rinpoche (Skt. Padmasambhava), the eighth-century figure who is credited with bringing Buddhism from India to Tibet. The mytho-histories connected to him include many descriptions of how he left marks on Tibetan ground.

As described in several sections of this chapter, Nepal's increasing geopolitical allegiance to and economic reliance on China and its implications for the future of the country cannot be underestimated. I am fortunate to have a friend in General Sir Sam Cowan, a (now retired) four-star general in the British Army. His *Essays on Nepal*, based on more than four decades of military and diplomatic experience as well as his ongoing study of these issues, provide invaluable resources and analysis for me (and others) as we work to track these developments in real time.

For more on "the Mustang incident" described in the section "Border Consciousness," see Cowan's chapter of the same title in *Essays on Nepal*. For more on the consequences of roads and food shortage areas in northern Nepal, see my former Dartmouth student Jocelyn Powelson's photo essay on Humla, "Life and Livelihood in Remote Nepal" in the *Nepali Times*.

In relation to hiring outside laborers to help with planting and harvest in Mustang, rates for non-skilled contract workers have continued to rise. In fall 2018, the rate was at least Rs. 800/day, plus food and alcohol, and by summer of 2019, this had risen to between Rs. 900–1,000. When I refer to the five elements in relation to environmental change, I am speaking of water (*chu*) and wind (*lung*), earth (*sa*) and fire (*mé*), and consciousness (*namkha*), each of which bears on the health and well-being of individuals and environments.

An Al Jazeera special, *Nepal: The Great Plunder*, released in 2018, describes the issue of heritage theft in Mustang. Luczanits's work details some of the controversies over efforts to restore Lo's artistic treasures. My 2004 article, "A Tale of Two Temples," provides a transnational perspective on some of these dynamics of heritage and cultural ownership.

Fidel Devkota's PhD thesis and his film, *Winds of Change in Lo Mustang*, chronicle issues of environmental precarity in the village of Dhe, with some comparative focus on Samdzong. Coverage of climate-related events in the village of Lubrak include a photo essay on "Belonging and Transformation in Mustang, Nepal" (Tsewang et al. n.d.).

Many scholars of Tibet and the Himalaya have documented the phenomenon of deities of place relocating. A favorite is Ann Armbrecht's description of this process in *Thin Places*.

On trees as symbols of taming Tibet, see Emily Yeh's book of the same title. I am grateful to Ulrike Roesler for sharing her forthcoming work on Reting. In considering trees, and Ursula Le Guin's work that I quote, her thinking seems a precursor to what has been called the "ontological turn" in anthropology and multi-species ethnography.

I use the phrase "temporary protected status" to describe some of the dynamics that this chapter evokes, with respect to precarity and uncertainty, land and home. Officially, Temporary Protected Status (TPS) is an immigration designation given by the U.S. government to eligible nationals of designated countries who have been affected by armed conflict or natural disaster. This status allows persons to live in the U.S. for limited periods of time. After the 2015 earthquakes, the Obama administration extended TPS status to Nepalis. The Trump administration attempted to revoke Nepali TPS status, but that termination is currently suspended due to legal action being taken against the administration.

For more on vampires in Tibetan culture, see Charles Ramble's work on the topic. In considering what to call the section of "The Ground beneath Our Feet" in which my companions and I encounter a snow leopard, I took inspiration from wildlife biologist George Schaller's *Stones and Silence*. He wrote this book about the same trip to Dolpo that inspired Peter Matthiessen's *The Snow Leopard*.

PART VI

I have benefited from descriptions of old age and death in Himalayan communities in Geoff Childs's *Tibetan Diary* and Robert Desjarlais's *Subject to Death*. It has also been helpful to return to Charles Ramble's articulation of Mustang's "civil religion" from his ethnography *The Navel of the Demoness* to consider how social structures, including those that govern death, are retained and transformed through the *khora* of migration. Yana Stainova has helped me to understand enchantment as anthropological theory and method.

In relation to the section "Release of Consciousness" in the chapter "Between Presence and Absence" and the cross-cultural encounters with death described therein, I note the late Sogyal Rinpoche's bestselling interpretation of the *Bardo Thödol* for Western audiences, *The Tibetan Book of Living and Dying*, as well as the role that Buddhism has continued to play in palliative care movements, such as through the teaching and writing of Pema Chödron and Roshi Joan Halifax.

In 1996, I was a participant-observer in the Lubrak Dö Gyab at the invitation of Charles Ramble, as was fellow anthropologist Nicolas Sihlé. In Tibetan language, this ritual is spelled *mdos rgyabs*, with *mdos* indicating a ritual effigy usually made of thread and string and *rgyabs* meaning to throw, expel, toss. An effigy is "hunted" with arrows and daggers before it is eventually ritually cast out of the village at the apex of the event. The Lubrak school described in this chapter is a community institution that has support from both the Nepali government and foreign donors. It includes a private hostel, Tibetan language instruction, and a focus on Bön religion and culture.

# BIBLIOGRAPHY

Adams, V., S. R. Craig, and A. Samen. 2016. "Alternative Accounting in Maternal and Infant Global Health." *Global Public Health.* https://doi.org/10.1080/17441692.2015.1021364.

Adams, V., S. Miller, J. Chertow, S. Craig, A. Samen, and M. Varner. 2005. "Having a 'Safe Delivery': Conflicting Views from Tibet." *Health Care for Women International* 26(9): 821–51.

Adhikari, J., and M. Hobley. 2015. "'Everyone Is Leaving—Who Will Sow Our Fields?' The Livelihood Effects on Women of Male Migration from Kothang and Udaypur Districts, Nepal, to the Gulf Countries and Malaysia." *HIMALAYA* 35(1): 11–23.

Aengst, J. 2011. "Reproductive Politics at the Border: Pronatalism, Intermarriage, and Moral Movements in Ladakh, India." PhD diss., University of California, Davis.

———. 2013. "The Politics of Fertility: Population and Pronatalism in Ladakh." *HIMALAYA* 32(1): 23–34.

Ahearn, L. M. 2001. *Invitations to Love: Literacy, Love Letters, and Social Change in Nepal.* Ann Arbor: University of Michigan Press.

Ahmed, S. 1999. "Home and Away: Narratives of Migration and Estrangement." *International Journal of Cultural Studies* 2(3): 329–47.

Åkesson, L. 2011. "Remittances and Relationships: Exchange in Cape Verdean Transnational Families." *Ethnos* 76(3): 326–47.

Aldenderfer, M. 2011. "Peopling the Tibetan Plateau: Insights from Archaeology." *High Altitude Medicine and Biology* 12(2): 141–47.

Andrugtsang, G. T. 1973. *Four Rivers, Six Ranges: Reminiscences of the Resistance Movement in Tibet.* Dharamsala, India: Information and Publicity Office of H.H. the Dalai Lama.

Armbrecht, A. 2010. *Thin Places: A Pilgrimage Home.* New York: Columbia University Press.

Aziz, B. N. 1978. *Tibetan Frontier Families.* Delhi: Vikas Publishing House.

Baldassar, L., and L. Merla, eds. 2014. *Transnational Families, Migration and the Circulation of Care: Understanding Mobility and Absence in Family Life.* New York: Routledge.

Basso, K. H. 1996. *Wisdom Sits in Places: Landscape and Language among the Western Apache.* Albuquerque: University of New Mexico Press.

Bauer, K. M. 2004. *High Frontiers: Dolpo and the Changing World of Himalayan Pastoralists.* New York: Columbia University Press.

Behar, R. 1997. *The Vulnerable Observer: Anthropology That Breaks Your Heart*. Boston: Beacon Press.

Berlant, L., and K. Stewart. 2019. *The Hundreds*. Durham, NC: Duke University Press.

Biehl, J. 2005. *Vita: Life in a Zone of Social Abandonment*. Berkeley: University of California Press.

———. 2007. *Will to Live: AIDS Therapies and the Politics of Survival*. Princeton, NJ: Princeton University Press.

Biehl, J., B. Good, and A. Kleinman, eds. 2007. *Subjectivity: Ethnographic Investigations*. Berkeley: University of California Press.

Biehl, J., and P. Locke, eds. 2017. *Unfinished: The Anthropology of Becoming*. Durham, NC: Duke University Press.

Bista, T. "Redefining the Bakhu—And the Great American Road Trip—Through Self-Portraiture." *The Picture Show*, October 15. https://www.npr.org/sections/pictureshow/2018/10/15/655786133/redefining-the-bakhu-and-the-great-american-road-trip-through-self-portraiture.

Brah, A. 1996. *Cartographies of Diaspora: Contesting Identities*. London: Routledge.

Brown, T. M. 2011. *Raising Brooklyn: Nannies, Childcare, and Caribbeans Creating Community*. New York: New York University Press.

Brubaker, R. 2005. "The 'Diaspora' Diaspora." *Ethnic and Racial Studies* 28(1): 1–19.

Buffetrille, K. 2015. "A Controversy on Vegetarianism." In *Trails of the Tibetan Tradition: Papers for Elliott Sperling*, edited by Roberto Vitali, 113–27. Kathmandu: Vajra Publications.

Buffetrille, K., and H. Diemberger. 2002. *Territory and Identity in Tibet and the Himalayas*. Proceedings of the Ninth Seminar of the International Association for Tibetan Studies, Leiden, 2000. Leiden: Brill.

Butler, K. D. 2001. "Defining Diaspora, Refining a Discourse." *Diaspora: A Journal of Transnational Studies* 10(2): 189–219.

Campbell, B. 2018. "Communities in the Aftermath of Nepal's Earthquake." In *Evolving Narratives of Hazard and Risk: The Gorkha Earthquake, Nepal 2015*, edited by L. Bracken, H. A. Ruszcxyk, and T. Robinson, 109–23. Cham, Switzerland: Palgrave Macmillan.

Carsten, J. 2000. *Cultures of Relatedness: New Approaches to the Study of Kinship*. Cambridge: Cambridge University Press.

———. 2004. *After Kinship*. Cambridge: Cambridge University Press.

Childs, G. 2003. "Polyandry and Population Growth in a Historical Tibetan Society." *History of the Family* 8:423–44.

———. 2004a. "Cultural Change in the Name of Cultural Preservation." *HIMALAYA* 24(1–2): 31–42.

———. 2004b. *Tibetan Diary: From Birth to Death and Beyond in a Himalayan Valley of Nepal*. Berkeley: University of California Press.

———. 2008. *Tibetan Transitions: Historical and Contemporary Perspectives on Fertility, Family Planning, and Demographic Change*. Leiden: Brill.

Childs, G., and N. Choedup. 2018. *From a Trickle to a Torrent: Education, Migration, and Social Change in a Himalayan Valley of Nepal*. Berkeley: University of California Press.

Childs, G., S. Craig, C. M. Beall, and B. Basnyat. 2014. "Depopulating the Himalayan Highlands: Education and Outmigration from Ethnically Tibetan Communities of Nepal." *Mountain Research and Development* 34(2): 85–94.

Childs, G., S. Craig, D. N. Dhakal, M. Donohue, and K. Hildebrandt. 2018. "Narrating Disaster through Participatory Research: Perspectives from Post-earthquake Nepal." *Collaborative Anthropologies* 10(1–2): 207–36.

Childs, G., M. C. Goldstein, and P. Wangdui. 2010. "An Entrepreneurial Transition? Development and Economic Mobility in Rural Tibet." *HIMALAYA* 30(1–2): 51–62.

Clifford, J. 1994. "Diasporas." *Cultural Anthropology* 9(3): 302–38.

Coburn, B. 2017. "Preaching on High." *Nepali Times*, August 25–31. http://archive .nepalitimes.com/article/nation/preaching-on-high,3904.

Cohen, J. 2018. "Negotiated Intimacies: A Study of Gendered Labor and Cross-Cultural Care in New York City." Undergraduate thesis, Department of Anthropology, Dartmouth College.

Conboy, K., and J. Morrison. 2002. *The CIA's Secret War in Tibet.* Lawrence: University Press of Kansas.

Constable, N. 2014. *Born Out of Place: Migrant Mothers and the Politics of International Labor.* Berkeley: University of California Press.

Cowan, S. 2018. *Essays on Nepal: Past and Present.* Kathmandu: Himal Books.

Craig, S. R. 2002. "Place, Work and Identity between Mustang, Nepal and New York City." *Studies in Nepali History and Society* 7(2): 355–403.

———. 2004. "A Tale of Two Temples: Culture, Capital and Community in Mustang, Nepal." *European Bulletin of Himalayan Research* 27:11–36.

———. 2008. *Horses Like Lightning: A Story of Passage through the Himalayas.* Boston: Wisdom Publications.

———. 2009. "Pregnancy and Childbirth in Tibet: Knowledge, Perspectives, and Practices." In *Childbirth across Cultures: Ideas and Practices of Pregnancy, Childbirth and the Postpartum*, edited by H. Selin and P. K. Stone, 145–60. New York: Springer.

———. 2010. "'Not Found in Tibetan Society': Culture, Childbirth, and a Politics of Life on the Roof of the World." *HIMALAYA* 30(1–2): 101–14.

———. 2011. "Migration, Social Change, Health, and the Realm of the Possible: Women's Stories between Nepal and New York." *Anthropology and Humanism* 36(2): 193–214.

———. 2012. *Healing Elements: Efficacy and the Social Ecologies of Tibetan Medicine.* Berkeley: University of California Press.

Craig, S. R., G. Childs, and C. M. Beall. 2016. "Closing the Womb Door: Contraception Use and Fertility Transition among Culturally Tibetan Women in Highland Nepal." *Maternal and Child Health Journal.* https://doi.org/10.1007/s10995-016-2017-x.

Craig, S. R., and N. T. Gurung. 2018. "The *Khora* of Migration: Everyday Practices of (Well) Being between Mustang, Nepal, and New York City." In *Global Nepalis: Religion, Culture, and Community in a New and Old Diaspora*, edited by D. N. Gellner and S. L. Hausner, 271–300. Oxford and New Delhi: Oxford University Press.

Davis-Floyd, R. E., and C. F. Sargent, eds. 1997. *Childbirth and Authoritative Knowledge: Cross-Cultural Perspectives.* Berkeley: University of California Press.

Dennis, D. 2016. "Fifty-Three Kilos." *Anthropology and Humanism* 41(2): 206–11.

Des Chene, M. 1996. "In the Name of *Bikas*." *Studies in Nepali History and Society* 1(2): 259–70.

———. 2014. "Development or Destruction?" *The Record*, October 11. www.recordnepal .com/perspective/development-or-destruction/.

Desjarlais, R. 2003. *Sensory Biographies: Lives and Deaths among Nepal's Yolmo Buddhists*. Berkeley: University of California Press.

———. 2016. *Subject to Death: Life and Loss in a Buddhist World*. Chicago: University of Chicago Press.

Devkota, F. 2016. "Climate Vulnerability and Adaptation to Climate Impacts in the Himalayan Region of Nepal." PhD diss., Institute of Social and Cultural Anthropology, Free University of Berlin.

Dhompa, T. W. 2016. *Coming Home to Tibet: A Memoir of Love, Loss, and Belonging*. Boulder, CO: Shambhala Publications.

Dhungel, R. K. 2002. *The Kingdom of Lo (Mustang): A Historical Study*. Kathmandu: Tashi Gephel Foundation.

"Discovery of Uranium Could Change Nepal's Energy Scenario." 2014. *Nepal Energy Forum*. www.nepalenergyforum.com/discovery-of-uranium-could-change-nepals -energy-scenario-experts/.

Fisher, J. F. 1986. *Trans-Himalayan Traders: Economy, Society and Culture in Northwest Nepal*. Berkeley: University of California Press.

———. 2017. *Trans-Himalayan Traders Transformed: Return to Tarang*. Bangkok: Orchid Press.

Fisher, W. F. 2001. *Fluid Boundaries: Forming and Transforming Identity in Nepal*. New York: Columbia University Press.

Fjeld, H. 2008. "When Brothers Separate: Conflict and Mediation within Polyandrous Houses in Central Tibet." In *Conflict and Social Order in Tibet and Inner Asia*, edited by F. Pirie and T. Huber, 241–61. Leiden: Brill.

Fouratt, C. E. 2017. "Love for the Land: Remittances and Care in a Nicaraguan Transnational Community." *Latin American Research Review* 52(5): 792–806.

Fürer-Haimendorf, C. von. 1975. *Himalayan Traders: Life in Highland Nepal*. London: J. Murray.

Gellner, D. N., and S. L. Hausner, eds. 2018. *Global Nepalis: Religion, Culture, and Community in a New and Old Diaspora*. Delhi: Oxford University Press.

Ghodsee, K. 2011. *Lost in Transition: Ethnographies of Everyday Life after Communism*. Durham, NC: Duke University Press.

Gidwani, V., and K. Sivaramakrishnan. 2003. "Circular Migration and the Spaces of Cultural Assertion." *Annals of the Association of American Geographers* 93(1): 186–213.

Glick Schiller, N., L. Basch, and C. Szanton Blanc. 1995. "From Immigrant to Transmigrant: Theorizing Transnational Migration." *Anthropological Quarterly* 68(1): 48–63.

Goldfarb, K. E., and C. E. Schuster. 2016. "Introduction: (De)materializing Kinship— Holding Together Mutuality and Difference." *Social Analysis* 60(2): 1–12.

Goldstein, M. C. 1971. "Stratification, Polyandry, and Family Structure in Central Tibet." *Southwestern Journal of Anthropology* 27(1): 64–74.

———. 1987. "When Brothers Share a Wife." *Natural History* 96(3): 109–12.

Gomberg-Muñoz, R. 2017. *Becoming Legal: Immigration and Mixed-Status Families.* Oxford: Oxford University Press.

Gurung, N. T., R. Perlin, D. Kaufman, M. Turin, and S. R. Craig. 2018. "Orality and Mobility: Documenting Himalayan Voices in New York City." *Verge: Studies in Global Asia* 4(2): 64–80.

Gurung, P. D., and N. D. Bhotia. 2018. "On the Road: Commodities, Trade, and Transportation in Northwest Nepal." *HIMALAYA.* https://himalayajournal.org /photo-gallery/road-commodities-trade-transportation-northwest-nepal/.

Gurung, S. H. 2015. *Nepali Migrant Women: Resistance and Survival in America.* Syracuse, NY: Syracuse University Press.

Gutiérrez Nájera, L. 2010. "*Hayandose:* Zapotec Migrant Expressions of Membership and Belonging." In *Beyond El Barrio: Everyday Life in Latino/a América,* edited by G. M. Pérez, F. A. Guridy, and A. Burgos Jr., 63–80. New York: New York University Press.

Gutschow, K. 2010. "The Extension of Obstetrics in Ladakh." In *Medicine between Science and Religion: Explorations on Tibetan Grounds,* edited by V. Adams, M. Schrempf, and S. R. Craig, 185–214. London: Berghahn.

Gyatso, J. 1987. "Down with the Demoness: Reflections on a Feminine Ground in Tibet." *Tibet Journal* 12(4): 38–53.

Haas, B. M. 2017. "Citizens-in-Waiting, Deportees-in-Waiting: Power, Temporality, and Suffering in the U.S. Asylum System." *Ethos* 45(1): 75–97.

Hall, S. 1990. "Cultural Identity and Diaspora." In *Identity: Community, Culture, Difference,* edited by J. Rutherford, 222–37. London: Lawrence & Wishart.

Hannaford, D. 2016. "Intimate Remittances: Marriage, Migration, and MoneyGram in Senegal." *Africa Today* 62(3): 93–109.

Harris, T. 2013. *Geographical Diversions: Tibetan Trade, Global Transactions.* Athens: University of Georgia Press.

Harrison, J., C. Luczanits, C. Ramble, and N. Drandul. 2018. *A Blessing for the Land: The Architecture, Art and History of a Buddhist Convent in Mustang, Nepal.* Kathmandu: Vajra Publications.

Harvey, D. 1980. *The Condition of Postmodernity.* Cambridge, MA: Basil Blackwell.

Herzfeld, M. 2015. "The Village in the World and the World in the Village: Reflections on Ethnographic Epistemology." *Critique of Anthropology* 35(3): 338–43.

Heydon, S. 2010. "'The Greatest News': Khunde Hospital (Nepal) and Childbirth in a Sherpa Community." In *Health, Illness, and Modernity: Social Studies of Medicine in Tibetan Contexts,* Proceedings from the XIth International Association of Tibetan Studies Seminar, edited by M. Schrempf, S. R. Craig, F. Garrett, and M. Cuomo, 279–305. Bonn: Central Asian Seminar Series.

Hildebrandt, K., G. Childs, S. Craig, D. N. Dhakal, M. Donohue, and B. R. Gautam. 2018. "Narrating Disaster in the Aftermath of the 2015 Nepal Earthquakes: Linguistic and Sociocultural Perspectives." *Contributions to Nepalese Studies* 43(1): 1–15.

Hindman, H., and R. Oppenheim. 2014. "Lines of Labor and Desire: 'Korean Quality' in Contemporary Kathmandu." *Anthropological Quarterly* 87(2): 465–95.

Höfer, A. 1979. *The Caste Hierarchy and the State in Nepal: A Study of the Muluki Ain in 1854*. Khumbu Himal: Ergebnisse des Forschungsunternehmens Nepal Himalaya, Band 13/2. Innsbruck: Universitätsverlag Wagner.

Holmberg, D. H. 1989. *Order in Paradox: Myth, Ritual, and Exchange among Nepal's Tamang*. Ithaca, NY: Cornell University Press.

Holmes, S. M. 2013. *Fresh Fruit, Broken Bodies: Migrant Farmworkers in the United States*. Berkeley: University of California Press.

Huber, T. 1999. *The Cult of Pure Crystal Mountain: Popular Pilgrimage and Visionary Landscape in Southeast Tibet*. New York: Oxford University Press.

Jackson, D. P. 1984. *The Mollas of Mustang: Historical, Religious and Oratorical Traditions of the Nepalese-Tibetan Borderland*. Dharamsala, India: Library of Tibetan Works and Archives.

Jiao, B. 2001. "Socioeconomic and Cultural Factors Underlying the Contemporary Revival of Fraternal Polyandry in Tibet." PhD diss., Case Western Reserve University.

Kapstein, M. T. 2006. *The Tibetans*. Malden, MA: Blackwell.

Knaus, J. K. 2000. *Orphans of the Cold War: America and the Tibetan Struggle for Survival*. Washington, DC: Public Affairs.

Kusserow, A. 2002. *Hunting Down the Monk*. A. Poulin Jr., New Poets of America, vol. 24. Rochester, NY: BOA Editions, Ltd.

Kwon, J. H. 2015. "The Work of Waiting: Love and Money in Korean Chinese Transnational Migration." *Cultural Anthropology* 30(3): 477–500.

Le Guin, Ursula K. 1985. "She Unnames Them." *The New Yorker*, January 21.

Levine, N. 1981. "The Theory of Ru Kinship, Descent and Status in a Tibetan Society." In *Asian Highland Societies in Anthropological Perspective*, edited by C. von Fürer-Haimendorf, 52–78. New Delhi: Sterling.

———. 1988. *The Dynamics of Polyandry, Kinship, Domesticity, and Population of the Tibetan Border*. Chicago: University of Chicago Press.

Levine, N. E., and J. B. Silk. 1997. "Why Polyandry Fails: Sources of Instability in Polyandrous Marriages." *Current Anthropology* 38(3): 375–98.

Levitt, P. 1998. "Social Remittances: Migration Driven Local-Level Forms of Cultural Diffusion." *International Migration Review* 32(4): 926–48.

———. 2001. *The Transnational Villagers*. Berkeley: University of California Press.

Levitt, P., and N. Glick Schiller. 2004. "Conceptualizing Simultaneity: A Transnational Social Field Perspective on Society." *International Migration Review* 38(3): 1002–39.

Lock, M. 2001. "The Tempering of Medical Anthropology: Troubling Natural Categories." *Medical Anthropology Quarterly* 15(4): 478–92.

Lokshin, M., M. Bontch-Osmolovski, and E. Glinskaya. 2010. "Work-Related Migration and Poverty Reduction in Nepal." *Review of Development Economics* 14(2): 323–32.

Lopez, D. S., Jr. 1998. *Prisoners of Shangri-La: Tibetan Buddhism and the West*. Chicago: University of Chicago Press.

Lord, A. 2016. "Citizens of a Hydropower Nation: Territory and Agency at the Frontiers of Hydropower Development in Nepal." *Economic Anthropology* 3(1): 145–60.

Luczanits, C. 2013. Review of *Wonders of Lo: The Artistic Heritage of Mustang*, edited by E. Lo Bue. *Tibet Journal* 38(3–4): 161–67.

——. 2014. "Bringing a Masterwork to Life?" *Orientations* 45(2): 184–86.

Maharjan, M. R. 2015. "Emigrants' Migrant Wives: Linking International and Internal Migration." *Studies in Nepali History and Society* 20(2): 217–47.

March, K. S. 2002. *"If Each Comes Halfway": Meeting Tamang Women in Nepal.* Ithaca, NY: Cornell University Press.

Martin, E. 2001. *The Woman in the Body: A Cultural Analysis of Reproduction.* Boston: Beacon Press.

McConnell, F. 2013. "Citizens and Refugees: Constructing and Negotiating Tibetan Identities in Exile." *Annals of the Association of American Geographers* 103(4): 967–83.

McGranahan, C. 2010. *Arrested Histories: Tibet, the CIA, and Memories of a Forgotten War.* Durham, NC: Duke University Press.

——. 2018a. "Ethnography beyond Method: The Importance of an Ethnographic Sensibility." *Sites* 15(1): 1–10.

——. 2018b. "Refusal as Political Practice: Citizenship, Sovereignty, and Tibetan Refugee Status." *American Ethnologist* 45(3): 367–79.

——, ed. 2020. *Writing Anthropology: Essays on Craft and Commitment.* Durham, NC: Duke University Press.

McKay, A., ed. 2013. *Pilgrimage in Tibet.* Abingdon, UK: Routledge.

McKinnon, S., and F. Cannell, eds. 2013. *Vital Relations: Modernity and the Persistent Life of Kinship.* Santa Fe, NM: School for Advanced Research Press.

Messerschmidt, D. A. 1978. *"Dhikurs*: Rotating Credit Associations in Nepal." In *Himalayan Anthropology: The Indo-Tibetan Interface,* edited by James F. Fisher, 141–66. The Hague: Mouton.

Miller, D. 2007. "What Is a Relationship? Is Kinship Negotiated Experience?" *Ethos* 72(4): 535–54.

Mulmi, S., and S. Shneiderman. 2017. "Citizenship, Gender and Statelessness in Nepal: Before and After the 2015 Constitution." In *Understanding Statelessness,* edited by T. Bloom, K. Tonkiss, and P. Cole, 135–52. London: Routledge.

Murton, G. 2017a. "Border Corridors: Mobility, Containment, and Infrastructure Development between Nepal and China." PhD diss., University of Colorado Boulder.

——. 2017b. "Making Mountain Places into State Spaces: Infrastructure, Consumption, and Territorial Practice in a Himalayan Borderland." *Annals of the American Association of Geographers* 107(2): 536–45.

——. 2018. "Nobody Stops and Stays Anymore: Motor Roads, Uneven Mobilities, and Conceptualizing Borderland Modernity in Highland Nepal." In *Routledge Handbook of Asian Borderlands,* edited by A. Horstmann, M. Saxer, and A. Rippa, 315–24. Abingdon, UK: Routledge.

Narayan, K. 1994. *Love, Stars, and All That.* New York: Gallery Books.

——. 1999. "Ethnography and Fiction: Where Is the Border?" *Anthropology and Humanism* 24(2): 134–47.

——. 2007a. *My Family and Other Saints.* Chicago: University of Chicago Press.

——. 2007b. "Tools to Shape Texts: What Creative Nonfiction Can Offer Ethnography." *Anthropology and Humanism* 32(2): 130–44.

———. 2012. *Alive in the Writing: Crafting Ethnography in the Company of Chekov.* Chicago: University of Chicago Press.

———. 2016. *Everyday Creativity: Singing Goddesses in the Himalayan Foothills.* Chicago: University of Chicago Press.

Narayan, K., with U. Devi Sood. 1997. *Mondays on the Dark Night of the Moon: Himalayan Foothill Folktales.* New York: Oxford University Press.

*Nepal the Great Blunder.* 2018. https://www.youtube.com/watch?v=noyKxj3KS3E&vl=en.

Ogden, L. A. 2018. "The Beaver Diaspora: A Thought Experiment." *Environmental Humanities* 10(1): 63–85.

Ong, A. 1999. *Flexible Citizenship: The Cultural Logics of Transnationality.* Durham, NC: Duke University Press.

Parashar, U. 2014. "Scientists Finds[*sic*] Large Uranium Deposit in Nepal." *Hindustan Times,* June 10. https://www.hindustantimes.com/world/scientists-finds-large -uranium-deposit-in-nepal/story-6icA8HZqskhIpUaWFwxpJP.html.

Parreñas, R. 2005. "Long Distance Intimacy: Class, Gender and Intergenerational Relations between Mothers and Children in Filipino Transnational Families." *Global Networks* 5(4): 317–36.

Peissel, M. 1967. *Mustang: A Lost Tibetan Kingdom.* Delhi: Book Faith India.

Peletz, M. G. 1995. "Kinship Studies in Late Twentieth-Century Anthropology." *Annual Review of Anthropology* 24:343–72.

Pigg, S. L. 1992. "Inventing Social Categories through Place: Social Representations and Development in Nepal." *Comparative Studies in Society and History* 34(3): 491–513.

———. 1997. "'Found in Most Traditional Societies': Traditional Medical Practitioners between Culture and Development." In *International Development and the Social Sciences,* edited by F. Cooper and R. Packard, 259–90. Berkeley: University of California Press.

———. 2019. "The Penstocks." *Roadsides.* https://roadsides.net/pigg-002/?fbclid =IwAR2KHIEXyVjwSUnZrK2bTIXlD92_4JYe5zm3IwvuiOzqn2ZVjdhRZAvWk3A.

Pine, A., and M. Turin. 2017. "Language Revitalization." In *Oxford Research Encyclopedia of Linguistics,* edited by M. Aronoff. New York: Oxford University Press. https://doi.org/10.1093/acrefore/9780199384655.013.8.

Pinto, S. 2008. *Where There Is No Midwife: Birth and Loss in Northern India.* New York: Berghahn Books.

Powelson, J. 2018. "Life and Livelihood in Remote Nepal." *Nepali Times,* September 28. https://www.nepalitimes.com/banner/life-and-livelihood-in-remote-nepal/.

Pribilsky, J. 2004. "'Aprendemos A Convivir': Conjugal Relations, Co-Parenting, and Family Life among Ecuadorian Transnational Migrants in New York and the Ecuadorian Andes." *Global Networks* 4(3): 313–34.

Ramble, C. 1997. "Tibetan Pride of Place: Or, Why Nepal's Bhotiyas Are Not an Ethnic Group." In *Nationalism and Ethnicity in a Hindu Kingdom: The Politics of Culture in Contemporary Nepal,* edited by D. N. Gellner, J. Pfaff-Czarnecka, and J. Whelpton, 379–413. Amsterdam: Harwood Academic Publishers.

———. 2008a. *The Navel of the Demoness: Tibetan Buddhism and Civil Religion in Highland Nepal.* Oxford: Oxford University Press.

———. 2008b. *Tibetan Sources for a Social History of Mustang, Nepal.* Vol. 1, *The Archive of Te.* Halle: International Institute for Tibetan and Buddhist Studies.

———. 2015. "Trouble with Vampires: Or, How the Layout of this Book Came to be Done." In *Tibetan and Himalayan Healing: An Anthology for Anthony Aris,* edited by C. Ramble and U. Roesler. Kathmandu: Vajra Publications.

———. 2017. "A Century of Trade and Tension: Stakeholders in the Kali Gandaki Salt Route, Mid-Nineteenth to Mid-Twentieth Centuries." In *Commerce and Communities Social Status and the Exchange of Goods in Tibetan Societies,* edited by J. Bischoff and A. Travers. Berlin: EB-Verlag.

Ramble, C., and N. Drandul. 2016a. *Tibetan Sources for a Social History of Mustang, Nepal.* Vol. 2, *The Archives of the Tantric Lamas of Tshognam.* Halle: International Institute for Tibetan and Buddhist Studies.

———. 2016b. *Tibetan Sources for a Social History of Mustang, Nepal.* Vol. 3, *The Archive of Baragaon.* Halle: International Institute for Tibetan and Buddhist Studies.

Ramble, C., and M. Vinding. 1987. "The Bem-chag Village Record and the Early History of Mustang District." *Kailash* 13(1–2): 5–47.

Rankin, K. N., T. S. Sigdel, L. Rai, S. Kunwar, and P. Hamal. 2017. "Political Economies and Political Rationalities of Road Building in Nepal." *Studies in Nepali History and Society* 22(1): 43–84.

Rapp, R. 2000. *Testing Women, Testing the Fetus: The Social Impact of Amniocentesis in America.* New York: Routledge.

Ratanapruck, P. 2007. "Kinship and Religious Practices as Institutionalization of Trade Networks: Manangi Trade Communities in South and Southeast Asia." *Journal of the Economic and Social History of the Orient* 50(2/3): 325–46.

Reichman, D. R. 2011. *The Broken Village: Coffee, Migration, and Globalization in Honduras.* Ithaca, NY: Cornell University Press.

Roesler, U. 2007. "A Palace for Those Who Have Eyes to See: Preliminary Remarks on the Symbolic Geography of Reting (Rwa-sgreng)." *Acta Orientalia Vilnensia* 8(1): 123–44.

———. 2009. "The Place Is the Message: Sacred Space and Identity in Reting Monastery, Tibet." Paper presented at Tibetan Pilgrimage Workshop, University of Oxford, February 14.

Rosaldo, R. 2013. *The Day of Shelly's Death: The Poetry and Ethnography of Grief.* Durham, NC: Duke University Press.

Rozario, S., and G. Samuel. 2002. "Tibetan and Indian Ideas of Birth Pollution: Similarities and Contrasts." In *Daughters of Hariti: Childbirth and Female Healers in South and Southeast Asia,* edited by S. Rozario and G. Samuel, 182–208. London: Routledge.

Sadiq, K. 2009. *Paper Citizens: How Illegal Immigrants Acquire Citizenship in Developing Countries.* Oxford: Oxford University Press.

Samuel, G. 1993. *Civilized Shamans: Buddhism in Tibetan Societies.* Washington, DC: Smithsonian Institution Press.

Sato, S. 2016. "Yolmo Women on the Move: Marriage, Migrant Work, and Relocation to Kathmandu." *European Bulletin for Himalayan Research* 47:69–95.

Saxer, M. 2016. "Pathways: A Concept, Field Site and Methodological Approach to Study Remoteness and Connectivity." *HIMALAYA* 36(2): 104–19.

Scarry, E. 2012. *Thinking in an Emergency.* New York: W. W. Norton & Company.

Schaller, G. B. 1988. *Stones and Silence: Journeys in the Himalaya.* Chicago: University of Chicago Press.

Schrempf, M. 2011. "Re-production at Stake: Experiences of Fertility, Family Planning and Reproductive Health among Amdo Tibetan Women." *Asian Medicine—Tradition and Modernity* 6(2): 314–39.

Schuler, S. 1977. "Migratory Traders of Baragaon." *Contributions to Nepalese Studies* 5(1): 71–84.

———. 1978. "The Women of Baragaon, Vol. II Field Study." In *The Status of Women in Nepal,* edited by L. Bennett and M. Acharya. Kathmandu: Centre for Economic Development and Administration, Tribhuvan University.

———. 1987. *The Other Side of Polyandry: Property, Stratification, and Nonmarriage in the Nepal Himalayas.* Boulder, CO: Westview Press.

Seddon, D., J. Adhikari, and G. Gurung. 2002. "Foreign Labor Migration and the Remittance Economy of Nepal." *Critical Asian Studies* 34(1): 19–40.

Sharma, J. R. 2018. *Crossing the Border to India: Youth, Migration, and Masculinities in Nepal.* Philadelphia: Temple University Press.

Sharma, S., et al. 2014. *State of Migration in Nepal.* Kathmandu, Nepal: Centre for the Study of Labour and Mobility.

Sherchan, S. 2018. "Indigenous Practice in Climate Change Adaptation: A Case Study from Annapurna Conservation Area, Dhey Upper Mustang." MA thesis, School of Environmental Science and Management, Pokhara University.

Shneiderman, S. 2014. "Living Practical Dharma: Chomo Khandru and the Himalayan Bon Tradition." In *Buddhists: Understanding Buddhism through Biography,* edited by T. Lewis, 246–56. Chichester, UK: Wiley-Blackwell.

———. 2015a. "Regionalism, Mobility, and 'The Village' as a Set of Social Relations." *Critique of Anthropology* 35(3): 318–37.

———. 2015b. *Rituals of Ethnicity: Thangmi Identities between Nepal and India.* Philadelphia: University of Pennsylvania Press.

———. 2017. "The Properties of Territory in Nepal's State of Transformation." In *Trans-Himalayan Borderlands: Livelihoods, Territorialities, Modernities,* edited by D. Smyer Yü and J. Michaud, 65–83. Amsterdam: Amsterdam University Press.

Shrestha, T. 2014. "Working the Paper: Nepali Suffering Narration, Compassion, and the US Asylum Process." PhD diss., Cornell University.

———. 2015. *"Kāgaj Banāune: A Collective Moral Practice of Suffering in the Asylum Experiences of Nepalis in the United States." Studies in Nepali History and Society* 20(1): 5–30.

Sijapati, B., A. S. Lama, J. Baniya, J. Rinck, K. Jha, and A. Gurung. 2017. "Labour Migration and the Remittance Economy: The Socio-Political Impact, Nepal." Research report funded by USAID and the Asia Foundation. Kathmandu, Nepal: Centre for the Study of Labor and Migration, Social Science Baha.

Silko, L. M. 2006. *Ceremony.* New York: Penguin Classics.

Simpson, A. 2007. "On Ethnographic Refusal: Indigeneity, 'Voice' and Colonial Citizenship." *Junctures* 9:67–80.

Simpson, E. 2013. *The Political Biography of an Earthquake: Aftermath and Amnesia in Gujarat, India.* London: Hurst and Company.

Smith, R. C. 2006. *Mexican New York: Transnational Lives of New Immigrants.* Berkeley: University of California Press.

Smyer Yü, D., and J. Michaud, eds. 2017. *Trans-Himalayan Borderlands: Livelihoods, Territorialities, Modernities.* Amsterdam: Amsterdam University Press.

Snellgrove, D. 1989. *Himalayan Pilgrimage: A Study of Tibetan Religion by a Traveller through Western Nepal.* Boston: Shambhala.

Speck, S. 2017. "'They Moved to City Areas, Abroad': Views of the Elderly on the Implications of Outmigration for the Middle Hills of Western Nepal." *Mountain Research and Development* 37(4): 425–35.

Stainova, Y. 2019. "Enchantment as Method." *Anthropology and Humanism* 44(2): 214–30.

Stewart, K. 2007. *Ordinary Affects.* Durham, NC: Duke University Press.

———. 2012. "Precarity's Forms." *Cultural Anthropology* 27(3): 518–25.

Stoller, P. 1989. *The Taste of Ethnographic Things: The Senses in Anthropology.* Philadelphia: University of Pennsylvania Press.

———. 2002. *Money Has No Smell: The Africanization of New York City.* Chicago: University of Chicago Press.

———. 2004. *Stranger in the Village of the Sick: A Memoir of Cancer, Sorcery, and Healing.* Boston: Beacon Press.

———. 2014. *Yaya's Story: The Quest for Well-Being in the World.* Chicago: University of Chicago Press.

Thapa, M. 1992. *Mustang Bhot in Fragments.* Kathmandu: Himal Books.

Toffin, G., and J. Pfaff-Czarnecka, eds. 2014. *Facing Globalization in the Himalayas: Belonging and the Politics of Self.* Thousand Oaks, CA: Sage Publications.

Tournadre, N. 2014. "The Tibetic Languages and Their Classification." In *Trans-Himalayan Linguistics: Historical and Descriptive Linguistics of the Himalayan Area,* edited by T. Owen-Smith and N. Hill, 105–30. Berlin: De Gruyter Mouton.

Tsewang, Y., T. Gurung, Y. Gurung, K. Thibeault, and E. Amburgey. n.d. "Belonging and Transformation in Mustang, Nepal." *HIMALAYA.* https://himalayajournal.org /photo-gallery/belonging-transformation-mustang-nepal/.

Tsing, A. L. 2005. *Friction: An Ethnography of Global Connection.* Princeton, NJ: Princeton University.

Tucci, G. 1977. *Journey to Mustang: 1952.* Kathmandu: Ratna Pustak Bhandar.

Tulachan, P. V. 2003. "The Lobas of Monthang: Loba Ethnography and Tourism as Development." PhD diss., University of Southern California.

Turin, M. 1997. "Too Many Stars and Not Enough Sky: Language and Ethnicity among the Thakali of Nepal." *Contributions to Nepalese Studies* 24(2): 187–99.

———. 2013. "Globalization Helps Preserve Endangered Languages." *YaleGlobal Online,* December 3. https://yaleglobal.yale.edu/content/globalization-helps-preserve -endangered-languages.

———. 2014. "Mother Tongues and Language Competence: The Shifting Politics of Linguistic Belonging in the Himalayas." In *Facing Globalization in the Himalayas:*

*Belonging and the Politics of the Self*, edited by G. Toffin and J. Pfaff-Czarnecka, 371–96. New Delhi: Sage Publications.

"Uranium Found in Mustang." 2016. www.youtube.com/watch?v=e4EIr7dTsog.

van Spengen, W. 2000. *Tibetan Border Worlds: A Geohistorical Analysis of Trade and Traders*. London: Routledge.

Vinding, M. 1998. *The Thakali: A Himalayan Ethnography*. London: Serindia Publications.

Watkins, J. C. 1996. *Spirited Women: Gender, Religion, and Cultural Identity in the Nepal Himalaya*. New York: Columbia University Press.

Wiley, A. S. 2004. *An Ecology of High-Altitude Infancy: A Biocultural Perspective*. New York: Cambridge University Press.

Yamanaka, K. 2000. "Nepalese Labour Migration to Japan: From Global Warriors to Global Workers." *Ethnic and Racial Studies* 23(1): 62–93.

Yeh, E. T. 2013. *Taming Tibet: Landscape Transformation and the Gift of Chinese Development*. Ithaca, NY: Cornell University Press.

# CREDITS

# INDEX

# ADDITIONAL RESOURCES FOR COURSE USE

Materials compiled by Sienna Craig are available on an *Ends of Kinship* website for instructors, including:

- Writing prompts
- A visual glossary
- Video conversations with Professor Craig
- And other related resources

https://sites.dartmouth.edu/endsofkinship

# GLOBAL
# SOUTH
# ASIA

Padma Kaimal
K. Sivaramakrishnan
Anand A. Yang
SERIES EDITORS

GLOBAL SOUTH ASIA takes an interdisciplinary approach to the humanities and social sciences in its exploration of how South Asia, through its global influence, is and has been shaping the world.

CPSIA information can be obtained
at www.ICGtesting.com
Printed in the USA
BVHW070457200920
589133BV00004B/10

9 780295 747699